# THE FATE OF COMMUNION

# THE FATE OF COMMUNION

*The Agony of Anglicanism and the Future
of a Global Church*

Ephraim Radner *&* Philip Turner

*Foreword by Stanley Hauerwas*

WILLIAM B. EERDMANS PUBLISHING COMPANY
GRAND RAPIDS, MICHIGAN / CAMBRIDGE, U.K.

Wm. B. Eerdmans Publishing Co.
2140 Oak Industrial Drive N.E., Grand Rapids, Michigan 49505 /
P.O. Box 163, Cambridge CB3 9PU U.K.

Paperback edition 2007

Printed in the United States of America

12  11  10  09  08  07      7  6  5  4  3  2

**Library of Congress Cataloging-in-Publication Data**

Radner, Ephraim, 1956-
   The fate of Communion: the agony of Anglicanism and the future
  of a global church / Ephraim Radner & Philip Turner.
     p.    cm.
  ISBN  978-0-8028-6327-0
  1. Lord's Supper — Anglican Communion. 2. Lord's Supper.
  3. Christian Union. 4. Ecumenical movement. 5. Christianity —
  Forecasting.   I. Turner, Philip, 1935-  II. Title.

  BX5149.C5R33   2006
  283.09' 0511 — dc22

                            2006004252

www.eerdmans.com

*For Andrew, Chris, Don, and Peter*
*our companions in the struggle*
*over the fate of the Anglican Communion*

# Contents

# Foreword

Even if you have no interest in the Episcopal Church of America or Anglicanism; even if you have no interest in Christianity; even if you have no interest in the disputes surrounding homosexuality in our culture at large; you should benefit from this book. You will benefit from reading the book because Philip Turner and Ephraim Radner have refused to let their account of the turmoil in the American Episcopal Church or Anglicanism be determined by the unhappy liberal/conservative alternatives. Instead, they have written a book that explores and engages, interestingly enough, fundamental questions in political theory and practice. By doing so they remind us that theology, and in particular ecclesiology, is never separable from political questions surrounding what constitutes having a life in common.

Turner's and Radner's exploration of the foundational questions surrounding the relation of power, authority, unity, and truth is necessary because they see quite clearly that the conflict occasioned by the ordination of a bishop who is openly gay and in a committed partnership has only made apparent the prior accommodation of the church to America. That accommodation has taken the form of the church's imitation of the development of American democratic political arrangements. That the church has become a mirror image of the national government is not surprising because it has always been difficult for Christians to resist the habits of the wider social and political world.

For example, as a Texan I have long wondered: "Who started to look and act like whom first? Did Texas politicians first begin to look and act like Southern Baptist pastors in Texas or did Southern Baptist pastors start to look and to act like Texas politicians?" I do not know which came first but I do know they are carbon copies of one another, particularly when it comes to manipulating the people they allegedly serve. That the church, even the Baptist church in Texas, has found it hard to resist taking into her own life secular political arrangements is not new nor is such imitation always problematic. But Turner and Radner help us see how by taking into the church's life the practice of authority that dominates American politics we have cut short the kind of debate we must have as Christians.

In particular Radner and Turner help us see how the modern democratic attempt to keep civic peace by accommodation to pluralism cannot be a polity for the church. More strongly they argue that such a politic cannot help but corrode the communion that should characterize what it means to be church. Even more controversially, and I should say that this is a conclusion I draw explicitly that they did not, the basic mistake made by the ordination of the bishop in a same-sex relationship was that the decision was put to a vote.

Christians in America seem to have forgotten that voting can be a coercive and even violent practice. Voting is not the mark of democracy. Rather, voting is the mechanism used in the hope of encouraging the discussion and debate for a community to discern the goods they have in common. Too often democracies domesticate conflict by establishing allegedly procedural rules of fairness to avoid substantive conflict and debate. When the church adopts such a strategy for her life, Radner and Turner argue, the church will be less than the communion she is called to be.

Perhaps nowhere is the radical discontinuity between democratic politics and the church more apparent than in Turner's and Radner's contention that the politics of communion must also be a politics of holiness. This may explain why I was asked to write this foreword. I am, after all, a Methodist even though I am now a communicant at the Church of the Holy Family (ECUSA) in Chapel Hill, North Carolina. However, my recent identification with the Church of the Holy Family is certainly not sufficient to give me standing to enter debates in contemporary Episcopal life. Yet Methodists, at least on some readings of Methodism, do represent the concern for holiness that Radner and Turner rightly emphasize as central for a recovery of the conciliar character of our Anglican polity. Of course, they quite rightly note that the significance of holiness was not a peculiar insight of the Wesleys', but rather has always been at the heart of the Church of England.

I, therefore, find myself in deep sympathy with the theological politics Radner and Turner develop in this book. I should like to think that I have developed similar themes in my own work over the years. I have, for example, criticized accounts of democratic politics that assume that through procedural mechanisms a society may achieve justice even though the people are not formed to be just. Like Radner and Turner I do not believe it possible to be a good society without people being good. It turns out, moreover, without good people authority cannot be other than the arbitrary imposition of power because the conditions are absent that allow authority to be exercised for the good in common.

Radner and Turner, moreover, locate the virtue of patience as crucial for the formation of an ecclesial politics of holiness capable of sustaining the conflicts we need to have. Only through patience is it possible for truth and unity not to conflict. Moreover, the unity truth makes possible is a unity that takes time. And taking time is what Christians can do because they have the conviction that time is but another name for God's patience. I cannot refrain from observing that Radner's and Turner's account of time and patience is quite similar to John Howard Yoder's understanding of the patience required for the practice of Christian nonviolence.

I have tried to direct attention to those aspects of this book that I think make it not just a book about the current controversy in the Episcopal Church in America. Although anyone caught up in that controversy will also find here a reconfiguration of the scriptural and theological questions raised by the debate that offer, I believe, a way forward for the communion. Turner and Radner are clearly in the opposition to the current policy of ECUSA, but I hope those who are on "the other side" will discover that this book helps us avoid being on a "side." Turner and Radner have written an extremely intelligent love letter to the church. I hope it will be read as such.

STANLEY HAUERWAS

# Acknowledgments

This volume is the result of a decade of collaborative effort by a group of scholars both in the United States and the United Kingdom meeting under the auspices of the Anglican Communion Institute (ACI). The conversations we have had with the various members of this group have contributed in essential ways to both the content and tone of these essays.

In the meetings and conferences sponsored by ACI we have sought, along with the other members and participants, to engage our various denominations in a debate over the nature and calling of the church. The debate has been occasioned in the first instance by the struggles set off by a host of moral issues that face all the churches in the West and increasingly in the Global South as well. As these issues have been struggled over and debated, it has become increasingly clear that they have caused differing views of the mission and character of the church to surface. The essays collected here are a representative sample of essays written during the past five years by two people who have been part of this group. Each essay seeks to display the calling and nature of the church within a global setting.

We would like, in particular, to express our thanks to The Rev. Don Armstrong, The Rev. Dr. Christopher Seitz, The Rev. Dr. Andrew Goddard, and The Rev. Dr. Peter Walker, all of whom have been our colleagues at ACI. Their critical judgment has been of enormous help to us, and their companionship has sustained us in the midst of what has proven a very difficult time in the life of the churches. In gratitude, we dedicate this volume to them.

We would also like to express our thanks to the editor of *First Things* for permission to print amended versions of two articles, "ECUSA's God" and "The End of the Church and the Triumph of Denominationalism," that appeared in that journal under the titles "An Unworkable Theology" and "The Episcopalian Preference," respectively. We would also like to thank the editor of *Pro Ecclesia* for permission to print an amended version of "Episcopal Authority within a Communion of Churches" and the editor of *Journal of Anglican Studies* for permission to print an amended version of "Diversity and Integrity: The Challenge of Life Together."

Finally, would like to express our thanks to Andrew Hoogheem of Eerdmans Publishing Company for the help he has given in getting this volume to press.

EPHRAIM RADNER

PHILIP TURNER

# Unity, Obedience, and the Shape of Communion

*Philip Turner*

## I

These essays lead their readers down two paths. One passes through the landscape of decline and disarray that characterize the life of America's once prominent "mainline" denominations. The other leads along a track that (possibly) leads not only to the rebirth and reform of these once proud institutions but also to an ecumenical vision of the nature and calling of the churches that is both rich and broad. Honest observers of the present religious scene in America find it difficult to ignore either the decline of "mainline" Protestantism or the ever-increasing balkanization of America's denominations. One way both to understand and address a situation of this sort is to mount a multi-denominational study intended to yield both the causes of decline and its remedy. Another way is to take a single, (one hopes) well-chosen example of a general phenomenon, and draw from it conclusions that cast light well beyond its own circumference.

We have chosen the second of these possibilities both because we believe it yields a clearer and more accurate picture, and because we, as Episcopalians and members of the Anglican Communion, have actually struggled through the events and issues our essays record. For over two decades we have been immersed in a church struggle with both domestic and international dimensions. In the process, we have been forced not only to assess the reasons for this struggle but also to search for a godly way through it.

These essays comprise a selection of the many we have written seeking an answer to these questions.

For Episcopalians and (more broadly) members of the Anglican Communion, what can only be called a crisis of identity that threatens the very existence of both denomination and communion has been occasioned by the confluence of two historical shifts. One is the increasingly secular and plural character of American culture. The other is the close of the colonial period that has issued in the independence of a host of churches spawned originally by the nineteenth-century missionary movement.

The increasingly secular and pluralistic character of American culture exposed what might well be called the Achilles' heel of Episcopalianism (and perhaps Anglicanism in general), namely, a penchant for over-adaptation to its environing culture. English literature is filled with examples, both poignant and satirical, of this proclivity within the Church of England. The temptation to over-adaptation followed members of that church to England's colonies. As a consequence, Episcopalians in the new world have from the beginning searched for an identity suited to a new environment. As the essays "The End of a Church" and "ECUSA's God" suggest, the latest expression of this quest for cultural acceptance is espousal of the goals and values of liberal culture as an alternative to what many Episcopalians tend to perceive as the dogmatism and moralism of both Roman Catholicism and Evangelical Protestantism. So identified, Episcopal clergy have launched out in new and "prophetic" directions unhindered by the strictures of past times and (in their view) less enlightened cultures. Further, in doing so, they have aligned themselves, as the essay "Children of Cain" suggests, with a strain of American culture common to all that country's denominations — a desire somehow to deny or at least escape the Fall and maintain a state of primordial integrity, a new beginning in the Land of Nod on the East of Eden where one can begin afresh.

In any case, the close identification of the Episcopal Church (ECUSA) with liberal culture has prompted her leadership (though not always her membership) to espouse beliefs and practices that, when compared to the long history of Christian thought and practice, can only be called "novelties." The most controversial of these new directions are the blessing of unions between persons of the same gender and the ordination of persons who have sexual partners of the same gender. These moral shifts have been accompanied by theological revisions of a radical sort — revisions that on the one hand downplay the need for redemption from sin and on the other emphasize God's non-judgmental and loving acceptance of all people, in a sense, without regard to their moral state.

Needless to say, such shifts in theology and ethics have set off internal battles not only among Episcopalians but also among Christians from across the spectrum of America's denominations. America's "culture wars" have produced bitter conflict not only within the denominations but also across their boundaries. They have also produced alliances between Christians from denominations that previously held each other to be outside the realm of acceptable belief and practice — witness for examples the joint statements by "Evangelicals and Catholics Together."

Of greater significance, however, is the fact that these new directions in belief and practice have, among Anglicans (and other denominations as well), ignited an international firestorm. For many, probably most, Christians from the Global South (shaped as they have been by the evangelical thrust of the nineteenth-century missionary movement) the changes they observe within the churches in America and Europe suggest at best spiritual sickness, and at worst apostasy. Thus, the recent actions on the part of ECUSA and the Anglican Church of Canada giving legitimacy both to sexual relations between people of the same gender and to the ordination of people engaged in such relations are in the minds of most Christians from the Global South both compromising and scandalous. As a result, events that have revealed fault lines in and between denominations within America have as well caused chasms to appear between the member churches of the Anglican Communion.

Thus, the recent consecration of an ECUSA bishop living with a partner of the same gender has produced tendencies toward division within ECUSA, and outright breaks in communion between some of the Anglican provinces of the Global South and ECUSA. It is, we believe, an open question as to whether either ECUSA or the Anglican Communion will survive the present upheaval. The question, however, is an open one. No conclusion is foregone; and this for a very good reason. Buried in the issues of division and survival is another, namely, what it might mean to be incorporated by water and the Spirit into the body of Christ. If a satisfactory answer is given to this question, the present struggles and divisions might well produce not further fragmentation and bitterness, but a more unified and obedient church.

It is this hope toward which these essays press. Though when compared to the doctrines of God and Christ, the doctrine of the church must

3

be considered derivative rather than central, it is nonetheless of great importance. In this case, rightly or wrongly, at the moment it comprises, among Anglicans, the center of the storm. Arguments over sexual ethics have in fact sparked a fierce debate over the nature of the church. Is it to be understood as a "communion of churches" in which the "autonomy" of each is properly exercised only within the constraints of a wider fellowship of common belief and practice; or is it best understood as a "federation of churches" in which each member church is autonomous in a way that makes it uniquely responsible for its stewardship of God's self-revelation in Christ? We have undertaken to defend the first of these possibilities and to offer what we believe to be trenchant criticism of the second. We have also undertaken to chart a way ahead through the storm of division that now characterizes the internal life of America's "mainline" denominations.

In defending the view that the church should address disputed issues as a communion rather than as a federation, we have aligned ourselves with the theological position taken in recent years by all the consultative bodies of the Anglican Communion. Two primary documents (the Virginia Report and the Windsor Report) have been produced by international Anglican consultative bodies over the past decade. Both documents address the threats of division faced by the communion with what can fairly be called a "communion ecclesiology," rooted in a reading of the Epistle to the Ephesians. As the essays on these two documents contained in this collection make clear, as a communion, Anglicans have taken the view that unity is a prime aspect of the nature of the church itself — one that manifests God's purpose to unite all things in heaven and earth in Christ. The unity of truth and love the church is called to manifest in its common life is thus to be understood not simply as a fond hope but as an effective sign of God's providential purposes for both human and natural history. For this reason, the way in which division is addressed within the common life of the church is not tangential to the Gospel's proclamation but central to it. In respect to the gospel, therefore, truth and unity are not distinct realities but necessary aspects of one and the same thing — in this case the gospel of God in Christ.

## II

The difficult question arises when, in the course of history, disagreements over the truth of the Gospel reach a point where unity threatens truth and truth unity. It is at this point that the church struggle in which Anglicans find themselves becomes a matter of concern to all Christians. The sad history of church division from the Great Schism, through the Reformation, to the present proliferation (both national and international) of denominations shows what must be considered an entrenched inability on the part of Christians to maintain the necessary connection between truth and unity. Put another way, the failure of Christians to love one another has rendered them incapable of agreeing on the very thing that is supposed to unite both their minds and their hearts.

The question presented by the current struggle over sexual ethics thus concerns more than the way in which Christians order their sexual desires and activities. It raises the question of how, within the changes and chances of history, truth and unity are to be bound together within the common life of God's people. There are any number of answers that have been given to this question. They range from the highly centralized system of authority within the Roman Catholic Church, through the confessionalism of the magisterial churches of the Reformation, to one or another version of congregationalism (whose adherents hold that God provides each gathered company of Christians all the gifts they need to remain both faithful to God and at peace with one another).

The essays "The Scriptual Community: Authority in Anglicanism" and "Conciliarity and the American Evasion of Communion" suggest that the "conciliar economy" that continues to evolve within the Anglican Communion is different in important ways from any of these. It is a means of ordering the life of the church in which a host of interlocking bodies maintain their unity in Christ not by reference to a principle or structure of authority that is in some way independent of the communion it is to guard, but by the practice of "mutual subjection" within the living relations of a body of people. Conciliarism is a model of church order different from any of those just mentioned. Mere distinctiveness, however, is not the reason this way of maintaining the bond between truth and unity demands ecumenical attention. A conciliar economy, defined as it is in this case by the practice of mutual subjection, provides a way to maintain the tensed congruence between unity and truth in which the means of apprehending truth takes the very form of truth itself. Such an economy is rooted in a series of practices (rather than principles or structures of authority) that manifest the very form of the sacrifice of Christ. Thus, mutual subjection within the Body of Christ requires of each of its members a

5

range of graces or virtues (if you will a degree of holiness) that serve to create a space in time for the peaceful resolution of conflict. As the essay "Diversity and Integrity" contends, these graces include the Christ-like qualities listed in Ephesians 4, namely, lowliness, meekness, patience, forbearance, eagerness for unity, truthfulness, kindness, tenderheartedness, forgiveness, love — and we would add a willingness to suffer as the ultimate expression of each and all these virtues.

If truth and unity are to remain bound together, space must be created for the resolution of conflict. No such space can exist (no matter how adequate the confession or how strong the political structure) apart from the presence of the above-mentioned graces and practices. These give expression to the love of God as seen in the life of Christ Jesus. They do not, however, exhaust the practices necessary for the successful functioning of this form of church order. The essay "The Scriptual Community: Authority in Anglicanism" places "scriptural immersion" by a people also at the base of a communion ordered in a conciliar manner. Truth bound to unity and unity bound to truth require the presence of a common mind. A common mind that conforms to the truth of God in Christ comes to be within a communion only when the members of that communion have been formed by constant exposure to the first-order language of the Bible as read within the context of worship and the ancient prayers of the church. These essays build upon Thomas Cranmer's insistence on the priority of scriptural knowledge on the part of the people that is not inhibited either by pre-existent confession or unchallengeable pronouncement. A conciliar economy holds that the meaning of the Bible is perspicuous when sought in the midst of common practice, prayer, and worship. Consequently, the effectiveness of a conciliar economy rests upon a sanctified people whose belief and the shape of whose life have been formed by immersion in the holy scriptures and the context of worship and prayer in which they are appropriated.

## III

As the essay "Diversity and Integrity" contends, however, neither the presence of the communion generating and sustaining virtues nor scriptural immersion on the part of the people precludes open and free debate of disputed issues. Indeed, true communion requires that Christ's followers "thoroughly comprehend what the will of the Lord is" (Eph. 5:17). The issue is how this effort at comprehension is to take place in a manner that serves both truth and unity. A conciliar means of maintaining the bond between truth and unity begins first with "scriptural immersion" and the presence of those graces that give shape to the love of Christ. However, these two aspects of life together in communion are not divorced from a particular view of the nature and function of authority within a polity or social order that takes the form of a communion. Given the fact that both finitude and sin continue to inhabit the common life not only of peoples and nations but of the churches as well, effective authority is necessary if the space provided by time is in fact to be one in which reconciliation can occur. Constructive argument requires a peaceful and ordered space if it is to remain constructive in a way that renders a people who are of one mind. The essays on "Diversity and Integrity," "The Virginia Report," and "The Windsor Report" provide an extensive account of the way in which authority within a conciliar economy is conceived and of why it is such a vital aspect of maintaining the bond between truth and unity.

Authority, as classically understood, exists to strengthen and further the common beliefs and practices that give a people identity. It is a means of sustaining what is common in ways that allow a people to meet with integrity the changing circumstances that history inevitably brings. Behind this view lie two assumptions. One is that there exists a common set of beliefs and practices. The other is that there exist persons who have the virtues necessary both to understand and sustain this "common good." The pluralism that increasingly characterizes the contemporary period calls into question both these assumptions. Pluralism challenges both the existence and value of a common good and the value of an exemplary life. As a result, a new view of authority has emerged in the present era. According to this view, authority exists not to further what is common but to ensure that each in their difference is accorded their fair share of the goods and services provided by social cooperation. Further, those vested with authority need not lead exemplary lives. They need only see that everyone gets their fair share.

The upshot of what might be called the "new authority," however, is not equity but a struggle for power in which, more often than not, authority (even ecclesial authority) is used neither to further what is common nor to establish equity. It is used in fact to further a particular point of view and a particular set of interests. To accomplish this end, authority lays claim not to a common heritage but to a "prophetic," "pneumatic" warrant that justifies itself on the basis of supporting the justice of a particular claim. The way in which the consecration of a gay bishop came about within ECUSA provides a graphic example of the triumph of what can fairly be called "the new authority." This claim of direct prophetic anointing has, not unexpectedly, set off similar claims on the part of people in authority throughout the Anglican Communion who see things differently.

## IV

The results of these "pneumatic wars" within the Anglican Communion are proving chaotic. Prophet meets prophet and they seem to occupy no common ground upon which to establish the legitimacy of their claim. It is significant, however, that precisely in the midst of this prophetic warfare the "instruments of unity"[1] of the Anglican Communion have begun to reaffirm a classical view of authority in which bishops seek to establish an order that supports a common good by the practice among themselves of "mutual subjection." Thus, all the instruments of unity within the Anglican Communion have stated quite clearly that the recent actions of both ECUSA and the Anglican Diocese of New Westminster in Canada have acted against the principles that tie Anglicans together as a communion. The instruments of unity from the Archbishop of Canterbury to the Anglican Consultative Council have made it clear that Anglicanism is defined in part by a conciliar polity in which each member waits upon the other in patience until, in respect to divisive matters, a common mind is reached.

It is, however, just at this point that what might be called the Anglican experiment in conciliarity faces its most severe test. The threat takes two forms. The first arises from a glaring omission in the documents (the Virginia Report and the Windsor Report) that go such a long way toward de-

---

1. The term "instruments of unity" is used by Anglicans to refer to international bodies that claim no jurisdictional authority beyond the limits of their own jurisdiction but do have moral authority within the communion as a whole. Increasingly, they have become instruments by means of which, in particular, the bishops of the communion seek a common mind in respect to disputed issues. The instruments of unity recognized by the Anglican Communion are the Archbishop of Canterbury, the Lambeth Conference of Bishops, the Meeting of the Primates, and the Anglican Consultative Council (the only instrument of unity comprised of lay persons and clergy as well as bishops).

fining the conciliar economy the Anglican Communion as a whole seems to take as part of its self-definition. Because of a longstanding commitment on the part of Anglicans to the "autonomy" of each of the communion's member provinces, there is, in the documents produced for and by its instruments of unity, no discussion of the place of discipline in a conciliar form of church polity.[2] The question of discipline within a communion governed in conciliar fashion cannot, however, be avoided unless, of course, one simply wants to give up the experiment as a failure. Those presently holding authority within ECUSA and the Diocese of New Westminster have made it clear that they believe their actions in respect to sexual ethics lie within their prerogative. It is unlikely that they will change course despite the admonitions of all the instruments of unity.

This intransigence confronts the Anglican Communion as a whole with a dilemma. If, in the name of honoring the "autonomy" of one province, the instruments of unity impose no discipline in a case thought not to be a matter of indifference, Anglicanism becomes by default a federation of churches rather than a communion. On the other hand, if Anglicans maintain a conciliar polity rather than one in which there is a form of jurisdiction (like that of Roman Catholicism) that extends across provincial boundaries, the question arises as to the form such discipline ought to take. How is discipline to be imposed when there is no jurisdictional authority to do so?

At present, two answers to this question seem to vie one with another. One is to pronounce a break in communion. In reaction to ECUSA's action a number of provinces from the Global South have done precisely this. Understandable as their actions may be, they in fact represent a denial of the very principle of mutual subjection the primates of these provinces have affirmed. They have not waited on one another until a common mind has been reached. Rather they have taken independent action. As a result, one is left with some provinces claiming communion with the Archbishop of Canterbury (until now the defining mark of membership in the Anglican Communion) who are not in communion with other provinces claiming the same thing. There is furthermore now a threat that Canterbury itself will lose its connective role altogether. This anomaly makes clear how

---

2. It is well to note, however, that the Anglican Communion Institute submitted for consideration an extensive document on this very subject. See *Communion and Discipline: A Submission to the Lambeth Commission by the Anglican Communion Institute* (Colorado Springs: The Anglican Communion Institute, 2004).

fragile the communion of Anglicans is and how fledgling is its conciliar economy.

Within a conciliar form of church order, actions of such a grave sort cannot result from the private judgment of a single person or province if indeed the polity is to remain conciliar. Further, a premature pronouncement of broken communion gives insufficient time for error to be recognized and repented. In addition, once communion is broken, as the sad history of the churches makes painfully clear, it becomes extraordinarily difficult to mend what has been severed. Thus, as a second option, what might be called a mediating form of discipline has been suggested in the essays on the Virginia Report and the Windsor Report. The Archbishop of Canterbury has one form of trans-jurisdictional authority recognized by all Anglicans. He has authority to gather the bishops of the communion in council. If he has this authority he has authority also not to gather them or to gather them with differing status. The form of discipline implied by the authority to gather provides a way to protect and further the unity of belief and practice that defines a communion that is less severe than broken communion and so more open to reconciliation. By creating an asymmetry in the status of bishops in relation to the Archbishop of Canterbury, a province or bishop can be in a way reduced in stature but not expelled from communion until recognized by all as clearly intransigent.

This seems a promising form of discipline for those whose common life is built upon the virtues listed in the letter to the Ephesians as definitive of unity in Christ Jesus. It is this remark that presents the second test this form of church governance faces. What are those to do who live within a church whose governing bodies and authorities act in ways clearly opposed to the common belief and practice that define a communion? This is one of the most perplexing and serious of the issues that face all the churches. An answer that has, as it were, become a part of the DNA of the churches perhaps from the time of the Great Schism, and certainly from the time of the Reformation, is to break away and form another church or (latterly) to join a church whose belief and practice more clearly match one's own. In these essays, and particularly in the essay "The Humiliation of Anglicanism" we suggest another way. It is the way of conformation to Christ's cross through patient and obedient suffering. This way of addressing the strained relationship between truth and unity does not pit one against the other and ask for a choice for one or the other. It does not seek to place the future of the truth and unity revealed and established by

Christ within human hands but within the providence of God. It allows for the fact that God may place his church under judgment so severe that it may appear to die; and it insists that no one should seek to place themselves outside that judgment by flight to or creation of a purer church. A communion bound by a conciliar form of government, if its foundation is indeed scriptural immersion, must allow for the possibility of its own defection from God's purposes. If such proves to be the case, and if it indeed is a communion, can its members exempt themselves from God's economy of judgment and redemption? Our contention is that communion is maintained not only by the obedient practice of mutual subjection, scriptural immersion, holiness of life, and godly discipline but also by submission to divine judgment. Such judgment is intended by God not as an exit visa from one church and an entrance visa to another, but as another, though not preferred, way in which God maintains the truth professed by his people and the unity to which they are called.

# PART I

# THE CHALLENGE OF
# THE PRESENT MOMENT

# CHAPTER ONE

# The End of a Church and the Triumph of Denominationalism: On How to Think About What Is Happening in the Episcopal Church

*Philip Turner*

## I

On August 5, 2003, the House of Bishops of The Episcopal Church USA (ECUSA), following an initial action by the House of Deputies of ECUSA's General Convention, gave its consent (by a ratio of roughly 60/40) to the election of the Rev. Gene Robinson to become the next bishop of the Episcopal Diocese of New Hampshire. Gene Robinson is an outspoken gay man who has lived openly with his partner for over a decade. He is also the divorced father of two children. At a later point in the same convention, delegates gave a *de facto* permission for the blessing of gay unions in dioceses that may choose to grant clergy license to perform these services.

How is one to understand and respond to this event — an event being watched closely by most other American denominations because the event (along with reactions to it) is generally considered a bellwether? Before any attempt is made at interpretation or prognostication, it is well to note that there are few if any dispassionate observers of these developments. Everyone seems to have a strongly held opinion. From my perspective, it seems most clarifying to say that, by its action, ECUSA has confirmed a decision taken unconsciously some time ago to find its primary identity as a liberal but liturgical option within the spectrum of Protestant denominations that make up America's religious kaleidoscope. In making this decision, ECUSA has at one and the same time (perhaps again unconsciously) made marginal for its self-understanding the significance of its membership in a worldwide communion of churches that jointly claim to be a part of the One, Holy, Catholic, and Apostolic Church. In fact, it has placed its membership in the Anglican Communion under threat, and, rather recklessly, brought that communion itself to the verge of a split between the churches of the Global South and those of the North. This is my point of view, and the best way to make it understandable (and defensible) is first off to recount, even if all too briefly, certain key aspects of ECUSA's more recent history.

## II

The U.S. Constitution guarantees a right to the "free exercise" but prohibits the "establishment" of any religion. The right to free exercise and the prohibition of establishment provide, in the American context, legal and social space for the birth and growth of a plethora of religious beliefs and practices. In America, "churches" became "denominations" — named organizations, each of which occupies a particular niche in a religious marketplace. Thus, when Episcopalians found *establishment* beyond reach, they presented themselves within the American religious market as a "bridge church," incorporating the best elements of both Protestantism and Catholicism. This self-presentation proved both pretentious and fatuous, and in time lost its hold on the imagination. In its place came another, namely, that the Episcopal Church provides an enlightened alternative to the moral and theological rigidities of both Roman Catholicism and Evangelical Protestantism. Emboldened by this new self-image, Episcopal clergy embraced new learning and new experience. They preached an enlightened religion attuned to the latest movements of liberal culture.

The power of this new self-image over the mind of the Episcopal Church showed its strength clearly as far back as 1966 when the late Bishop James Pike was accused of heresy for stating in *Look Magazine,* "The Church's classical way of stating what is represented by the doctrine of the Trinity is . . . not essential to the Christian faith." For reasons that will become apparent, the presiding bishop of ECUSA, despite pressures to the contrary, wished to avoid a heresy trial; and so managed to have the matter referred to an ad hoc committee rather than to a panel of judges. The committee concluded that a heresy trial would be widely viewed as a "throw back" to a previous century in which both church and state sought to penalize "unacceptable opinion." As such, a trial would give ECUSA an "oppressive image." The committee did say, however, that they rejected "the tone and manner" of the bishop's statements, and that they wished to dissociate themselves from many of the bishop's comments. His utterances were, they said, "irresponsible" for one holding Episcopal office. The bishops then censured Bishop Pike; but, despite the fact that he did not renounce his heresy, did nothing to inhibit him in the exercise of his Episcopal office. To charge him with heresy in the minds of the church's leadership would be to risk compromising ECUSA's position within the spectrum of American Christianity. Thus it would appear that the bishop's fault was a certain degree of irresponsibility and a lack of tact rather than false doctrine.

This view was certainly held by a group of bishops who opposed Bishop Pike's censure. They wrote a minority report in which they gave voice with stark clarity to the new self-image of the Episcopal Church. "We believe it is more important to be a sympathetic and self-conscious part of God's action in the secular world than it is to defend the positions of the past, which is a past that is altered by each new discovery of truth." So the doctrine of the Trinity became a position of the past that is altered by each new discovery of truth. In the minority report, Bishop Pike was not viewed negatively as a heretic, but positively as "a casualty (martyr?) of the Christian mission in our day."

Throughout this struggle, all sides sought to present ECUSA as an enlightened denominational option on the American religious scene. In this struggle can also be seen the birth of the notion that Episcopal office is to be used as a "prophetic" lever to pry people loose from the encrusted positions of the past. This notion of Episcopal office appeared in even more pronounced form during the battle over the ordination of women that took place during the decade of the 1970s.

Before recounting this tale, I feel compelled to make it clear that I am a staunch, even fierce, supporter of the ordination of women. However, the way in which the practice was introduced into ECUSA has (sadly) served both to weaken its structures of order and authority, and to further strengthen its self-identity as an "enlightened" denominational alternative.

In 1974, after the General Convention had twice refused to approve the ordination of women to the priesthood, three retired bishops ordained 11 female deacons as priests. The reason given by the bishops was that their act was an "obedient" and "prophetic" protest against oppression and an act of solidarity with those who are oppressed — in this case women. Once more there was an attempt to bring the offending bishops to trial, but once again the attempt was foiled. The matter was referred at various times and in various ways both to the House of Bishops and to a special committee. The bishops decried the action and went on at a later date to censure the bishops involved. The special committee found that the offending bishops were in fact guilty of canonical offenses, and that their acts involved "teaching publicly a doctrine contrary to that held by the church." Further, the committee posed in clear terms a fundamental question, namely, "whether this church's understanding of the nature of the church and the authority of the episcopate permits individual bishops, appealing solely to their consciences, to usurp the proper functions and other duly constituted authorities in this church." Another advisory committee put the point even more pointedly by saying that "a bishop is not free to appropriate the sacramental structure of the church to his own views."

Despite these admonitions, warnings, and actions, in October of 1975 Bishop George Barrett, another bishop without diocese, ordained four more female deacons to the priesthood. The women involved stated as the reason for their action that to wait for the General Convention to give approval to women's ordination was to affirm in principle the concept that discrimination against ordaining women to the priesthood may be practiced in the church until the majority changes its mind and votes. Once more a leading cultural trend, this time women's rights, showed itself as the dominant force within a defining moment of ECUSA's common life. Once more, a majority of ECUSA bishops decried what had been done, but acceded to its legitimacy by failing to take effective disciplinary action.

Looking back over the history that stretched from the "Pike affair" to the struggle over the ordination of women, one can see by the end of the process certain things firmly in place — ECUSA's espousal of enlightened culture and progressive cultural trends, the use of Episcopal office to further "prophetic causes," and the inability of the governing structures and authorities of ECUSA to restrain independent action on the part of its bishops. All these factors revealed themselves plainly when, in 1977, just two years after Bishop Barrett's blatant defiance of his fellow bishops, Bishop Paul Moore of the Episcopal Diocese of New York ordained a professed and practicing lesbian to the priesthood. In response, the House of Bishops did no more than express "disapproval" of Bishop Moore's action. The next General Convention, which met in 1979, passed a resolution that said among other things that the delegates believed "it is not appropriate for this Church to ordain a practicing homosexual or any person who is engaged in heterosexual relations outside marriage."

On the surface, it appeared as if the General Convention had legislated against the practice initiated by Bishop Moore; but surface appearances can be deceiving. The resolution that labeled these practices "inappropriate" began with the phrase "We recommend." Twenty dissenting bishops immediately signed a letter saying that they took the action of General Convention to be "recommendary and not prescriptive." These twenty Bishops also announced that in the name of "apostolic leadership" and "prophetic witness" they would not implement the resolution in their diocese.

It is unlikely that the General Convention resolution was intended to do no more than recommend against a practice, but over time political forces within ECUSA have in fact managed to establish the resolution as "recommendary" rather than "prescriptive."

In 1989, 1990, and 1991 the Episcopal Dioceses of Newark and Washington D.C. ordained open and practicing homosexuals to the priesthood. The justification for these ordinations was "new experience" and "new learning" that serves to "contextualize" the negative biblical witness. The ordination of sexually active homosexual persons then became a "justice issue" that must be furthered by a "prophetic" episcopate. In the face of these claims, it is perhaps not surprising that charges of heresy later brought against one of the bishops of Newark (Walter Righter) were turned down on the grounds that the bishop's action was not contrary to the "core doctrine" of the Episcopal Church.

After the Righter trial, the way was open for bishops to ordain sexually active homosexual persons if they so chose. It was clear that no disciplinary consequences would follow. It was at this point that the policy of a bishop or diocese to ordain or not ordain, to bless or not to bless, came to be known within Episcopal circles as the "local option." It was asserted, quite rightly, that "local option" is the *de facto* practice of ECUSA. The election of Gene Robinson to succeed the incumbent bishop of New Hampshire was thus only the most radical assertion of a policy that had been firmly in place in respect to ordinations and blessings since the time of the Righter trial. Not only was it now permissible within ECUSA for clergy and bishops to be openly gay, not only was it permissible to bless gay unions, it was also the case that these novelties were hailed by their supporters as evidence that God is "doing a new thing." The cultural recogni-

tion and integration of gay and lesbian people into the American mainstream was read as an act of God. The Episcopal Church, so the claim goes,
is taking a lead in calling attention to the finger of God in history and giving prophetic support to divine providence.

## III

It is possible that people from outside ECUSA who oppose these measures
will at this point simply throw up their hands and say, "Well, what else
would you expect from the Episcopalians? They've always been a little long
on style and a little short on substance." A reaction of this sort might provide some self-satisfaction, but would miss the significance for the rest of
the churches in America of what has happened in the Episcopal Church.
The Robinson election in fact serves to highlight the primary challenge all
the churches in America face, be they Catholic, Orthodox, "mainstream"
Protestant, Evangelical, or Charismatic. I speak of the subversion of Christian belief and practice by the logic of autonomous individualism, and
their transformation into simulacra. For one should make no mistake!
What has happened in ECUSA is not the particular problem of a once
(overly) proud denomination. Rather, it provides an exemplary case of the
sort of subversion and transformation that, in one way or another, threatens all American denominations.

To display this point with some clarity, I will freely borrow from the
account Alasdair MacIntyre has given of the tradition of liberalism in
*Whose Justice? Which Rationality?* The present economic and political cultures of America plainly stem from this tradition, and it is this tradition
that currently is bringing all its force to bear (in a hostile way) on more
traditional forms of Christian belief and practice. MacIntyre notes that the
tradition of liberalism cannot allow for a single notion of good to possess
"the public square." Liberal society must remain neutral in respect to the
good. What one can express in public are not notions of *good* but *preferences*. Of course, some way must be found to order preferences both in respect to individual life and to social policy. No rational way can be found
to achieve this goal, however, because there is no common notion of good
to which appeal can be made when it comes to sorting out conflicting
claims. Thus, the way in which one establishes preference in the public
arena, if it cannot be done by force, is by bargaining. Everything, both in

respect to private and public life becomes a "trade-off." Social life becomes a sort of free trade zone for preferences. All one needs to be able to play the game is the ability to bargain.

There are two things in particular to be noted about this form of social economy. The first is that theories of justice abound. They must for the following reason. To have one's preferences excluded is to have one's rights denied. Then the question arises of how one person's right to his or her preference is to be balanced against a contrary right claimed by someone else. At this point, some theory of justice must be invoked, but in a liberal social economy of preferences, no one theory can establish itself. Theories of justice simply multiply exponentially and interminably. Given this social reality, one can see easily why supporters of gay rights hold ordination and the blessing of gay unions to be matters of justice. One can see also why supporters of Gene Robinson hold that his election was above all "a justice issue."

The dominance in America of a liberal social economy also provides another reason for regarding the Robinson election and the permission given for gay blessings to be more than an Episcopal anomaly. Within a liberal social economy there comes to be a view of moral agency that gives special significance to sexual preference and sexual satisfaction. The denizens of a social order based upon competing preferences think of themselves not as inhabitants of a pre-established moral order but as *individuals* who are utterly unique, as *selves* that have particular personal histories and needs, and as *persons* who have rights that allow them to express their individuality and pursue their personal well-being within the social world they inhabit. For moral agents who think of themselves as *individuals, selves,* and *persons,* sexuality becomes, along with money, both a marker of identity and a primary way of expressing the preferences that define identity.

It is precisely this notion of moral agency and personal identity that makes the Robinson election so understandable. Here is a unique *individual,* who is a *self* with a particular history and a *person* with a right to express his preferences and put his talents to work in the social world he inhabits. To deny him that right on the basis of sexual preference is, at one and the same time, to deny his personal identity. This notion of moral agency also makes understandable why the issues of abortion and euthanasia take their place alongside self-chosen sexual expression as centers of moral controversy both within the churches and without. At the basis of each of these arguments lies the characterization of moral agents as *indi-*

*viduals, selves,* and *persons* who have the right to pursue the preferences that provide them with personal identity. In the culture wars that rage over abortion, euthanasia, and sexuality defenders of more traditional Christian teaching and practice often miss the fact that they must confront American culture on a deeper level than any of these specific issues. If they are to be effective, they must take on the very way in which Americans think of themselves as moral agents. The "socio-logic" that stands behind ECUSA's recent action beckons thinking to an even deeper level than the sad history of this church's search for a distinctive place on the spectrum of America's denominations. It calls Christian thought to confront a perception of moral and social life that runs counter to the very foundations of Christian thought and practice. It raises the question of whether we inhabit a moral universe with an order we are called upon to understand and to which we are required to conform, or whether the moral universe we inhabit is properly the creation of preference-pursuing *individuals, selves,* and *persons* who create a social world suited to their self-defined goals through an elaborate process of moral bargaining.

## IV

The Robinson election in fact manifests the social forces that at present erode the ability of America's denominations to act like churches: that is to say, to form people in a pattern of belief and a way of life which may run against preference but nonetheless accords with what Christians have, through the ages, held to be the truth about God and his intentions for human life.

It is important to recognize these social forces, but it is important as well not to conclude that the recent actions of ECUSA can be adequately explained by the play of these forces alone. Christians through the ages have faced social forces that threaten to compromise the truth they have been given to live and proclaim, but they have not always succumbed to them. To think well about what is happening in ECUSA one must ask why the sirens of modernity have sung so sweetly in ECUSA's ears.

My belief is that a religious rather than historical or sociological answer must, in the end, be given to this question. The English theologian P. T. Forsyth once wrote, "If within us we have nothing above us we soon succumb to what is around us." The history recounted above suggests that the internal life of ECUSA may well lack a transcendent point of reference — one that can serve as a counterbalance to the social forces that play upon it. A certain vacuity at the center is suggested also by an analysis of the theology that currently dominates ECUSA's pulpits. The standard sermon in outline runs something like this: "God is love, God's love is inclusive, God acts in justice to see that everyone is included, we therefore ought to be co-actors and co-creators with God to make the world over in the way he wishes."

Here is *the* theological projection of a society built upon preference — one in which the inclusion of preference within common life is the be-all and end-all of the social system. ECUSA's God has become the image of this society. Gone is the notion of divine judgment (save upon those who may wish to exclude someone), gone is the notion of radical conversion, gone is the notion of a way of life that requires dying to self and rising to newness of life in conformity with God's will. In place of the complex God revealed in Christ Jesus, a God of both judgment and mercy, a God whose law is meant to govern human life, we now have a God who is love and inclusion without remainder. The projected God of the liberal tradition is, in the end, no more than an affirmer of preferences. This view of God is, furthermore, acted upon by an increasing number of ECUSA's clergy who now regularly invite non-baptized people to share in the Holy Eucharist. It's just a matter of hospitality — of welcoming difference. An inclusive God, it would seem, requires an inclusive sacramental system.

Judaism has always held that idolatry is the greatest of all sins. In the end, the actions of ECUSA must be traced to idolatry, to the creation of a god made in our own image, rather than to the play of social forces. It is this observation that brings me to the final remark I wish to make about how to think about what is happening in the Episcopal Church. A majority of the bishops of the Global South are of the opinion that some form of discipline must be imposed upon ECUSA if the Anglican Communion is to maintain its claim to apostolicity and catholicity. Contrary to the assertions of many liberal Episcopal clergy and bishops, the concern of the bishops from the Global South does not stem from the fact that they have not as yet lived through the Enlightenment. It stems rather from a perception that some form of idolatry has infected ECUSA, and that this infection has led to forms of gross disobedience that compromise not only Anglican but also Christian identity.

Time will tell whether ECUSA's presiding bishop will manage to convince these bishops from the Global South that an international "local option" is the enlightened way for the Anglican Communion as a whole. The attempt is certainly being made. It is entirely likely, however, that the bishops of the Global South will say to ECUSA that membership in the Anglican Communion requires conformity to the faith and practice of a worldwide fellowship of churches — even if that conformity runs against the grain of the culture in which Christians happen to find themselves. ECUSA will then have to decide if it wants to remain in its denominational niche or if it wants to affirm its identity as a church that is part of a worldwide communion of churches. This is the issue now facing the bishops, clergy and people of ECUSA. The issue calls into question ECUSA's self-identity, and for that reason alone one may expect a long and sadly bitter struggle. Further, if my analysis of the relation of the churches to American culture is accurate, one may expect as well that this sad, bitter struggle will characterize the internal history of each for some years to come.

# CHAPTER TWO

# Children of Cain:
# The Oxymoron of
# American Catholicism

*Ephraim Radner*

> *"There is plenty of emptiness, as much as you need, to define*
> *yourself against, as American souls seem to do."*
>
> Saul Bellow, *The Dean's December*

In the current crisis of the Episcopal Church USA, and of the Anglican
Communion, a couple of things at least have become clear. First, American
Episcopalians do not understand who they are as Americans, and as a result their understanding of what is and ought to be the Christian Church
in America is woefully obscured and perverted. At the same time, it has become increasingly obvious that those outside America looking in on and
being swept up in this crisis — Africans, Asians, and even the British — do
not understand what drives the American religious psyche, and hence they
cannot grasp why it is that Americans do not comprehend the church's demands upon them. These non-Americans have thrown up their hands in
dismay and disgust; or, in a few cases, have lulled themselves into thinking
there must be some mistake that will soon be made right. Very few seem
willing to face the fact that for Americans the Church of Christ is fundamentally in a struggle of titanic proportions, one that it is in the interests
of the world to see virtuously engaged.

And in fact, the stakes of this interest are great. As American Episcopalianism has come into conflict with worldwide Anglicanism, this very
drama has managed to bring into relief a parallel dynamic at work in the

relationship between American Roman Catholicism and the Roman Catholic Church as a whole. Obviously, people have sensed for a long time that Catholicism in America is peculiar and faces peculiar challenges. There has been a steady literature on this topic for some time.[1] And certainly many factors of late have made this confrontation evident. But the Anglican agony has played a particular role in making clear that "American Catholicism" is an intrinsic problem for a worldwide church in the context of the Tradition writ large. Transitions in the papacy have encouraged numerous popular analyses on the ways in which the American church in particular represents a difficulty in the face of the Vatican's vision of a revitalized orthodoxy; and many of the traits that characterize this difficulty are those shared, in a special way, with American Episcopalianism, only recently exposed to wide popular scrutinizing in the wake of the ordination of gay bishops.[2]

There are those who would probably be content to allow Anglican (certainly) and Roman (perhaps) versions of "American Catholicism" (a category whose distinctions many, I realize, would reject) to disintegrate and disappear. These religions represent, it may seem, such a corrupted instance of western secularized transpositions of the gospel as to merit nothing else than abandonment. But it may also be the case — such is the argument here — that American "Catholicism," of whatever kind (if there is

---

1. See among many: John Tracy Ellis, *American Catholicism* (Chicago: University of Chicago Press, 1969); David J. Alvarez, ed., *An American Church: Essays on the Americanization of the Catholic Church* (Moraga, Calif.: Saint Mary's College of California, 1979); Stephen J. Vicchio, "The Origin and Development of Anti-Catholicism in America," in *Perspectives on the American Catholic Church, 1789-1989*, ed. Stephen J. Vicchio (Westminster, Md.: Christian Classics, 1989); John T. McGreevy, *Catholicism and American Freedom: A History* (New York: W. W. Norton, 2003); John T. McGreevy, "Thinking on One's Own: Catholicism in the American Intellectual Imagination, 1928-1960," *Journal of American History* 84 (June 1997), 97-131; Jay P. Dolan, *In Search of an American Catholicism: A History of Religion and Culture in Tension* (New York: Oxford University Press, 2002). More broadly, Peter Steinfels, *A People Adrift: The Crisis of the Roman Catholic Church in America* (New York: Simon and Schuster, 2003); George Weigel, *The Courage to Be Catholic: Crisis, Reform and the Future of the Church* (New York: Basic Books, 2002); Andrew Greeley, *The Catholic Imagination* (Berkeley: University of California, 2000).

2. Cf., among many, David C. Steinmetz, "The new pope and the archbishop of Canterbury," *Orlando Sentinel*, April 27, 2005. See also the official communication from December 2004 by Cardinal Kaspar to Archbishop Williams regarding the Windsor Report. Within the general realm of these kinds of cultural comparisons, see Lauri Goodstein, "Catholics in America: A Restive People," *New York Times*, April 3, 2005.

more than one kind), is a vocation to be pursued, for the sake of every church and all churches together.

The establishment of a vital and stable American Catholicism is an important work to be accomplished, a long effort to be expended, for the sake of living into and demonstrating the necessary Christian alternative to the violence of continual self-rejuvenation that our American churches have so readily embraced, and shared with the world at large. The secular outplaying of this violence is well known, if perhaps not deeply appreciated. It can be seen in the longstanding conflict in America between the idealists and realists of political and social renewal; between, that is, those convinced of the possibility of immediate or progressive embodiments of virtue in our social lives, and those by contrast convinced of the ingrained need for pervasive self-protections one from another. The political scientist Robert Kagan made much of this not long ago in his extended essay on the differences between Europeans and Americans in the present day, and amid our tragic struggles over global order — the Europeans favoring an idealism of universal peace founded on universal capacities and rights; and the Americans working out of an almost Hobbesian vision of the savage world of conflicting instincts and depredations, demanding imposed restraint and caution.[3] What Kagan doesn't address is the way these two attitudes actually lie *together* at the heart of American social expectation itself, and how both inevitably lead to their own forms of uncontrollable violence.[4]

The Christian experience, in America especially, embodies in its own spirit these two conflicting and violence-laden orientations. They mark the present conflicts of our denominations, not only in the pragmatic choices seemingly offered to distraught members, but they even inform the issues at the root of the conflicts themselves, for example, sexuality

3. Robert Kagan, *Of Paradise and Power: America and Europe in the New World Order* (New York: Random House, 2004). Not everyone, of course, has accepted Kagan's thesis. Cf. Anthony Padgen, "Imperialism, Liberalism, and the Quest for Perpetual Peace," *Daedalus* 134:2 (Spring 2005), 46-57, who suggests actually reversing the characterizations. But since both aspects vie with each other in the American social psyche, the argument is perhaps moot.

4. Cf. Christopher Lasch's *The True and Only Heaven: Progress and Its Critics* (New York: W. W. Norton & Co., 1991), which marked an attempt, from a social-scientific vantage, to chart out an alternative. See especially his discussions of Orestes Brownson, nineteenth-century American transcendentalist turned Roman Catholic, pp. 184-97, and of Reinhold Niebuhr and Martin Luther King Jr., pp. 369-411, as explicators of his final statement on pp. 527ff.

and how Scripture's authority functions. And the muted struggle for some lived alternative to these two warring and war-prone ways of understanding human life and history marks one of the great Christian vocations of the present era. The alternative is both possible and demanded precisely because it represents the vocation of Christ and the form of Christ within a world where the unanticipated "violence of innocence" — crouching at the door (Gen. 4:7) — and the accepted violence of conscious corruption find temporal redemption in the Body of Christ Jesus, and in the history of the one New Man of reconciled Jew and Gentile in him. There is, in other words, a divine vocation for Catholicism in America; but one bound up with the passage of Jesus Christ through the Cross; thus a vocation both necessary, because it belongs to Jesus first; and one whose outcome in the world moves only by "faith," as a stranger and an exile, through a world whose contours color the display of such a faith as given in the painful limits of Christ's own subjected body. Thus, we cannot run away, American or African or British; for here, in the context of this vocation, the world as a whole is offered the chance to observe the redeeming work of God.

If there is something oxymoronic about being both "Catholic" and "American," then, it is bound up with the paradox of the God-Man himself and with the life of his body as the Church. This is true for Anglicans, and if Anglicanism has any purpose in America, and others have any stake in its presence, it lies in the way its fate can help explicate this life. Surely it is true as well for Lutherans, or Methodists, or Roman Catholics, as much as anyone, for reasons that will come clear through the image of the Anglican Catholic whose embrace extends, if only by desire, to the full range of our denominations. The following comment on this image, then, speaks to a common struggle.

There is a danger in this kind of analysis by exemplar, in that the conclusions inevitably come across as assertions rather than demonstrated deductions. And this is so, first, for the sake of simplifying (and thereby perhaps distorting) complex historical detail. But, secondly, such assertion is permissible because we know from the start that these details *must* somehow conform to the reality of Jesus Christ in the world, and therefore the risk of simplification and distortion is one we must assume: we know that the created world and its future must "look like him" (cf. 1 John 3:1ff.). Our theological responsibility is to apprehend this shape within the welter of details that otherwise would overwhelm in their disparate diversities.

## What Is American?

Our national character has been a longstanding American and European interest — from the more limited self-criticisms of Puritan settlers to the political polemics and justifications of the Revolutionary period, through the more analytical observations that flourished in early-nineteenth-century descriptive writing of Tocqueville, Crèvecoeur, and even James Fenimore Cooper.[5] Such reflections flourished among American moralists like the transcendentalists and abolitionists in the mid-nineteenth century and among English travelers like Dickens and Trollope later; and so it has continued among political commentators to this day, in an era of intense concern with America's role in the world.

We can enter this tradition with an assertion, as it were, by taking as an indicator of the specifically *religious* aspect of our national character a comment made by Thoreau in his 1863 *Atlantic Monthly* essay "Life without Principle."[6] Thoreau has been lamenting the passivity of Americans in the face of material demands — consuming their existences in "earning a living." And he comments on the way that American religion encourages this by inculcating a sense that we "merely come into the world as the heir of a fortune," fated with this or that set of resources, which we use or lose, and try to increase or regain as the case may be. He links this to Americans' obsession with original sin, which somehow locks us into a limited existence we are continually struggling against: "Thus men will lie on their backs, talking about the fall of man, and never make an effort to get up."[7]

Thoreau's comment, inclusive of those he criticizes, seems to me emblematic of a deep-seated American imperative: "We must do something about the Fall." "Do something" in the sense of govern our actions according to its purported reality — by rejecting it (as Thoreau does), or by figuring out the key to its resolution, or by embracing it. Certainly the impera-

---

5. A brief bibliographical essay on such literature is given by Ray Allen Billington in *America's Frontier Heritage* (Albuquerque: University of New Mexico Press, 1974), pp. 285-88. The Library of Congress provides a digital collection of several hundred volumes under the title "American Notes: Travels in America 1750-1920," available online at http://www.memory.loc.gov/ammem/ammemhome.html.

6. In Perry Miller, ed., *The American Transcendentalists* (Garden City: Doubleday, 1957), pp. 308-29.

7. Thoreau, in Miller, *The American Transcendentalists,* pp. 313-14.

tive has been posed before, as well we know: in the early centuries of the church, it became an ordering issue when it was pressed from a decidedly particular origin — that is to say, what we call Gnosticism.[8] The resemblance is significant. Historically, and in the context of Christian language, "gnosticism" represents a range of different ways of "doing something about the Fall."

Among the early Gnostics, this fixation upon a moment or experience of human fallenness and release led to a bypassing of the church and her history in the world. Within the American context also, this bypassing has proven endemic, although with peculiar reasons of origin. First, the anti-historical and anti-ecclesial attitude rooted in American Christianity is a product of a particular Protestant set of theological habits that have informed most Christian immigrants to America (and have clearly now influenced Roman Catholicism in America as well); habits which spring from a kind of primitivist restorationism that defines the descendents of the Reformation *ab initio*. [9] In America, however, this basic Protestant impulse has been further shaped and expanded, perhaps even transformed, by something unique: the experience of an immovable, if variously traversed, geographical reality of landscape and social development, characterized at its heart by the inescapable experience of encounter with new

---

8. It seems undeniable that the Gnostic challenge was primary in pressing the Church to focus with increasing clarity on the "Fall," bringing into some ordered articulation the concerns of Paul in particular. But the concern was peculiar, in the first place, to the Gnostics themselves, whose experiential anxieties over "imprisoned spirit" involved them in an eventual obsession with the character and history of corruption. In this, I side in the debate over a "Gnostic religion" with traditionalists like Filoramo over and against revisionists like M. A. Williams. Cf. Giovanni Filoramo, *A History of Gnosticism,* trans. Anthony Alcock (Cambridge, Mass.: Blackwells Publishing, 1990), esp. pp. 87-100, a discussion of a representative "creation and fall" perspective, including the problem of Adamic progeny, which might even bypass Cain and Abel altogether (in favor of the race of Seth) in an attempt to evade material history's violence; Michael Allen Williams, *Rethinking 'Gnosticism': An Argument for Dismantling a Dubious Category* (Princeton: Princeton University Press, 1999), esp. the conclusion, which gives away perhaps more than was intended once "biblical demiurgy" is made the single common characteristic of the Gnostic mindset.

9. Cf. Ephraim Radner, *The End of the Church: A Pneumatology of Christian Division in the West* (Grand Rapids: Eerdmans, 1998), pp. 82-93. The point is not simply that Protestantism sought a "reform" that would reproduce the early purity of the first Church; rather its reform was a kind of unveiling of the "original" Church that had existed from Adam's first progeny: the Church of Abel in conflict with the Church of Cain. The Reformation, that is, finally sought a re-integration into the "first moment" of history itself.

sights, new opportunities, new peoples — the land, the spaces, the rocks, the rivers, the Indians, the beasts.[10]

This observation represents a well-established view of the political-social self-understanding and hope of Americans in a *novus ordo seclorum* ("a new order of the ages") — as our national seal puts it[11] — bound up with the all-encompassing experience of a "new world" both in fact and in yearning. This consciousness has been extended by commentators to explain an entire cultural grasp of reality that is meant to characterize our national outlook, perhaps the most famous being Frederick Jackson Turner's thesis regarding the formative force of the persistent adaptation to "frontier" living in a constant reinvention of civilization from its barbarian beginnings.[12] Although Turner's theory has been attacked on various specific grounds, its explanatory reach remains inescapable.[13]

In religious terms, this has taken the many forms of re-creationism. (And Turner's theory, we need to recall, was less about the "progressivist" spirit of America, than it was about incessant generation and regeneration.) As Joseph Needleman said, in the context of an examination of the Shakers, "America is the land of zero. Start from zero, we start from nothing. That is the idea of America."[14] And from an explicitly Christian perspective, that outlook has impelled among Americans a consideration of human existence not in historically shaped terms, but in terms of permanent "originals," of Adam and of Adam's family. Here, then, I simply assert the scriptural character of American religion in practical terms: as the

10. The confluence of identifiable theological pursuits and a temporally traceable encounter with a documented landscape means that we can indeed study it historically as a "national" character.

11. This portion designed by Charles Thomas for the final version of the seal in 1782, was perhaps based on *Eclogue* IV:5 of Virgil.

12. Frederick Jackson Turner, "The Significance of the Frontier in American History" (1893), in Frederick Jackson Turner, *The Frontier in American History* (New York: Dover Publications, 1996, repr. of orig. 1920 edition), pp. 1-38.

13. Ray Allen Billington's *America's Frontier Heritage* (Albuquerque: University of New Mexico Press, 1974), is devoted as a whole to a description and analysis of the debate over Turner's thesis (which was not, in itself, wholly novel at the time of its influential circulation). More recent critics, e.g. Stephen Aron (*How the West Was Lost: The Transformation of Kentucky from Daniel Boone to Henry Clay* [Baltimore: Johns Hopkins University Press, 1996]), despite their objections, continue to work within the circuit of Turner's larger claims.

14. In Robert Kaplan, *The Nothing That Is: A Natural History of Zero* (New York: Oxford University Press, 1999), p. 202.

experienced enactment of this consideration and search for the "primordial," however defined, the American religious character has involved itself in the constant tracing and retracing of the figure, not of the Christian Church's life, not of the Body of Christ, itself a renewal of the human race in time, but of Adam's progeny, of Cain and of the children of Cain.[15] The very fixation of American experience on beginnings and re-creation represents a return to the moment in which humanity stands on the brink of violence, to choose it or, in ignoring it, to be captured by it anew.[16] Anne Bradstreet's Puritan "contemplations" of human existence tellingly hovers over this event, universalizes it, and declines to move into even the outplaying of divine election's process in time:

> Who fancyes not [Cain's] looks now at the Barr,
> His face like death, his heart with horror fraught,
> Nor Male-factor ever felt like warr,
> When deep dispair, with wish of life hath sought,
> Branded with guilt, and crusht with treble woes,

15. The phrase "children of Cain" has a long history of theological application, from Philo (see pp. 55-56) to the present, as a figure of human internecine violence. Cf. Tina Rosenberg's *The Children of Cain: Violence and the Violent in Latin America* (New York: Morrow/Avon, 1991). The figure of Cain has, furthermore, been particularized more recently as the peculiar *religious* bearer of human violence, a paradigm of "monotheistic" pressures towards exclusivism and antipathy. Cf. Regina Schwartz' *The Curse of Cain: The Violent Legacy of Monotheism* (Chicago: University of Chicago Press, 1997). My own use of the phrase is meant to point to the figural contrast between the progeny of the "old Adam" and the "new Adam" of the Body of Christ. It is a contrast whose resolution we are privileged to witness, perhaps, with our own eyes.

16. It is worth contrasting (in the manner of Robert Kagan) American primordialism in this scriptural sense with e.g. paradigmatic European interest in human origins within a scriptural context. Kant's brief reflection of 1786, "Conjectural Beginning of Human History," makes use of the Cain and Abel story as mythic markers of the development of human society from pastoral and agrarian and urban forms of life. His interest in considering the "origin of humanity," however, lies not in re-apprehending this primordial moment, but in noting its continuity with the present with respect to human capacity, unadorned and freely-willed, whose uniform rationality can be autonomously used for ill or, as Kant would hope, for the gradual progress of civilization. For Kant, Cain is but a learning moment within the historical appropriation of human reason, to be noted today and reasonably built upon in the ongoing task of human betterment. See Immanuel Kant, *On History,* trans. Lewis White Beck, Robert E. Anchor, Emil L. Fackenheim, and ed. Lewis White Beck (Indianapolis: Bobbs-Merrill, 1963), pp. 53-68, esp. pp. 63ff.

A vagabond to Land of Nod he goes.
A City builds, that wals might him secure from foes.

Who thinks not ofte upon the Fathers ages [. . .]
How Adam sigh'd to see his Progeny,
Cloath'd all in his black sinfull Livery,
Who neither guilt, nor yet the punishment could fly.[17]

A recognition of this ineluctable fascination can open religious knowledge to a striking and honest vision of the self; even while its attraction may well pull us into the vortex of a kind of self-immolation.

## What Is Catholic?

We will return to this matter in a moment. But first let us observe the contrast between "Cainite" primordialism and the very concept of catholicism. However we might define the concept in detail, catholicism represents a reality of "wholeness" and "completeness" which is meant to embrace the reach of Christ's active redemption across time and space, and to establish our own religious experience within the apprehension of this context, and none other. Although the term is not itself scriptural, its root cognates in the New Testament are used in a way directly continuous with later patristic definition: the *holos* of "cat-holic" is the faith and teaching and mission that embrace a "whole" region or the "whole" world with the truth of Christ and his life (in the Synoptics and Paul, e.g. Matt. 26:13; Mark 6:55; Luke 8:39; 11:34ff.; 13:21; Acts 15:22; Rom. 1:8; 16:23; etc.). It becomes with St. Cyril of Jerusalem the full extension of a divine creative and redemptive reach:

> [The Church] is called Catholic then because it extends over all the world, from one end of the earth to the other; and because it teaches universally and completely one and all the doctrines which ought to come to men's knowledge, concerning things both visible and invisible, heavenly and earthly; and because it brings into subjection to godliness the whole race of mankind, governors and governed, learned and un-

17. Cited from Harrison T. Merole, ed., *Seventeenth-Century American Poetry* (New York: New York University Press, 1968), p. 14.

learned; and because it universally treats and heals the whole class of sins, which are committed by soul or body, and possesses in itself every form of virtue which is named, both in deeds and words, and in every kind of spiritual gifts.[18]

This is catholicism as the description according to which the sheer sovereignty of the Creator God redeems his work through the very propagation of the Body of Christ within the history of the world, as his church. Historical continuity, reach, power, and interpenetration stand as marks of such a vision, and are inherently pressed beyond life and death, beyond personal locations and national boundaries, and even beyond the simple choices of individuals to fathom and order their own lives. We can turn to an extended illustration here, that has pertinence in our analysis of American Catholicism in particular.

When in late 1839 John Henry Newman wrote of the phenomenon and growth of an "Anglican" American church in the nineteenth century, he did so on the basis of a renewed vision of catholicism that seemed to him to be drawing America into the realm of an expanding history of hope within the wider world.[19] For Newman, the American church was not some newly created wonder, but the fruit of a universal providence — the grasp of the Body of Christ — that had long been at work to gather all of humanity. Newman had read an account of the young Protestant Episcopal Church in the United States written by an English priest, Henry Caswall.[20] Caswall's volume offered the first lengthy analysis of the American "Anglican" church (and an early account of Mormonism too!), and was based on a decade of pastoral work in, among other places, the Ohio

18. Cyril of Jerusalem, *Catechetical Lectures*, XVIII:23, trans. E. H. Gifford, in *Nicene and Post-Nicene Fathers, Second Series*, Vol. 7 (Peabody, Mass.: Hendrickson Publishers, 1994), pp. 139ff.

19. "The Anglo-American Church," in *British Critic* (October 1839); reprinted, with a note of comment from his Catholic perspective, in J. H. Newman, *Essays Critical and Historical* (London: Longmans, Green, and Co., 1871), vol. 1, pp. 309-86.

20. Henry Caswall, *America, and the American Church* (London: J. G. & F. Rivington, 1839; repr. New York: Arno Press, 1969). Caswall later returned for an extended tour, including Canada, in 1851, and published an account *(The Western World Revisited)*. A useful discussion of both Caswall and the Tractarian and later English interest in the American Episcopal Church can be found in H. G. G. Herklots, *The Church of England and the American Episcopal Church: From the First Voyages of Discovery to the First Lambeth Conference* (London: A. R. Mowbray and Co., 1966), pp. 127-65.

frontier. Newman was now approaching the end of his own Anglican Tractarian phase and, having glimpsed in the Monophysite separation from the "orthodox" a mirror image of Anglicanism's separation from Rome, he was beginning to falter in his convictions regarding Anglican integrity.[21] He was perhaps already, and unconsciously, searching for reasons still to hope in the "catholic" character of the Church of England. Caswall's volume both provided him some, as well as struck deeper notes of an already resonating anxiety. It is instructive to hear both aspects in order to get a sense of what "catholicism" might mean to someone deeply committed to its apprehension.

Newman begins his extended essay on the "Anglo-American Church" with a lamentation over the desultory state of the Church of England, which he describes primarily in terms of her isolation and barrenness among the "nations." Although in this the English Church resembles all the other scattered pieces of "Christendom broken up," the Anglican Church has suffered particularly in her loneliness from the assaults of State and infidelity (pp. 310ff.). "She has been solitary. She has been among strangers; statesmen, lawyers, and soldiers frisked and prowled around; creatures wild or tame have held a parliament over her, but still she has wanted some one to converse with, to repose on, to consult, to love" (pp. 311f.). This is the lack that the rise of the American Anglican church has filled, according to Newman. "This friendly Church is a daughter of ours, and is our pride as well as our consolation. The daughter is the evidence of the mother's origin; that which lives is the true Church; that which is fruitful lives; the English Church, the desolate one, has children. . . . [The] day of rebuke is passed. The English Church has fulfilled the law which evidences her vitality" (pp. 312f.).

Newman here outlines the primary character of "catholicity" as being the providentially attested "life" that grows to include the "nations," and that draws them into the single life of God's redemptive work in Christ, as an organic and mutually entwined Body. Much of the rest of the essay's comments on the American church's hopeful existence play upon this organic image of growth — the words "vitality," "energy," and "vigor" reappear frequently as Newman reiterates Caswall's account of the remarkable growth, from a condition of near ruin, of nineteenth-century

---

21. J. H. Newman, *Apologia pro Vita Sua,* Part V (London: J. M. Dent and Sons Ltd., 1912), pp. 101-146.

Episcopalianism in numbers and resources. And this account Newman ties to his vision of embodied catholicity: American Episcopalianism, bound to the Prayer Book's exemplified faith as given through the Church of England, represents a lived connection of the actual church with the world's unfolding history.

Although Newman makes much of the Americans' adoption of the formal elements of "Catholic" life in the shape of apostolic "succession" of bishops and of a realist eucharistic devotion (cf. pp. 336-42), these aspects are essential as being expressive of this deeper historical connection — something he calls a "creative principle" (p. 335) at work in the Episcopal Church's very being, like a seed growing from some invisible source into the fullness of her divine nature. Her external form and her doctrine stand together (cf. his discussion on pp. 364ff.) as the articulation of the scriptured figuration of this history, given in the narrative of the Fall, Redemption, and Consummation of the human race, explicated through Israel and enacted within the temporal experience of the nations and peoples brought within the sway of this divine work. As it moves and is apprehended backwards and forwards, this history itself displays the Body of Christ — and the Episcopal Church is exemplifying it!, Newman enthuses.

And so Newman began his essay with an almost ecstatic claim: "Few passages in the history of the church are better calculated to raise the Christian heart in admiration and gratitude to the giver of all good, than her fortunes in the United States, fortunes which have a still greater promise in the future, than a present accomplishment." But not all is well. For by the end of his long reflection, the "promise" seems blighted by the particular constraints America herself has placed upon this hope. Newman adopts a phrase of Caswall to describe these constraints in terms of "extraneous influences," working from the social context of the Episcopal Church's life and in a sense corrupting the outworking of the grand "catholic and apostolic idea" that was sown in its heart (cf. pp. 342ff.). These "influences," in Newman's analysis, derive from the religious character of the United States itself — the multiplication of sects; and from the adaptation of American Anglicanism to the national dynamics of economic and intellectual life — self-preservation, material security, and reciprocal restraint against the intrusion of others.

In one of the most telling passages of this "negative" accounting, Newman describes the confluence of a number of these peculiarly American influences, and unveils the full potential force of their work upon the spiritual witness of Episcopalians. Growing up within a culture of political and religious choice, in which proliferating denominational allegiances are encouraged and protected, the "catholic" principle is reduced to a religious "preference," and with this comes the whole undercutting of the historical unity and embracing thrust of the Gospel's witness. Newman points to the debates at the founding conventions of the Episcopal Church in the 1780's, in which numerous representatives worried over the "divisive" potential of a strongly "creedal" form of Christianity, that might somehow press for an embodied unitary faith amid the new Republic's valorization of diversity (cf. pp. 344ff.). "Socinianism," as Newman calls the anti-creedal and Unitarian impulse of this outlook, inevitably becomes entrenched among a people whose concern is to maintain a realm of security for individuals whose public mission is transferred from evangelical goals to economic ones. "Secure from all her foes," as Bradstreet wrote. There is, as Tocqueville also noted, a kind of paradoxical relationship between a fixation upon individual meaning and individual life amid the threats of a vast and unwelcoming world, and the search for a place of "generalized" benevolence and departicularized demand. "A trading country is the *habitat* of Socinianism," Newman notes (p. 347). For

> commerce is free as air; it knows no distinctions, mutual intercourse is its medium of operation. Exclusiveness, separations, rules of life, observance of days, nice scruples of conscience, are odious to it. . . . A religion which neither irritates their reason nor interferes with their comfort, will be all in all in such a society. Severity whether of creed or precept, high mysteries, corrective practices, subjection of whatever kind, whether to a doctrine or to a priest, will be offensive to them. They need nothing to fill the heart, to feed upon, or to live in; they despise enthusiasm, they abhor fanaticism, they persecute bigotry. . . . Reason teaches them that utter disregard of their Maker is unbecoming; and they determine to be religious, not from love and fear, but from good sense. (pp. 348ff.)

Whether all this springs up in a field as it were forcibly "cleared," politically, for commerce, or the reverse, Newman does not say. But he details the frightening consequences of such a social ordering of individual religious preference for the sake of unobstructed and self-assertive material advancement. In the first place, the continuities of human life in Christ are ignored and even destroyed: in such a society as this, the poor are written off and the deep yearnings of the desperately needy, which can be fulfilled only through a substantive, particularistic, and exclusive (because focused) Gospel of redemption, are covered over so that common human failing can be repulsed from the self's consciousness. "If [the trading person] thinks of religion at all, he will not like from being a great man to become a little one; he bargains for some or other compensation to his self-importance, some little power of judging or managing, some small permission to have his own way" (p. 348). And "his own way" means the veiling of the world's poor and humble in favor of personal "comfort" and material ease, which themselves are but the mask of a frightened self hiding from the encroachments of death and sin. Although congratulating, with Caswall, the material advancement of the Episcopal Church in building and financial resources, Newman realizes that, in the end, such success and celebration may be a sign of a terrible disease, rather than of blessing.[22]

Secondly, by so restricting religious meaning to the support of individual security, the very power of God in Christ to save, to work for the redemption of the world and her peoples, is obscured and finally denied. If salvation is tied to a personal preference, it is also reduced to a moment and confined in a corner. In the one place where Newman avails himself of some other perspective upon America than Caswall's, he turns to James Fenimore Cooper's novel *The Pioneers,* and its description of an Anglican divine seeking to establish a congregation in the eighteenth-century forests of upstate New York. In two episodes of this book, Cooper recounts how the priest's attempts to use the Prayer Book liturgy and to communicate a vital knowledge of the Christian mysteries of salvation to frontiersmen and Native Americans are inevitably circumscribed by a perception of their superficial value as "mere forms" of religious self-expression. The frontier families respond to the preacher and to his personal style, not to the prayers of the catholic church that draw together the living and the dead; the Indian meets his death at the end of the novel on his own terms, turning to his own "great Spirit," which is judged "right for him" by his American friends, even as Mr. Grant, the Anglican minister who stands beside the dying warrior, proffering him the truths of the ancient gospel, is

---

22. Cf. Caswall's extended and finally grating emphasis upon quantifiable figures — money raised, buildings constructed, the form and "elegance" of Episcopal parishes, membership statistics, higher social classes represented.

left visibly ignored, prattling uselessly, in the paltry comforts of his own beliefs.[23] In the context of the "primeval" forests and the passions of "uncivilized" settlers and indigenous peoples, the church here stands in Newman's eyes not only accused, but convicted and, from the American perspective, openly accepted as being neither catholic nor apostolic in the power of its life.

Newman perceives, with Tocqueville, that the "democratic" character of American society is somehow tied to all of this, and he expresses an almost shrill concern over the Episcopal Church's subjection of episcopal council at diocesan and national conventions to agreement with lay and clerical deputies (pp. 360ff.), individuals with neither the office certainly, nor the grace, to govern the church's formal life. And with Tocqueville he raises the possibility that "Catholicism" as he defines it stands as the only real alternative to the creeping "pantheism" that must finally take hold of the democratic search for individual freedom within the "cleared field" of mutual self-protection. Tocqueville, for his part, saw this as an opportunity for Catholicism's growth in America[24] — Protestantism would prove too empty a draught in the end for truly spiritual thirsts — but Newman at this stage is not so sure. Indeed, although the later "Roman Catholic" note he appends to his essay on the "Anglo-American Church" makes clear that a "worldly vitality" among this or that Protestant and Anglican church means little in comparison with the true "life" that (Roman) Catholicism spreads and embodies around the globe, he voices an overall anxiety that local or regional influences so characterize a church — even a purportedly "catholic" one — that it becomes but the expression of the individual, and not the history of the race in God's hands. Thus he remarks of all churches but the Roman that "they depend on time and place for their existence, they live in periods or in regions. They are children of the soil, indigenous plants, which readily flourish under a certain temperature, in a certain aspect, in moist or in dry, and die if they are transplanted" (p. 384).[25] Can Catholicism be "localized"?

American Catholicism, in its Anglican form at least, Newman hesi-

---

23. Cf. James Fenimore Cooper, *The Leatherstocking Tales* (New York: The Library of America, 1985), vol. 1, *The Pioneers*, pp. 8-11, 38-41, 95-130, 420-31, 454-65.

24. Alexis de Tocqueville, *De la Démocratie en Amérique* (Paris: Garnier, 1981), vol. 2, I:6-7 (pp. 39-42).

25. Cf. also *Apologia*, pp. 108f., where the "future of Anglicanism" in general is discussed in similar terms.

tantly predicts, is threatened with a kind of horrible desiccation of faith, fixated upon self and locality and personal need, "disguising" histories and commonalities and continuities of need and redemption, and so veiling with its own "disguise" God himself in his reality of Christ and Cross. The result? A "drying up of the seas" (pp. 348-50), that is, of the sea of God's own mysterious abysses and sovereign purposes; and with it the very death of Christianity through the obscuring of the redemptive scope of Christ in the Church as it reaches into the dark depths of human life.

To summarize Newman's vision of "Catholicism," detailed through its American dangers, we see something close enough to Cyril's definition: the grasping of commonalities in the redemptive power of Christ within and across the nations; a grasp, furthermore, that demands an attention to the reality of these peoples impinging upon oneself; a going out of self and a transformative encounter with "the other" (as we say today) — the Indian, the poor, the English, the immigrant — each one given particularistically in Christ; the encounter of these and other particularities in Christ that strips the self to such a point that at last it can be apprehended by God's own depth; and finally the reality of "grace" as involving the giving of one's self over to a history embracing the very world, and not just touching a place nearby, and hence, in a way, grace as leaving one's own powers dangling in time for another's use.

## American Concerns with the "Catholicism" of Newman's Stripe

We have elsewhere, and in a way congruent with this broad sense of "Catholicism," described "communion" in an ecclesial sense as the Body of Christ, in the integrity of its temporal life and witness, expressing itself in mission; and in the course of this mission, subjecting itself to the demands of such an encounter with new members of the Body and to the changes wrought in Christ through it.[26] The context of this description was precisely the conflicts and estrangements that have arisen within Anglicanism over the past months, which have pitted American and African or Asian — we might even note in some cases, white American and African American

26. *Communion in Discipline,* esp. Part IV (Colorado Springs: Anglican Communion Institute, 2004), pp. 29-40.

— against one another. The character and imperative of "conciliarism" as an alternative way of life, wherein decisions are made in subjection to the "whole," and wherein the "whole" is understood as the breadth of time's teaching in the Body in a way that extends beyond local borders and constricted epochs — all this is embedded in this kind of view of communion, as is a flexible and adjustable form of hierarchicalism that can order such "subjections in council" in a way that holds accountable the determining force of the Body's breadth.

But this is also exactly what seems so difficult to assimilate into the constraining focus of American sensibilities. Whether one came in search of a "new start" or was surprised by its possibility, or even the failure of its hopes, the land confronted Americans with something inescapable that seemed to truncate the continuities of historically forged bonds, such as the Catholic understanding the Body of Christ assumes. In its place, as we know from the imagery of American religion even in its unreflective start, history was rewritten by the landscape and its inhabiting peoples and their mutual encounter, in terms of "wilderness" or "Eden." And these terms were ever re-injected with an astonishment at the sheer creative mystery of the terrain and tribes (again, whether barbaric or edenic) in such a way as to brush aside all conceptions of the *human* past in favor of some vision of actual and immediate generation. One can still catch something of this sense, for instance, by traversing the strange landscapes of Utah, where it seems as if the cover of the world has been stripped away so as to glimpse into the workshop or laboratory of the Creator himself, as he invents new and seemingly alien wonders. This is a passing response that nonetheless replicates the enveloping perceptions of immigrants and explorers from their first encounter five hundred years ago, and informed the very construction of the "new nation."[27]

The search among immigrants for "new beginnings," religious and economic, that were then inextricably bound to the imposed vision of geo-

27. Cf. the classic popular account in Howard Mumford Jones, *O Strange New World. American Culture: The Formative Years* (New York: Viking Press, 1952), chapters 1, 2, and 10, with some of its rich primary source references; Frederick W. Turner, *Beyond Geography: The Western Spirit Against the Wilderness* (New York: Viking Press, 1980), for a more sweeping social-psychological theory ; Max Oelschlaeger, *The Idea of Wilderness from Prehistory to the Age of Ecology* (New Haven: Yale University Press, 1991), esp. ch. 4, pp. 97-132, on the European philosophical categories that began to offer intellectual ballast for these views of "wild nature."

graphical newness, created a potion of almost boiling anxiety over enslavement of the self to a human past — to the "old Europe," for instance, of the Puritans' disdain and fantastical nightmare; as well as to a charted human future that could somehow transcend the powers of immediate creation. I have already suggested that the proper way to describe religiously this outlook is that of "primordialism," given in either innocence or Fall: loosened from the Fall, or still struggling in its first and unrehearsed meaning. Either way, the self in this religious need demanded some space of release from time.

We are familiar with the eighteenth-century political forms of this contrast, for example, in the anti-Federalist search for a society of regenerated and purely held local virtue uncorrupted by the impediments and burdens of past (or vast) cultures, a vision of the nation's purpose that was held in bitter argument with the Federalist constitutional ordering of checks and balances, designed to protect sinners one from another (and from the "constitution of human nature" itself, as Hamilton put it[28]), even while freeing them for productive life under the emerged guidance of a higher reason. We can even observe what at first appears to be the strange combination of the two visions, as in Washington's Farewell Address, where he perorates on the need for the virtuous citizen, even while he counsels a vigorous mistrust of other nations and peoples, and a policy of vigilant self-protection. But once the religious intuitions for this debate, deriving from different emphases of a more profound and single primordialist fixation, are noted, we can see that Washington, among others, was merely expressing, to a contentious audience, the imperatives of their common root.

And the more explicitly religious inventions of America — what Paul Conkin has called the "American Originals" of the Disciples, Unitarian-Universalists, Adventists and Witnesses, Mormons, Christian Scientists, and Pentecostal churches — each constitutes an offshoot from this common primordialist stock.[29] And each, through their various gnostic, hermetic, rationalist, or restorationist propheticisms, have attempted somehow to stake out a space within the wilderness for the experiment of

---

28. *Federalist Paper* 15.

29. Paul K. Conkin, *American Originals: Homemade Varieties of Christianity* (Chapel Hill: University of North Carolina Press, 1997). This is one of the best overviews of religious re-creationism in America, providing many useful elements for theological analysis (even though it offers none itself).

spiritual virginity. The "pantheist" temptation that Tocqueville suggested as being endemic to democratic societies, we can see, is not simply driven by the search for unity on the part of a multiplied and divided citizenry of discrete individuals, but is even more so the intuition of created commonality, inhabiting the first corners of a still-uncivilized, unsubjected world. If you are first, you hold the key to the life of everyone else, and of all other worlds.

Thus, from the beginning of the United States' religious self-reflection, "sectarianism" positively seen as the proliferation of various and unconnected local spiritual self-assertions, was understood to be a vehicle of truth as well as of self-protection. In all their ramifications and individual trivializations of doctrine and moral demand, America's endless stream of denominations could actually articulate their more common subterranean meaning, bubbling up from the springs of original reason, original encounter with God, original facing off of evil, original glory, so leading to the apprehension of the deeper truths of the divine life. This is what the ex-Unitarian and transcendentalist Theodore Parker meant when, on the one hand, he castigated Christians for failing to arrive at a clear understanding of the "first principles" of their faith — the "absolute morality and religion" of love for God and man — and on the other hand celebrated the intrinsically American pursuit of novelty, practicality, disdain for tradition, and temporal impatience. For these very characteristics that mark the nation's unsubsiding sectarianism will serve to strip away veneers and pretenses, and finally uncover the "universal truth" that marks pure religious knowledge: "The Roman Church has been all men know what and how; the American Church, with freedom for the mind, freedom for the heart, freedom for the soul, is yet to be, sundering no chord of the human harp, *but tuning all to harmony.*"[30] Sectarianism itself becomes a new kind of "Catholicism" — the "American Church" — the entry into the mysteries of original truth and the sentinel of religious "essence." (The religion of "diversity" is a direct, if pallid, offspring of this conviction.) It was a view already expressed by pre-revolutionary Protestants a century earlier, in the arguments against appointing Anglican bishops for America, when they

---

30. Theodore Parker, "The Transient and Permanent in Christianity" (1842), in *Theodore Parker: An Anthology,* ed. Henry Steele Commager (Boston: Beacon Press, 1960), pp. 38-62; and "The Political Destination of America and the Signs of the Times" (1848), in the same volume, pp. 169-83, esp. pp. 182ff.

claimed that "Catholicism" was not a term to be possessed by a single Christian group, but could only refer to the profession of Christianity's "essentials," something done by "Lutheran, Calvinist, Congregation, Consociated, Presbyterian, Baptist, Quaker *and all other churches of America*."[31]

All. All in their diversity, all in their localities, all in their burrowing into the heart of God's own original purposes, in the land of originals. One could analyze more systematically the theological interests of this common and focalized burrowing, and in doing so I think one area one would need to concentrate upon is its specifically "pneumatist" character, one that informs the restorationist, Gnostic, and transcendentalist embodiments of American religion together. It would include, even, the still-too-little understood character of so-called "Americanism" among Roman Catholics. And certainly the "sentimental" appropriation of pneumatic universalism by mainline Protestants, including Episcopalians right down to the present presiding bishop.[32] But we are here more concerned with the his-

---

31. *The Centinel No. 1,* from the *Pennsylvania Journal,* March 24, 1768, in John F. Wilson, ed., *Church and State in American History* (Boston: D. C. Heath and Co., 1965), p. 57.

32. Although it makes no pretence at systematic analysis, and leaving aside the inadequate predictive character of the book, I still consider Harold Bloom's *The American Religion: The Emergence of the Post-Christian Nation* (New York: Simon and Schuster, 1992) to be the most astute reflection on the lived shape of this pneumatic emphasis of American religious character. Leander Harding has acutely applied Bloom's thesis to the homosexual religious quest within, e.g. the American Episcopal Church, in his essay "Homosexuality and the American Religion," at www.anglicancommunioninstitute.org. On the odd story of the "Americanist" error and its pneumatist implications, see the Introduction by Joseph Chinnici to his anthology *Devotion to the Holy Spirit in American Catholicism* (New York: Paulist Press, 1985), pp. 3-90. The tendency, in the latter volume as among other commentators, has been to downplay the actual concerns of the Vatican on this matter, an impulse belied (it seems to me) by the evidence: Isaac Hecker's so-called "romantic" religious motives, pressing him into and through the formation of a particularly American Catholicism, included some very basic primordialist visions, in which the Holy Spirit clearly was seen as opening the individual human heart to a renewed entrance into the "Paradise" once lost, now regained. (Cf. Isaac T. Hecker, *Isaac T. Hecker, the Diary: Romantic Religion in Ante-Bellum America,* ed. John Farina [New York: Paulist Press, 1988], pp. 275ff.) This is not to imply some basic heresy at work. But even the defense of "traditionalism" by self-conscious "American" Roman Catholics in the mid-nineteenth century was sufficiently constrained by this vision that democratic ideals were transformable only within the context of this kind of primordialist pneumatism, now deployed in favor of some larger scheme (cf. the admittedly diverse efforts of Orestes Brownson, especially in his transitional period into Catholicism). Much of this is still embedded in contemporary American Roman Catholic sensibilities, despite the structural press, over the last century and renewed in the present day, for a clearly

torical, and thus intrinsically pragmatic, settlement of this attitude, where it has "landed" in the vision and expectation of inhabited experience. And this place, as our argument goes, is the land of beginnings, origins, and the encounter with those origins' demands and limits: Cain and his children, seeking some immediate reconstitution of the immediate "face of God,"[33] struggling with the closeness of family, with the malignity of heart and the forlornness of love destroyed, wandering to the edges of the earth, extracting from the earth gifts God does not accept, building cities within which to hold a peace that is found ever wanting.

The image of Cain, in fact, has had enormous appeal for Americans. It very quickly stepped out from the general Christian tradition (mainly Augustinian) of its use as a parsing of human and world history. Once confronting the image's sensed reality anew in the form, first, of Native Ameri-

---

ultramontane understanding of the church. One of the areas this has been most evident, perhaps oddly, is in the realm of biblical scholarship, where the embrace of historical criticism over the past decades has in fact been buttressed by a renewed hermeneutic pneumatism that allows for the continued application of the primordialist deconstruction of the biblical text into its "original" constituents. The alliance, for instance, of modernism with mysticism in the late nineteenth century, and of this with historical criticism, is telling. Cf. Gerald P. Fogarty, S.J., *American Catholic Biblical Scholarship: A History from the Early Republic to Vatican II* (San Francisco: Harper and Row, 1989), pp. 58-119, 140-170 (where this phenomenon is interestingly linked to Episcopalian scholarship in the person of Charles Augustus Briggs). On the Episcopal front, William Porcher DuBose's *The Reason of Life* (New York: Longmans, Green, and Co., 1911) offers an extended and classic explication of the pneumatic-evolutionary thinking that has come to be definitive of official American Anglicanism up to the present day (cf. the analysis, using somewhat different, although related categories, of the current ECUSA Presiding Bishop's theology, in the unpublished essay of Robert Sanders, "Mystical Paganism: An Analysis of the Presiding Bishop's Public Statements"; cf. also his "The Ecstatic Heresy"; both are available on his website: http://users.iglide.net/rjsanders/). The question of specifically American Episcopalian vs. British Anglican pneumatism is interesting; the former's more palpably-linked American Gnostic genealogy (via a context of richly saturated rationalist pietism [as Tocqueville and Newman sensed], later explicitly impregnated with Swedenborgian instincts) seems to me better attested than the latter's more philosophically idealistic-Hegelian origins (although the explicitly Gnostic character of Anglican spirituality via William Law and others remains to be charted).

33. This search for pristine "conversation with God" is the great "American" spiritual quest, noted by so many, and still deeply alluring. Cf. extended evaluative discussion of the Ephrata Community by Joseph Needleman in his neo-gnostic and highly popular *The American Soul: Rediscovering the Wisdom of the Founders* (New York: Penguin Putnam Inc., 2002), pp. 290-314.

can and then of slavery's peculiar curse (the Indian and African as "Cain," intractably and recalcitrantly in their midst), the image became indigenized in the United States and severed from its global context. In its face, ever struggling for a racialist purity that simply would not emerge, the figure of Cain was gradually transformed into some internalized explicator of unfulfilled innocence and repeated fall, some hoped-for and impossible regeneracy, that finally found its grand historical embodiment in the fratricidal conflagration of the Civil War. After which, quite simply, Cain becomes the tragic hero of all America and for all its time.[34]

And in the process, "catholicism," in the tradition of Augustine's world-embracing "City of Abel,"[35] is made the iconically slaughtered virtue of the American Religion itself. The world and her peoples totter and disappear behind the stage of the peculiar American destiny. Primordialism and provincialism, the Land of Nod as the tragic yet homely sect, become co-efficients. Anti-catholicism, in this sense, *is* embedded in the historical consciousness and lived understanding of the religious vocation of America. And if there is to be an "American Catholicism," it can only be one that finds its vocation within the landscape of Cain himself.[36]

34. On all of this, cf. Ricardo Quinones, *The Changes of Cain: Violence and the Lost Brother in the Cain and Abel Literature* (Princeton: Princeton University Press, 1991), esp. pp. 136-66 and notes. On the use of Cain as a figure of the "cursed" black (or sometimes Native American) race, see David M. Goldenberg, *The Curse of Ham: Race and Slavery in Early Judaism, Christianity, and Islam* (Princeton: Princeton University Press, 2003), ch. 13, "The Curse of Cain," pp. 178-82, and the extensive notes on pp. 357-62. On the racial conflicts involved in the "American Cain," cf. the poems of Phillis Wheatley ("On Being Brought from Africa to America") and Longfellow ("The Slave in the Dismal Swamp"); on the racialist search for purity this and other biblical images informed, cf. Eric Kaufmann, "American Exceptionalism Reconsidered: Anglo-Saxon Ethnogenesis in the 'Universal' Nation, 1776-1850," *Journal of American Studies* (1999).

35. Cf. Augustine's *City of God,* 15:1-8, 17ff.; 18:51.

36. Ray Allen Billington's *The Protestant Crusade, 1800-1886: A Study in the Origins of American Nativism* (New York: The Macmillan Co., 1938, repr. Chicago: Quadrangle Books, 1964) is the classic exposition of the religious, intellectual, and political meaning of nineteenth-century anti-catholicism in the United States. Despite criticisms that it is overly focused on religious attitudes as a root cause of American "nativism," the book deserves careful rereading, especially in the present. More recently, see Jenny Franchot, *Roads to Rome: The Antebellum Protestant Encounter with Catholicism* (Berkeley: University of California Press, 1994). See also the references in footnote 1 above. There is no question in my mind, on the basis of the wide literature of anti-Romanism — that includes journalism, fiction, biography, philosophy, theology, politics, and medicine from the seventeenth century

## Episcopal Catholicism

If we turn back to the actual character of Anglican "Catholicism" in America, we find matters constrained very much in the way Newman himself, for all his distance and abstraction, suspected; and furthermore for reasons that are peculiarly tied to the primordialist fixations of the nation as a whole. But it is this constraint within the bonds of these reasons that makes the catholic struggle within America so critical in a theological sense.

Newman's sense of "catholicism" as an organic connectionalism, the bonds of an expanding life and history that draw peoples together, and in doing so express the actual reality of God's absolute reach within the temporal order of redemption, is something repeatedly alluded to in Episcopalian apologetics from the early nineteenth century on. "Catholicism" meant a genetic link with the Church of England, with the character of her teaching and formal witness, and within the structure of her ordered and continuous life, embodied in the episcopacy.[37] "Apostolic succession" as an essential element of catholicity, while certainly an articulated focus of more High Church sensibilities early on, was nonetheless a given, by definition, in the general Episcopal Church's self-promotion within the spectrum of American religion.

But the claim to catholic apostolicity and connection was characterized in a special way by Episcopalian apologists, who were often eager to distinguish their history from England's as being somehow "purer" in its

---

on — that there is something almost pathologically deep-seated in the American psyche that revolts against Roman Catholicism's forms and figures. And American Roman Catholics share the disease!

37. This was a central principle of the Episcopal Church, enshrined in the Preface to its 1789 Prayer Book, and reiterated many times, e.g. at the 1814 Convention, by an explicit resolution of the House of Bishops (the House of Deputies concurring), that the Episcopal Church and the Church of England in America prior to the Revolution "are the same body," and share the same "religious principle, in doctrine, or in worship, or in discipline," despite their different "names," a distinction "induced" by the different civil arrangements under which they now live. Cf. Christopher Wordsworth and Hugh Davey Evans, *Theophilus Americanus; or Instruction for the Young Student concerning the Church, and the American Branch of It* (Philadelphia: H. Hooker, 1852), pp. 314-18, 351-54; or the representative and widely distributed apology by Arthur Wilde Little, *Reasons for Being a Churchman. Addressed to English Speaking Christians of Every Name* (Milwaukee: The Young Churchman Co., 1885), pp. 174ff.

form. This was most commonly described in terms of the American church's freedom from state control, an element worked out in the colonial arguments against Protestant fears over the shape of an American episcopacy,[38] but quickly embraced in the new church with a convert's enthusiasm: the "voluntary" character of American Episcopalianism, its immersion in the disciplines of individual freedom and democracy, made of its "catholic" inheritance a kind of ever-renewed grace, re-created by sheer desire and will, and without the heavy hand of government demand, at every moment.[39] This, of course, was articulated as a quintessentially "Anglican" form of catholicism itself, in contrast with the corruptions of Roman imperialism. It was an argument easily assimilated, several decades later, by the movement of historical criticism in scriptural studies which was tied, by Episcopalian apologists, to the Anglican freedoms of individually inspired readers, universally set loose in their own fields of personal religious scrutiny and discovery.[40]

More revealingly, this regenerate — and unoppressive! — Catholicism was ascribed to the peculiar history of the American nation itself. The story of the re-invention of Anglicanism after the Revolution's destruction of the colonial Church of England's *raison d'être* had already gained an almost mythic grandeur, as can be seen in Caswall's description.[41] But the politico-theological analysis to which this episode was subjected went beyond extolling an act of divine mercy in preserving a threatened church. Simply put, the Revolution had provided Catholicism in America a new and pristine birth, by tearing apart the relationship of church to (the Eng-

38. This was not an unambiguous debate even among American Anglicans. Cf. Nancy L. Rhoden, *Revolutionary Anglicanism: The Colonial Church of England Clergy during the American Revolution* (New York: New York University Press, 1999), esp. pp. 134ff. Some of the pre-revolutionary arguments with non-Anglicans over an American episcopacy can be found in standard documentary histories of American religion, e.g. David Turley, ed., *American Religion: Literary Sources and Documents* (Mountfield, U. K.: Helm Information, 1998), vol. 1, pp. 354ff.

39. Cf. New York bishop John Henry Hobart's essay *The United States of America Compared with Some European Countries, Particularly England* (London: John Miller, 1826).

40. Cf. Alexander V. G. Allen, *Freedom in the Church, or The Doctrine of Christ as the Lord hath commanded, and as this Church hath received the same according to the Commandments of God* (New York: Macmillan Co., 1907), pp. 30-41.

41. Caswall, *America, and the American Church,* pp. 161-98; the incident was reviewed by Newman himself with excitement, as one still committed to Keble's original call for a disentanglement of church and state in his influential 1833 sermon on "national apostasy."

lish) state, thereby reducing the church to a state of almost pure innocence: dioceses could be formed, councils gathered, bishops elected by the people, structures reordered from within an almost Rousseauian "state of nature," "not-quite-anarchy," as one writer put it admiringly, because there was always England, hovering somewhere on the other side of the sea, a memory and a justification, however and happily distant.[42]

This is Catholicism-as-Adam; but the Adam who himself creates and forges and figures out. Not the New Adam in whom all humanity is taken up through the lineaments of a self-giving and expansive Body; but the one who finds himself alone, in a strange land, impelled by the memories and the dangers of the divorce of Eden. And the mission of this Adam and his progeny, the mission of Cain, is to labor, to protect, to build, wherever he can find safety.

To look at the self-description of Episcopal missionaries in the nineteenth century, is to wonder at the energies expended, even while being taken aback at the self-limitations imposed. The great Daniel Tuttle, missionary bishop to Utah and the West, seems the epitome of both Newman's hopes and anxieties about American Anglican Catholics. Sent out as a young cleric, traveling the Platte, passing through Denver and the mountains, and finally after months to the Great Salt Lake, he set about building schools and hospitals. But the motive of these great efforts was surprisingly modest: to provide a socially acceptable instance of the catholic life, without impinging overly on the many other varieties of religious expression he found along the way. The Indians were too itinerant to deal with and required a "whole life" of going native to reach (something impossible for "builders" and perhaps best left to Roman Catholic celibates and eccentrics); the Mormons were too well-established to dare threaten, and were, in any case, sincere and well-meaning people; and the Methodists and Baptists were all earnest sorts better equipped for dealing with the lower classes in any case.[43] The diversity of Christian mission, for Tuttle, was part

42. Wordsworth and Evans, *Theophilus Americanus*, pp. 318ff., where the American editor of Wordsworth's English handbook inserts a lengthy essay on the origin of governments and of the Episcopal Church's in particular. Evans actually rejects Rousseau's theory of the "social compact": there is never a "literal state of anarchy" in history; rather only a moment when God creates some order within the midst of a kind of ethereal state between either nothingness and being or between "old and new."

43. D. S. Tuttle, *Reminiscences of a Missionary Bishop* (New York: Thomas Whittaker, 1906). Cf. pp. 104ff.; pp. 165ff.

of the "democratizing" spirit of the nation, in which catholicism itself ought to find its special place, its native root, its original spring; hence, it was inherently self-limiting in its manifestations.

Thus Anglican self-assertions regarding "apostolic succession," which in theory completely trumped the legitimacy of every other American denomination, in practice found their "integralist" pretensions met by the accepted impermeability of individual strivings, and devolved at most into a kind of cultural *hauteur* wed to a kindly *noblesse oblige*.[44] When William Ingraham Kip was sent out as a missionary bishop to California a decade earlier even than Tuttle, this scholarly East Coast intellectual proved his mettle by bunking and bedding with the roughest men in his train. But he despised the crudeness of the gold-seekers, lamented the ineffectual fruit of the Spanish Roman Catholics, and consigned the native Indians to some "better suited" missionary group, still to be identified. In doing so, he offered Episcopalian catholicism as a means of raising the spiritual sights of California's growing urban centers, and pointing to the "invisible realm" of divine life amid a too-rugged materialist and visible society.[45]

This too represented a hope for building some new "city on a hill" (San Francisco, in this case), one that would civilize the more barbarous forms of life the California frontier had unleashed. But however refined his vision, it was a version of catholicism bound to denominational "preference," embedded as a principle at the founding of the Episcopal Church after the Revolution,[46] and so disdained by Newman. And the "Whig" dismissal of any profound sense of the episcopacy that Voltaire himself observed while visiting England long before,[47] turned out to be an under-

44. Cf. my article "The Theological Accoutrements of Anti-Pluralism: The Confused Fate of American Episcopalianism," *Journal of Anglican Studies* 2.1 (June 2004), 22-39.

45. See Kip's account of his 1856 journey through the San Joaquin Valley, in *A California Pilgrimage* (Fresno: N.p., 1921), esp. pp. 27ff, 44ff. On Kip's religious role in bringing a catholic luster to California's barbaric shores, see Kevin Starr, *America and the California Dream, 1850-1915* (Santa Barbara: Peregrine Smith, Inc., 1981), pp. 83-85, 105-9; on the primordialist imagery held by the American religious missionaries to California, see Ch. 3 as a whole, pp. 69-109. Kip's *Double Witness of the Church* (Philadelphia: Richard McCauley, 1849) remains a classic exposition of American Episcopalian "catholic" ecclesiology.

46. Cf. the preface of William White's 1782 *The Case of the Episcopal Churches in the United States Considered*.

47. Cf. Voltaire, 5th of his *Lettres Philosophiques*, on "The Anglican Religion," where he begins with the statement that "This is the land of sects. An Englishman, since he is a free man, goes to Heaven by whatever route he wishes," and later points out that, while the Tories

lying pull even among High Church Episcopalians within the democratic United States, filled with the sowing and the reaping of original choices.

From the point of view of Episcopalians, then, American anti-Romanism was different in character than the English repugnance at political treason and irrationalism associated with "popery" in the sixteenth and seventeenth centuries. Roman Catholicism, for Episcopalians, was instead berated as a religion intent on limiting the creative energies, possibilities, and hopes of Americans, whoever they might be, and wherever they might choose to settle themselves. The Roman religion, it was asserted, drew individuals into a realm outside their own burrowing, encountering, deciding. It was not, of course, possible simply to dismiss Roman Catholics, as other Protestants did, since they at least had the appearance of some "apostolic form." And thus, a peculiar tension is seen in the Episcopalian depictions of Catholics, with an ambivalence far more profound than among most British Anglicans. Bishop Kip, for instance, was a historian before his election as a missionary bishop, and was one of the first Americans to study sympathetically from original documents the Jesuit missions in America (even before Parkman).[48] Thus, for Kip the "Jesuits" were worthy of reflection largely because of their astonishing personal sacrifice, even though they were guilty of a kind of oppression, their "superstitions and errors [breaking] a noble spirit" within the Indian who "might otherwise have lived for years, a light in the wilderness." These two elements — sacrificial energy and error — combined to paint a picture of worrying fanaticism.[49]

But for Kip it went beyond that. He could still recollect the Christian virtue of self-sacrifice for another's soul as something valuable from the past and from the universal store of Christian treasure and could also note its general absence from American religion as a lost artifact. He reminds

---

are for bishops, the Whigs care less about "apostolic succession" than about Parliamentary legitimation. Subtract the civil apparatus from this observation, and the American scene rises up with looming shadows.

48. William Ingraham Kip, *The Early Jesuit Missions in North America* [1846] (Albany: Pease & Prentice, 1866), p. xii.

49. Cf. Tuttle's view of the Mormons on this score. Admiring of many of their religious values (including their "sacramentalism"!), and of their utter commitment to the faith especially in terms of "missionary zeal," he is also repulsed by the "undemocratic" character of their polity and social life: "their priestly domination is un-American and anti-American." See his *Reminiscences,* with a long chapter devoted solely to the Mormons; citation from p. 355.

his readers, with a tone of special pleading, that Anglicans have their own missionary heroes (he mentions Henry Martyn and Bishop George Augustus Selwyn of New Zealand, a short enough list, and one without room for any Americans). Hence his unresolved admiration of the Jesuits — internally struggling in the same vein as Parkman and Prescott did in their vast histories of Catholic imperialism in the Americas. Nonetheless, Kip's final reaction was one of horror at the self-effacement of these "sons of Loyola," given that their labors bore so little permanent fruit in his eyes. Theirs was a sacrifice with little to show for it, inefficacious in its personal profligacy. It is almost as if he recoils at the impediments to human success strewn by the Fall itself, and taken up only through the suffering of a crucified Christ granted a history in the church.[50] Kip's turning away from this vista towards a more accessible and goal-oriented mission was not simply a mark of American shallowness; it was Cain's denial and escape. And in the conflicted catholicism of the Episcopal Church, it was finally enunciated in terms of a simple yet profound *distaste:* surely, such sacrifice for another people is neither necessary if without visible fruit nor, because of that, prudent.

The ironic devolution of the "catholic" sensibility of American Anglicans into "niche group" religion, which so defines contemporary Episcopalianism (as well as other denominations), represents, therefore, less an explicit denial of the catholic motive than it does an almost *pre*-catholic sensibility regarding the potential reach of Cainite efforts, each in their individual striving sustainable as an image of all others, even while recognizing its own demanded, and often regretted, limitations. Like the anti-Federalist "Brutus" (*Paper* 1), this kind of religion could indeed "extend across the continent" and "realize the golden age" of humankind through the propagation of "free" and protected individual choices and questing. This was not an anti-imperialist attitude at all, and could occasionally reach world-embracing proportions, much as Mormonism could; but always couched in the parochial terms of localized virtue. As Bishop McCoskry of Michigan said in a sermon at St. Paul's Cathedral in London

---

50. Cf. Kip, *The Early Jesuit Missions in North America*, p. xiv: "Greater devotion to the cause than theirs has never been seen since the Apostles' days. Why then was this result [of always coming to naught]? If 'the blood of the martyrs be the seed of the Church,' why is this the only instance in which it has not proved so? Must there not have been something wrong in the whole system — some grievous errors mingled with their teaching, which thus denied them a measure of success proportioned to their efforts?"

in 1852, while discussing the particular role of American Episcopalianism as one portion of the "household" of the "Church of God": "We, as part of this household, have no common responsibilities. Of late our territorial possessions have been greatly enlarged. California, New Mexico, and Oregon have been added. Sooner or later Mexico and South America must come under Saxon control . . . and become the kingdoms and nations of God and of His Christ . . . even the walls of that old spiritual Jericho, Rome, will fall flat."[51] It was not too much to think that the "Abrahamic Promise" of the original "nations," clothed in the "Saxon" garb of American Episcopalianism, would somehow sweep up the New World with its native virtue; a hope that Kip himself would uneasily share. It was not "too much"; it was merely vain.

## Why Should We Care?

None of this supremely Americanized catholicism — neither the self-limitations in religious industry nor its occasional self-revelation of potential power — represents anything that Thoreau himself would have understood as a positive response to his plea to "get up" and do something about the Fall. But Kip's conflicted American conscience is not, in fact, wholly discontinuous with Thoreau's own preferred direction of delving into the world of nature's abyss unhampered by the tools of civilized America. Thoreau too sought to dwell within the shadow of the first Tree, to relive the savor of its fruit, and to recapture a world still struggling with its taste. In doing so, he reveled in the thrill of the first choices, the first challenges, even the first sufferings of a humanity only a step from Eden. As Richard Slotkin has pointed out, when Thoreau himself reflects upon Jesuit self-sacrifice, he recasts its Christian virtue — in a way not wholly unrelated to Kip's reflection — as but the pale shadow of a deeper violence embraced and suffered by "natural" humanity, and only recently visible among the American Indian. And this desirous burrowing into the realm of a more original and wild virtue expressed itself, in Thoreau's case, by his own intellectual vio-

51. Cited in Herklots, *The Church of England and the American Episcopal Church*, pp. 157f. Cf. the highly popular anti-Roman Catholic and jingoistic work by Bishop William Montgomery Brown, later deposed for atheism and communism, *The Church for Americans* (New York: Thomas Whittaker, 1896), which argues, among other things, why the Episcopal Church is the appropriate religion "for our [American] race."

lence against outsiders to his preserve, against the past, and against the con-temporary world built upon it.[52] Not a few contemporary conservative Christians in America sound uncannily like Thoreau in this regard.

That Episcopalianism could never embrace such a whole-hearted abandonment of the nearby and developed world of men and women and of their history, and that the American Anglican Church needed in fact to find ways of holding on to such realities if only through the forms of stud-ied nostalgia, was an expression of a still-clinging catholicism struggling with the accepted forms of original man, of Cain still striving and hiding at once (much as Genesis depicts him). And the repeated failures of this cath-olic character have conversely embodied the violences of originality seek-ing its place in a world of self-assertion, unmasking in its wake the re-demptive promise as an unexpected act of grace, terrible in the breadth of its scope and of its form. To a people ever living on the outskirts of Eden — that is, to the human race still somehow in search of Christ, to the chil-dren of Cain, to Americans — the catholic vocation must seem both an as-sault upon their panting and straining hearts, and the embattled token of a truly realistic redemption.

The violences of disdain, of neglect, of hypocrisy are well-known vices of Episcopalians — whether they are directed at the poor, or the foreign, or the untutored, or the dying, they are of a piece with all the violences of the world, in which each of our churches and our selves have participated. But they are rendered brilliantly crimson through the fact that they clothe a specifically *catholic* claim. This catholic claim has provided for Episcopa-lianism's most outrageous self-debasement. The current "tearing of the fabric" of ecumenical and communion bonds that the Episcopal Church has accomplished with such supreme oblivion and abandon through her self-proclaimed autonomous propheticism — enacted unflinchingly in Convention, diocese, and episcopal office — stands as a great symbol of the anti-catholic magnet that marks her American identity. But it is the brilliance of the wound and the wonder of the current's force that render the victim, the catholic promise of Christ's redeeming Body in the world, in such starkly clear lines. She has become a spectacle, this church, so that the world can see that Cain is being dragged into the presence of the new Adam.

52. Richard Slotkin, *Regeneration Through Violence: The Mythology of the American Frontier, 1600-1860* (Middletown: Wesleyan University Press, 1973), pp. 518-38, esp. 523, 528.

For there is a sense in which catholicism itself — even if we are impelled to identify it with Roman Catholicism — may lose America as a whole (much as it lost what is now the Arab world), if it does not come to grips with America's own primordialist character as it embodies the still-striving character of fallen humanity. And if Catholicism loses America, it risks losing also its open capacity to speak peace to the heaving bodies of Cain's children throughout the world. Roman Catholics too, like the Anglicans, risk a "drying of the seas," in Newman's phrase, if they ignore this challenge. The vocation of American catholics like Episcopalians is critical precisely because of their brazenly conflicted condition, because of the openness of the "wound" that is displayed before the world much in the manner of Israel's fall in Lamentations: "Is it nothing to you, all you who pass by? Look and see if there is any sorrow like my sorrow which was brought upon me, which the Lord inflicted on the day of his fierce anger" (1:12). Stand, look, listen, and see. Surely this *is* a divine vocation.

"Catholic"-oriented churches like the Episcopal and Lutheran, along with elements of American Roman Catholicism itself, are being wrenched and dragged to this place, where we can observe each other's flailings, where we can be shaken into a kind of hearing and seeing as we are held to account by a larger world, where we can see the Abel in the other, and hope in his resurrection. This is a novel kind of conciliarism, a strange new ecumenism of histories joined and made fertile, of self-giving filiation.

And that, for a world that still builds walls and holes or dreamily waits in its garden as the walls of others are torn down, is an intonation of the gospel that we might all properly stay to hear. When this dragging is engaged as a missionary enterprise, where the diversities of such denominational agonies, the shattering of the niches as it were, are willfully linked and subjected to the larger world's hearing, to the nations themselves (as today in the turmoil of the Anglican Communion's restless rising), then this struggle for a true conciliar Church becomes the tracing of a Cross many will astoundingly gaze upon, no longer fleeing from city to city. The "mark of Cain" will fulfill its promise. As Philo the Jew wrote longingly at the end of his treatise on *The Posterity and Exile of Cain*, might not the citizens of each town yet learn rightly to bring an end to the violence within their midst? "For faction and sedition, if we must speak the truth, is the archetypal model of wars," and once gone, so will pass the imitations of these originals that so flood the earth, so that all humankind might enjoy the peace that is the true service of God."[53] The struggle for American Catholicism is the struggle of the world's redemption; but it must be a struggle — that is, it must embrace even the American repudiation of its truth within the form of our parochial denominations — if truly it redeems.

53. In *The Works of Philo,* trans. C. D. Yonge (Peabody, Mass.: Hendrickson Publishers, 1993), p. 151.

PART II

# QUESTIONS OF AUTHORITY

# CHAPTER THREE

## Apprehending the Truth: Anglican Conservatism and Common Discernment

*Ephraim Radner*

The catholic character of communion represents a special way of "knowing" God. This is so, in particular, because of the historical nature of such communion knowledge, embedded in the temporal struggles of Christians to be molded into the body of Christ as a living being within the outworking of God's purposes. The current struggle for ECUSA's future, and indeed for the whole Anglican Communion's, offers a unique opportunity to clarify a number of crucial challenges: what we understand the church's character in history to be; how we think it faithful and reasonable as a church to orient our decision-making process within time; and what we apprehend as being the ties linking God's creatures — including ourselves as ecclesial creatures in this whole mix — to God's unfolding providential actions within the world, actions we know to be aimed at the "reconciliation" of all things in Christ's own Body (cf. Col. 1:15-20; Eph. 1:10).

There is no doubt that some uneasiness accompanies the recent wide embrace (among ecumenists anyway) of what is called "communion ecclesiology." The uneasiness stems, in part, from a sense that the focus on communion represents an acquiescence to the ascendancy of "unity over truth," a willingness to dilute confessional clarity and commitment for the sake of some kind of set of mutual relationships possible only because grave differences in faith are glossed over or perhaps even set aside. Much of this worry over the "truth's" vulnerability to schemes of false unity is, as subsequent chapters of this volume will make clear, misplaced. But there *is* a sense in which life in communion reshapes our understanding if not of "truth" itself, at least of its apprehension. This is what the present chapter seeks to indicate: apprehending the truth from the perspective of Christian communion requires the cultivation and use of certain habits that simply do not cohere well with the claims to immovable dogmatic articulations that are frequently embraced as a stay against heresy and even apostasy. Even the claim to "orthodoxy" cannot be coherently sustained apart from a communal context whose substance as "communion in Christ" must necessarily transform the common usage of the term. The reflections that follow will not delve any further into the communion character of the Body of Christ; this is something that subsequent chapters will do. It will move, instead, within the realm of some rather abstracted historical categories, making use of political science as much as theology, for the sake of outlining, up front, some of the epistemological peculiarities of a communion orientation. These categories are illuminating of some of the choices that lie before those seeking to respond to the *vocation* of communion, choices that are often decided in a destructive manner because made without clear understanding. "Communion" cannot possibly be an open-ended arrangement of common life in respect to the knowledge of God; rather, it is a "conservative" reality when it comes to the truth. But "conservatism," as this chapter will show, is a dynamic reality when it comes to history, which is the only vessel through which communion takes its essential form.

## What Is Orthodoxy?

One of the great knots in the reflection on communion, then, is the meaning of "orthodoxy." The term is often used as a more precise and therefore useful explication of a Christian church's commitments than something like "traditionalist" or "mainline." Indeed, the argument is currently made by many that what is called "traditional" often masks a hidden *lack* of orthodoxy that has insinuated itself into present struggles over, say the Anglican Communion, in a pernicious way (e.g. those who oppose the church's permission of homosexual behavior, but who permit the ordination of women are simply not "orthodox," whatever "traditional" practices they may preserve in various areas; likewise those who oppose women's ordination are not "orthodox" to the degree that they permit remarriage after divorce; or again, those who accept revised Prayer Books cannot be "orthodox" whatever their views about the previous matters). To the degree that the Anglican Communion herself is not sufficiently consistent in her "orthodoxy," critics have alleged, the very notion of "communion" in this case is suspect. The challenge posed here is enormous, if there is to be in fact an embodied "communion" of any kind within the Church of Christ, since in practical terms the question of "orthodoxy" has proved over and again, in the modern world, a stumbling block of insurmountable breadth.

My own view, up front, is that the term "orthodox" is in fact *not* appropriately used to qualify the attitudes of most "traditionalists." But that is not because they are "*un*orthodox" so much as it is because the term itself is used with great doubt and some suspicion even within the current historical condition of Anglicanism and indeed many other Christian churches of the present. To be sure, the term has been loosely cast about by leaders of all kinds of traditionalist groups. But what does it really refer to, especially within an "Anglican context" defined by the character of "communion" that has emerged over the past century and a half?

The criterion of "orthodoxy" is not so much a "wax nose" in itself, as it is bound to plural sources of meaning that are hard to apply universally, especially in the midst of dispute. In some sort of basic etymological sense, the word refers to a measure for articulated belief in and praise for God, rightly ordered for human life in a divine relationship. But what is the traction such a sense holds for Christians in the world? Semantically, "orthodoxy"'s "measured" content is given by particular communities or recognized authorities, or — most powerfully — by the lived conjunction of both community and authority together. Regardless of whether one would accept the particulars of the Eastern Church's definition of "orthodoxy" as embracing the "Councils of the Holy Fathers and their traditions which are agreeable to divine revelation" (from the Liturgy for Orthodoxy Sunday), this conjunction of community and authority is exactly what makes possible such a general concept.

This was the case even when the term moved from its Eastern locale and became useful to seventeenth-century Lutheranism in the West. But as a general synonym for "Christian truth," which is how the word "orthodoxy" is now often loosely applied, the concept has lost its edge. Even as a contrastive category to "heresy" — which its Eastern usage often entailed — modern Protestant Christianity in its multiplied voluntaristic self-definition has blurred the New Testament linkage between the personal "choice" of the "heretical" teaching and the communal or ecclesial doctrinal "trust," apostolic in its origins, from which such a choice separates itself. (Hence, in the New Testament, "heresy" and "schism" or "faction" represent English translations of the same Greek word.) The point is, it is not really helpful to reduce "orthodoxy" and "heresy" simply to what is true and false, when in fact the terms' purchase is given in the communally authoritative context — the apostolic church that is the living Body of Christ — in which truth and falsehood are given articulate shape. When the identity of this church is in dispute, the very character of truth and falsehood will likely be thrown into question.

In situations, such as ours today, where multiple or overlapping Christian communities exist in some kind of relationship, or where diverse centers of authority hold sway, or where community life and articulate authorities do not mesh, it is extremely hard to apply criteria of "orthodoxy" in a clarifying manner. One might speak meaningfully of "orthodoxy" in a Roman Catholic context, or in a Mormon context, or in some small branch of a defined Reformed denomination, or even within the context of a given Eastern church. But these are by no means the same "orthodoxies," nor do they all cohere even within themselves to the same degree.

Furthermore, to use the term "orthodoxy" to refer to certain inter-communal (or even intra-communal) commonalities of belief is probably misleading. As theologians like Stephen Sykes have indicated, the search for Christian "fundamentals" or "essentials" or what has recently been called (following C. S. Lewis, who borrowed the phrase of the mild Puritan Richard Baxter) "mere Christianity" is precisely that — a *search* among separated or confused communities.[1] And the "essentials" articulated in this search were destined to be a tool for reconciliation or cooperation or mutual understanding on the part of individuals or groups explicitly aware that "orthodoxy," as understood by this or that group, is not in fact adequate to the task of forming or maintaining Christian community. Christian "fundamentals" have been proposed precisely as *alternatives* to orthodoxies no longer or not yet established, and are therefore hopes rather than working criteria.[2] This is true no matter how these hopes are described —

1. Cf. his well-known chapter on "The Fundamentals of Christianity," in *The Study of Anglicanism*, ed. John Booty and Stephen Sykes (London: SPCK, 1989), pp. 231-45. Sykes's essay demonstrates the difficulty of this search, although with a more sanguine sense of its usefulness than my own estimation affords.

2. What is called "fundamentalism," in its technical sense of referring to the early-20th-century movement of reasserting a set of defined (Reformed) "fundamentals" of the Chris-

the "Great Tradition," or "paleo-Christianity" or whatever, each of which designates some tactical or reactive alliance of those whose hopes are forged in the face of a sense of general Christian beleagueredness.

The term "biblical orthodoxy" is similarly unhelpful if, in fact, it does not arise from within an already established larger communal or authoritative orthodoxy of Christian belief itself. Clearly there is no common biblical orthodoxy, if this means some criteria of scriptural interpretation, application, or authoritatively defined scriptural teaching content, shared by, for instance, Calvinist groups and Eastern or Oriental churches together (even when creedally organized, as most famously disputes about the *filioque* demonstrate). There are, to be sure, certain shared *elements* of such interpretative content, but they do not and cannot constitute an "orthodoxy" precisely because they have no basis in a communal or authorized Christian life shared among such groups. They represent descriptions of overlap in teaching and no more (although such overlaps are not without significance for discerning the truth). This is especially true with respect to scriptural ethics, where there is no orthodoxy tied independently to scriptural moral teachings that is somehow embracing of diverse Christian communities in some defining and self-conscious fashion. No such common scriptural orthodoxy exists that constrains and forms Christians across denominations even in a recognizable and common way in areas of, for example, the use of wealth, war and peace, disciplines of worship and work, and sexual behavior.

None of this is meant to be an argument for the relativization of the reality of truth, including truth that is scripturally located. Rather, I simply want to stress that appeals to orthodoxy or the application of the claim to orthodoxy within conflicts like those within ECUSA now is semantically imprecise and probably confusing (as many people in fact intuit). The shape of God's truth, the search for this truth, and the application of what is true to the life of the Christian church cannot simply be resolved by an appeal to "orthodox belief" unless we are speaking within an already authoritatively ordered community. Otherwise, we must approach the matter of *divine* truth within a disputed context in some other fashion. We might therefore ask the question: is Anglican*ism*, or even ECUSA, such an authoritatively ordered community and has it ever been one?

---

tian faith, belongs both to this mindset and to another, more radically conservative outlook described below.

On the face of it, the present dispute and the nature of the questions involved in it, would seem to offer a preliminary and emphatic negative response. And this response itself indicates the breadth of the challenge before us. But without yet ceding this point, it is possible to answer "yes" to this question by initially referring only to the Church of England in particular and at some particular time, pointing perhaps to the *Book of Common Prayer* (of some specific edition) and to the Articles of Religion, for instance, conjoined to and upheld by Synods and Convocations, which together act(ed) as defining contours to such an authoritatively ordered community.

Still, even this is disputed and *has been* disputed since at least the late sixteenth century, by, for example, Puritans, Latitudinarians, Evangelicals, Tractarians, and others (and in different ways), so that it is hard to make the "orthodox" case for Anglicanism even before the present time, including particular churches that are a part of this phenomenon (like ECUSA), as well as including relationships between these churches. For the reality of a defined communal life and constraining authority either has been attenuated in practice (e.g., in America since the eighteenth century) or simply has existed without formal and clear, articulate expression (as is the case with "Anglicanism" itself). In each case, the recent search for uniting essentials or fundamentals or "core doctrine" testifies to the actual *lack* of community and authority by which meaningful orthodoxy might be articulated.

In the course of this search, to be sure, appeals have been made to *proposed* orthodoxies, especially ones founded on purported historical communities from previous generations: the "primitive" or "undivided church," the "first five centuries," the congruence of Reformed formularies with these previous entities or with other acknowledged "confessions," the sixteenth-century English formularies themselves within or without canonical orderings, the Caroline Divines, and so on. Any of these proposals may or may not once have had a lived integrity. What characterizes them all, however, is that such integrity is in each case *historical:* each represents for contemporary Anglicanism as a whole and for ECUSA in particular a "propositional community of the past," and each can therefore only be an imaginary community of the present, one that acts as a touchstone for something not yet established. (It should be noted that a similar and uncertain appeal to imaginary communities, although with very different contours, is at work within the struggles of the American Roman Catholic Church of the present.)

## Apprehension of the Truth in Time:
## The Nature of *Catalepsis*

The "not yet" here is critical with respect to the notion of an "Anglican orthodoxy." Something is happening within particular Anglican churches and among them that has made the "search for orthodoxy" more than an intellectual conundrum or endeavor. What has happened is the confluence of a set of events and hopes within churches, societies, and cultures that many Christians believe to be of divine ordering and demand. These events are calling, in a truly vocational sense, for the formation of a Christian community (and for an authoritative character within it) that in fact can sustain and express an orthodoxy of witness and teaching that reflects the Holy Spirit's witness to the Son's sending by the Father of all before the eyes of the world (cf. John 17:20-26). Is this not the calling of the Anglican "Communion" within a fractured human and ecclesial landscape? Is this not what we see as a kind of "groping after" in the slow and uneven and joyful evolution of Anglican plurality and common life within the world over the past two centuries?

Again, we need to emphasize that there *is* a measure of teaching about and praise for God rightly ordered for human life as God's creatures. But the measure can be articulated only as it is lived and embodied within a human society, only, that is, as it takes shape within an ordered life itself, gifted with common instruments for *measuring*. It is that life, with these instruments, that alone can frame what is "orthodox" in any meaningful (because commonly understood and enacted) sense; and it is this life, the life of Christ's own body formed and growing (cf. Ephesians 4), to which we must be attuned if we are to grasp what is orthodox itself. Is it possible, then, that the "not yet" of Anglicanism's orthodoxy is what we are suffering, simply because we are being pressed into apprehending; and that we are therefore not engaged in a conflict of propositions in the first place — propositions whose rootedness lies in the past, indeed in various pasts and not in the present — but that we are in the midst of a struggle over *apprehension*'s present form?

The character of "apprehension" in this case is not merely an ecclesiological detail, but rather it is bound up with the shape of Christian living itself. "Apprehension," in this sense, is an evangelical act, the original *catalepsis* (to use the transliteration of Paul's Greek) by which the active love of Christ works within a person or a community, transforming its lived contours into an image of the divine Son himself, the "outer" making the "inner" conform. (Cf. Phil. 3:12f., where "apprehending" Christ Jesus enacts the prior "apprehension" by Christ of Paul's own being; or Eph. 3:18, where the indwelling Spirit of Christ so strengthens the Christian church that she is able, "rooted" in love, to "apprehend the breadth, length, height, and depth" of Christ's love "along with all the saints.") Indeed, the significance of the distinction between historical propositions that may only wishfully define an orthodoxy of the present based on past propositional artifacts, and the shape of orthodoxy's present catalepsis or apprehension comes clear when we return to the current question of sexuality. In this context, the Rubicon that has been crossed with the affirmation of same-sex relations and unions is hard to explain purely in terms of some "orthodox" propositions now violated since — as many have pointed out — we have managed for some time now, with whatever easy or uneasy consciences, to violate many another proposition with a certain communal impunity (viz., divorce and remarriage). And it is not at all clear that homosexuality, as a topic, has sat at the top of anybody's list of Christian "essentials" until quite recently. Although one might mount an argument that sexuality looms large in a special way because of critically fundamental theological reasons and truths — creation and grace, providence and eschatology — it is hard to find their "orthodox" propositional contours prior to the reflection and argument itself (see below).

I myself would wish to pursue and affirm just such an argument; in fact, it is one that has been made with stunning persuasiveness and breadth by John Paul II in the discourses collected under the title "Theology of the Body." But just this example — papal talks, over a long period, with all their environing authoritative qualities, and that draw on an astonishingly rich exegetical and homiletic scriptural context that is informed by Patristic, scholastic, and modern philosophical tools — points to the way that the seriousness of the sexuality dispute within this or that denomination, including Anglicanism, cannot be tidily understood as to its inescapability or its import through the single lens of a set of simply ordered and prioritized propositions. It can be grasped only as part of a lived act of apprehension engaging a range of communal gifts and temporal extensions.

Rather, the Rubicon of the current debate and actions by ECUSA is given force, not by the application of such propositional hierarchies, but by an emerging and variously vocalized *common sense* within the Anglican Communion (and the larger Christian cultures of the nation and world) that this matter is Church-defining and touches upon the core of Christian identity. The *communion* itself is realizing that this is a Rubicon, and this realization is a part of the "not yet" of the communion's own common authority in witness and speech that is in the process of apprehension, that is, in New Testament terms, *cataleptic*. After all, on other matters like women's ordination, and to some extent divorce and remarriage, or even Prayer Book revision, all of which have been at the center of disagreements and even divergent practices, this communal awakening to the fact that a critical passage in the Church's teaching and witness is being pursued has not yet been noted and articulated. The only reason there is a Rubicon is that something called the Anglican Communion has perceived it as such through a range of conciliar instruments; and the communion has perceived it as such because, as an evolving communion, the process of apprehension of orthodoxy's contours has seen this emerging element rise up from the depths of its historical life.

The liberal argument that Anglican doctrinal instability, historically speaking, somehow justifies the kinds of changes in the teaching of sexual ethics we have been seeing, therefore, completely misses the point here. We are now talking, after all, about orthodoxy's apprehension by a communion in search of its own common measure of belief and praise of God, and not about the application of a completed set of historical propositions from the past that (as we know) have in fact had varied commitments over time. We are talking, that is, about the connection of this particularly apprehended reality, vitally bound, to the actual molding of Christ's body. And it is just because of this that we cannot simply relativize the content at issue according to historicized schemes. We approach the present dispute — or ought to — with a humble awe.

The matter of orthodoxy's apprehension, of catalepsis in its evangelical sense and not of orthodoxy itself, is what is at stake in the first instance in this dispute. And the differences in understanding the shape and character of such apprehension of orthodoxy are in part what distinguishes some of the major players within the current debate, not least the traditionalists' roundly assailed and purportedly compromised attitudes. Does apprehension itself have a set of distinct possible frameworks that, unlike the sets of doctrinal propositions specific to plural orthodoxies, can nonetheless illumine the alternative ways forward within a debate over truth, even over divine truth? If we are not simply to lapse back into vying orthodoxies of the past — imaginary communities that we would have invade the present from some distant temporal hills — we need to search elsewhere for help with this. And I suggest that, precisely because we are talking about the formation of communal authorities when we are speaking of apprehending orthodoxy, we are right to look for analogies within the specifically *political* realm. This, in itself, may be a peculiarly Anglican move.

## A Typology of Conservatism

The typology now proposed is exactly the one many commentators have claimed is theologically crude and unhelpful in the present struggles within Anglicanism, even though it is in fact the most frequently applied in common speech regarding our disputes; and that is the typology of "liberal" and "conservative." Although here, we should add to the dichotomy a third group, comprising the "radical conservatives." In each case, a particular stance is taken in relationship to the apprehension of "orthodoxy" itself. The critical bases for this typology, politically speaking, can be found in the work of Jerry Z. Muller[3] and in literary commentators like Lionel Trilling, as they have wrestled with the evolution of liberalism as an intellectual style.

Muller carefully distinguishes "conservatism" from "orthodoxy," and does so primarily on the basis of the former's engagement with "history" as an inescapably informing reality for discernment and decision-making. While orthodoxy, whatever its religious or philosophical location, is defined by a commitment to a given "metaphysical truth," conservatism's posture represents less an affirmation of some truth (which various conservatives may or may not themselves hold among themselves) than a pragmatic fashion of making one's way within a world where truths — whatever they may be — assert themselves most potently through temporal expressions and embodiments. Thus, whatever the "truth" may be for a conservative, it is grasped — apprehended — primarily through instruments that take historical reality and experience seriously and carefully. The paradox of this engagement with historical discernment, if such it is, is that discernment becomes tied to a valuation of time itself, of "taking time," of the landscapes of time, its institutions and traditions, its peoples;

---

3. Cf. his wonderful introductory chapter to his volume *Conservatism* (Princeton: Princeton University Press, 1997), pp. 3-31.

that is, the discernment of truth through time, for conservatives, becomes itself truth's self-assertion. Put in Christian terms, the "way" of orthodoxy's apprehension becomes the form of truth.

Just as orthodoxy reflects its own multiple authoritative communities, so too does conservatism tie itself to various temporal instruments. But Muller believes there is a broad and stable constellation of conservative "assumptions, predispositions, arguments, themes, images, and metaphors" that are shared among conservatives of a wide spectrum of commitments, whether political, religious, or philosophical. Most of these are tied to the historicist pragmatism of their common outlook. They include: a presumption of human imperfection — biological, cognitive, moral — as fundamental to individual and social existence (something borne out by simple historical experience and observation); "epistemological modesty" in the face of unavoidable limits in human knowledge regarding self, society, and the world; a presumption for "institutions," customs, and social prejudices as normed and ordered vehicles for a stable civic life within an otherwise generalized uncertainty of existence; the usefulness of "particularistic" (as opposed to universally organized or justified) social or religious realities, perhaps culturally specific and unique but also rooted historically for a given people, as a framework for conveying social goods; suspicion of theory or of over-riding principle in favor of pragmatic prudence; mistrust of functionalist or idealistic reform, as prone to the likelihood of unintended and negative consequences; the "veiled" character of human knowledge and experience, that both limits certainties of action, but that also provides a set of virtues conducive to moral life within such limited and limiting contexts. The reality of "continuities" — and the values and habits that maintain them — in fact brings "conservatism" into a kind of organic relationship with "communion" itself, understood in its Christian context.

Muller's conservative constellation of historical continuities, particular traditions, and general modesties stands in contrast to a "liberalism" that stakes its own discerning vision to the side of temporally-rooted experience and reality. This is important to note, because we are used to hearing liberals either affirm or be characterized by a kind of attunement to temporality in the specific form of "change" or even "progress." Conservatives do not deny the forces of change or even the eventualities of mutation; they simply do not view them as defined by an *a priori* virtue, of either direction or value. And here lies a significant distinction between conservatism and liberalism: not in the recognition of historical variation or evolution itself, but in its evaluation according to a rule. For conservatives, there is no such "rule" for the future or for the transformation of the present, and therefore we are constrained by simple humility to cling to what little we know, what little we are given, what little we have learned to manage. Whereas for liberals, time *is* governed by a rule, and furthermore a rule that is knowable and applicable to the decisions we make; therefore we are justified in creating and re-creating institutions, social orderings, practical moral frameworks for the sake and in confidence of a historically embedded truth. One might be permitted to wonder if liberalism, on this reading, is compatible at all with communion life.

Liberalism is fundamentally "principled" because governed by a sense of overriding direction; conservatism "unprincipled" because accepting of the limits of our internal and external controls and knowledge about the world and our very selves. Thus, Trilling's observation that the liberalism of the nineteenth century that was defined by a commitment to "continuity and justice" developed into an increasingly dedicated adherence to the second element as itself the definer of the first: history in its continuities *is* about the assertion of justice, increasingly and necessarily, within the experience of human society, and moral life is hitched to the momentum of this temporal truth. In a sense, for liberalism "orthodoxy" as a metaphysical "truth" is something that bypasses historical apprehension altogether, and rather determines historical choices from the start at any given moment.

It should be obvious, however, that this transformation of the historical process itself into a "principle" is and has been amenable to a variety of particular definitions within the liberal framework, to the point that one can properly speak of a dilution of liberalism into almost wholly transmuted forms. It might appear that there is little that holds in common the moral concerns of Matthew Arnold's battle against cultural "anarchism," for instance, and the almost nihilistic "postmodern" moral relativism of, say, "queer" philosophy. Yet both do share a conviction that time itself functions as the outworking of a kind of human "pleasure" — understood in almost contradictory ways, of course — and that the pursuit of this pleasure defines the political discernments, choices, and decisions a society ought to embrace in ways that span particular cultures and traditions. The distance from Arnold to Jeffrey Weeks (a celebrated queer theorist) is vast, obviously, but the migration of "justice" into the realm of malleable rights and finally to the assertion of subversive individual indulgences follows just the kinds of peregrinations that social discernment will make when riding through time upon the back of "principle."[4]

It is just this kind of mutation that conservatives would warn against and retreat from in their suspicion of principled history: when a principle, any principle, becomes the tool by which historical experiences and choices are hopefully and demandingly molded, the principle can only find itself warped by its unwilling subjection to the stranger and more mysterious forces of the human heart lurking within time. (Even if "conservatism" is not necessarily tied to Christian belief, its presuppositional sense of human perversity has clear Christian resonances.) This is why the third element in Muller's typology, "radical conservatism," has far less to do with conservatism itself than with the abduction of conservative predilections by the almost liberal-minded servility to principle — an often lethal combination. The radical conservative, according to Muller, is one who "believes that the processes characteristic of modernity have destroyed the valuable legacy of the past for the present, so that a restoration of the purported virtues of the past demands radical and revolutionary action."[5] This represents the decision, born of some sense of commitment or desperation, to turn history's unfolding into the image of whatever custom, habit, or prejudice a conservative outlook at a given time might valorize in the process of moral apprehension, and to do this by "radical" means, if necessary rupturing the very continuities that seem to be under threat or perhaps already destroyed. Thus, Moeller van den Bruck writes (from a radical conservative perspective) that "conservative means *creating things that are worth conserving*" (emphasis added). But the result of this kind of "taking the kingdom of God by violence" can develop into exactly the forms of fascistic coercion that seem to mirror the devouring historical principles that liberalism, generally although not always with less disjunctive demands, promotes.

It should be obvious, however, that orthodoxy as a vital reality stands

4. Arnold is sometimes classified with conservatives in the lineage of Burke (e.g. by Muller himself). But I tend to take his own self-description as a liberal more seriously, precisely because his argument seems far more deliberately "principled" than anything Burke would countenance. On Arnold's "liberal humanism," a principle that indeed saw him dispense with traditional Christianity for the sake of some deeper "core" in typical liberal fashion, see Trilling's Introduction to *The Portable Matthew Arnold* (Harmondsworth: Penguin Books, 1980 [1949]), pp. 3-10.

5. Muller, *Conservatism*, pp. 27ff.

in a diverse relationship to liberalism and radical conservatism, despite each of these outlook's common reliance on "principle" as human history's determinant. On the one hand, liberalism's principle (whatever it might be at a given moment) is itself the orthodox truth that drives its historical projects. But it is a truth that, as we said, bypasses the communal struggle for apprehension by constantly adjusting itself to the various and specific needs of the one apprehending. In other words, orthodoxy really has no intrinsic communal force within liberalism, but is something redefined by the plethora of experiences brought to bear upon the very shifting and self-orienting plural groups that liberalism's concerns tend to uphold and continually create. Whereas for radical conservatives, orthodoxy (in ways we have stated above) represents the character of an imaginary community, one already assaulted and probably past, that therefore requires re-creation. In this sense too, the radical conservatives' orthodoxy bypasses its own communal apprehension, by obligating a new community's invention — it stands outside both community *and* authority, and hence the effective character of orthodoxy's "measure," its comprehended articulation, and its ordering qualities are all absent. Radical conservatives, therefore, have historically slipped quite easily from principled action into forms of behavior that are simply overwhelmed by human instinct unmoored from communal and communally authoritative constraints altogether.

## The Nature of Christian Conservatism and Its Alternatives

The religious and specifically Christian application of this typology may or may not be immediately illuminating. But we must not suppose that the typology is itself extraneous to our ecclesial lives. Indeed, the particularly *political* shapes used to explicate its order are in fact of recent notice: late-eighteenth-century pre-Revolutionary and early-nineteenth-century post-Revolutionary reflection in England and France (e.g. Burke, de Bonald, Chateaubriand), within which the terms themselves were invented. Nonetheless, the historical exemplars from before this time are more appropriately located within the internal ecclesial struggles of the sixteenth and seventeenth centuries of Europe, and already in the late eighteenth century conservatives like de Maistre were able to perceive this pedigree. The specific application of each term to this or that group — who exactly represented "conservatives," "liberals," and "radical conservatives" among the players of Reformation, Counter-Reformation, and post-Reformation — is perhaps less interesting to our present purposes than being able to sense the vital and varying place of orthodoxy in the contexts in which various groups arose and flourished.

Within Roman Catholic contexts, for instance, liberal and radically conservative forces grappled differently with the same "orthodox" deposit: one need only observe the debates between Jesuits and Dominicans, not to mention the practical theology deriving from the culturally different areas of central Italy or Parisian France. The question of the relationship between orthodoxy and its apprehension or application is both pertinent and complex in these kinds of examples. More to the point of our own moment is the way that these and other varying forces have contributed to a currently conservative Roman Catholic Church (as I view it) that has managed somehow to appropriate institutionally liberal and radical aspects together of the eighteenth century as these impulses themselves have adapted slowly to a variety of historical evolutions. The character of contemporary Roman Catholicism as a world church is neither liberal nor radically conservative; but if neither of these, how are we to view its lived sense of orthodoxy? The answer to this is perhaps less obvious than some might think (except perhaps certain Eastern Orthodox theologians still instinctively critical of Rome).

With respect to Protestantism, we are probably correct in thinking that Paul Tillich's argument regarding its "principledness" rightly places much of the initial Reformation's thrust within a liberalistic dynamic of bypassing historical catalepsis in favor of a culturally malleable principle, in this case, of scriptural critique and/or gospel justification.[6] Within Anglicanism (and parts of Lutheranism to a lesser degree) this initial tendency was quickly constrained by a prior conservative outlook.[7] The English church remained, indeed until quite recently, a formative ecclesial vehicle for conservative values (more on this below), bound to a scriptural "principle" that was liberal in its continuous encouragement of critical inquiry. The amal-

6. Tillich's classic arguments can be found in his collection of essays *The Protestant Era* (Chicago: University of Chicago Press, 1948), esp. chapters 11-15 (pp. 161-233).

7. Hooker's "providential" argument regarding the Reformation in England at the end of Book IV of the *Laws* (IV:xiv) offers a crystalline exposition of a historical outlook that, once buttressed by the kinds of epistemological modesties provided by the eighteenth century, would inform Burke's own reading of English experience.

gam of these two elements has represented a peculiar attitude to the truth's apprehension within the modesties of communal constraint.

Within other spheres of Protestant life, however, the lack of this conservative container that gave a constricting set of forms to the scriptural principle permitted only direct confrontation between other alternative principles of, for example, interpretation, and the reactive responses to untethered liberal adjustments took the shape of what would later be called, in political terms, "radically" conservative attitudes. These were based on the embrace of one or another moment within the liberal continuum of change, each inventing its own communal vigor as an image of the past and insisting upon its necessary reestablishment. The separatist instincts of some forms of Protestantism, therefore, derive in part from the unequal paces and patterns with which ecclesial liberalism's inexorable dynamic of constant change has been accepted. As many contemporary observers have noted, the irreconcilably divisive contentions between parties in the Western Church today, when they arise, are not between genealogically unrelated groups, but between religious liberalism's generations and siblings. The radical conservative's rallying cry of "renewal by division" is a proverb proclaimed *within* liberalism's family, not from outside its fold.[8]

But is there not in fact a Christianly faithful evaluation that we can make of the terms of this fundamentally religious modern typology? Perhaps. And some would point to just those Christian communities where "orthodoxy" appears less disputed as appropriate lenses through which to make such an evaluation. Still, it is not clear that the vital and authoritative communal characters of Roman Catholic and Eastern Orthodox churches are particularly stable, and to them, just as to various well-defined Protestant groups, the question of cataleptic attitudes and their alternatives towards orthodoxy remains open, or is opening in new ways. How then might we assess the resolution to these questions on the basis of the Christian identity itself?

Israel's relation to the Law provides a potentially classic example. In a

---

8. Tocqueville's notion that *"ces sont les nuances qui querellent, pas les couleurs"* — the shades clash, not the colors themselves — fits, in different ways, the antagonisms between radicals and liberals, and radical conservatives and conservatives — although the difference between the latter two is, as I have been suggesting, greater than between the former pair. See Alexis de Tocqueville, *The European Revolution and Correspondence with Gobineau* (Garden City: Doubleday/Anchor, 1959), p. 21, in John Lukacs' excellent introduction dealing with Tocqueville's peculiar brand of "Christian conservatism."

foundational sense, the Law is presented as an immovable and defining deposit to which every aspect and moment of Israel's life is asked continually to conform and return. In light of this, the radical conservative's pattern of repeated ruptures for the sake of an arrested principle would seem in a way to describe Israel's prophetic vocation, consistently "called back" to an obedience previously compromised or abandoned.

However, the Scriptures also describe the pragmatic failure of this radical demand. The attempt — as with Jeroboam or with Josiah's "reform" — to reestablish a fixed appropriation of the Law, however necessary in terms of divine pressure, turns out to have been itself a moment in God's own refashioning of Israel in judgment and mercy. Jeroboam fails in faith and Josiah's people (with him as their representative) require a fall and penitence that only death and resurrection at God's hands — through destruction, exile, and return — can sustain. In this very process, the "Law" as an "orthodox system" of behavioral propositions is itself transposed into apocalyptic promise and divine incarnation. This historical transposition becomes the theological basis for the Gospel's "fulfillment" of the Law. On the one hand, certain providential constraints require the failure of the Law's radically and continually reasserted form; on the other hand, this providential ordering of Israel's life — which the Scriptures as a whole are now seen as actually embodying, and no longer acting merely as a commentary on the Law — becomes the very object of faith's (and God's people's) apprehension as "truth."

The Christian approach to Scripture has, in fact, never been primarily one of radical conservatism until recent times, even among those with the highest and most inerrantist view of its inspiration, as among the Fathers. This is so largely because Scripture has never, until after the Reformation, been understood as a fixed or in itself systematized body of propositions capable of being simply reasserted at times of perceived assault. Indeed, the early church's "assimilative" dynamic of cultural appropriation, to use Ramsay MacMullen's description of the expanding Christian community's relationship with a range of pagan customs and outlooks during its first centuries, stands in some tension with more modern forms of propositional orthodoxy.[9] Sociological descriptions of conversion have been helpful in sorting some of this out from a modern perspective, identifying the

9. See Ramsay MacMullen, *Christianity and Paganism in the Fourth to Eighth Centuries* (New Haven: Yale University Press, 1997), pp. 103-49.

various ways in which individuals and groups are able to maintain frameworks of practice and attitude that have divergent religious origins, for the
sake of an integrated and dynamically-oriented assimilation within new
communities of belief. The ways even that Paul sought to make sense of
continuities between Old and New Testaments, or between Law and Gospel, including the application of categories like natural law, for the sake of
"building up" his new charges, demonstrate how he too operated with a
kind of cataleptic approach to the truth that stands to the side of subsequent (real or imagined) stable orthodoxies.

It would certainly not do to call Paul a "conservative." (Nor, for that
matter, to assign to him any other station within the typology we have
been exploring.) But the question is whether aspects of his approach to the
truth are more or less amenable to conservative attitudes towards the
truth's apprehension. Paul made use of a range of exegetical tools and
philosophical appropriations, and he offered a number of different exemplary postures from his own adjustments to a disciplined but supple mission among Jews and Gentiles. Together they witnessed to a Messiah of Israel's "flesh," all the while also opening Israel to the mysterious providence
of God's purposes for the whole of creation, revealed through an incarnate
Son. In bequeathing to his followers a church whose shape reflected these
realities, Paul gave them a "tradition," to be sure, but one tied as much to
the character of his own life and sufferings bound to God's revealed purposes as to some single body of doctrines. (Cf. 1 Thess. 1:6ff.; 1 Cor. 11:1;
2 Tim. 1:8-14. Not surprisingly, people like Athanasius still would refer to
Paul's example more readily than to Jesus' own as a concrete determinant
of behavior for the church.) Yet more importantly, he offered to the young
church a rich and variegated engagement with the Scriptures whose authority was tied less to specific rules of exegesis and their defined outcomes
than to a historical molding by the forms of the tradition and by bodily examples themselves to which Scripture's hearing was to be bound (Romans
9-11 being a stunning model).[10] These examples, taken together, represented the very "communion" of the church *as* Christ's Body.

When churches of more deliberately and openly "conservative" habits
developed, like the Church of England, it was just in this area of scriptural

---

10. St. Augustine's *On the Morals of the Catholic Church* (see esp. chapters 29-35) provides a rich vision of the interaction of these means of learning and growing in the truth, a
kind of *cataleptic* primer for the period.

engagement that some of the most peculiar and telling aspects of their conservatism were manifested: by binding scriptural hearing within the communal appropriations of traditions — both devotional and intellective — these churches thereby subjected the hearing both to the pressures of history undergone by resilient and inherently prudent social forces and to the incrementally and cumulatively adaptive capacities of gathered spirits oriented towards God's purposes in Christ. The somatic character — something that should be seen as equivalent to its "communion character" — of the truth's apprehension within this context was one governed by the dynamics of members being constrained by and relating and accountable to each other in ways responsive to larger needs and callings of peoples over time. And this character itself bears a close relationship to the exampled traditionalism and reiterated self-implications in Scripture that Paul commended.

It is in the light of this understanding that the authors of this book consider ourselves to be Christian conservatives with respect to orthodoxy, rather than orthodox Christians *tout court,* the latter designation being one we believe too unstable to pin down usefully.

## Conservative Catalepsis and the Challenges of the Anglican Communion's Moment

Of course, we can and perhaps must continue to use the term "orthodox" to designate the cataleptic hope and commitment and even the tools used for attaining the full measure of our ordered speech and praise. We can use it, too, as a sign against the disdain many liberals feel towards such hope. And we can encourage the term's use by those who would maintain together such hopefulness. But we must take care that we are not seduced by the term's concreteness to cast aside the hopeful work of apprehension that is not, and cannot yet be, finished.

For within the American religious context, much of the cataleptic character of Christian understanding is difficult to make sense of, in large part because America has never had a rooted conservative culture in the particular fashion we have been using the term: as our last chapter argued, ours is a history of discontinuities rather than of continuities, and the religious landscape of the nation has been sown with variations of radical conservative experiments or liberal self-reconstructions from the beginning. The notion of "history" itself has always been problematic for Americans — it was hardly cherished or taught, well into the end of the nineteenth century, and remains the least grounded academic discipline to this day among American students. It is fair to say, I believe, that the implosion of American Anglicanism that we are seeing is a symptom of this experienced incoherence as Episcopalian liberalism simply morphs into its radically conservative counterpart of revolutionary imaginings, and the resultant and intractable struggles dismantle the church.

The catalyst for this reaction, for which the dispute over sexuality is *in fact* a Rubicon, is the specific awakening at this time, with this issue, of American experience to its location within a context far larger than its previously limited self-image. Whether sexuality is a more "essential" doctrine for the church than, for instance, the eucharistic presence is thus not really the point. The point is that it is at *this* time and with *this* matter that American Episcopalians are realizing that they do not live — or pray — within an independent arena, but are now part of a network of continuities, i.e. of "communion" itself, within world Anglicanism and Christianity. Liberalism has no means of clipping its principles to the reality of these emerged continuities, invisible until now to the conscience of self-referring cultural powers like the United States, but with the appearance of an astonishingly expansive church in non-Western and younger nations, no longer avoidable. Reactive liberalisms that take the shape of radical conservative movements of protest, seek to fabricate new entities that can somehow justify a continuity that has never in fact been experienced in America, as much because it never existed here as because it does not really describe the vital experienced grasp of truth within the new churches of the younger nations themselves.

The few conservatives that exist within the American Episcopal Church have been tentative in the face of the moment. They have awakened to this new network of connection in ways that perhaps were previously only theoretically considered, hoped for because of a general sense of our boundedness within the larger church's often misapprehended traditions, but never truly lived until recently. Conservatives are scrambling to maintain the lines of modest engagement that were always understood to underlie the life of the church, but were never really seen for what they were or might become. But far from undermining the sense of purpose that has driven them, they are seeing this crisis as a kind of cataleptic moment *par excellence*, although just because of that, one that requires an almost heroic effort at resisting overthrow and engaging the gifts of what is presently "at hand" through the life of the historic church of which we are a part. As I have emphasized earlier, it is the historical character of our apprehension that conservatives insist must govern our discernments and decisions, and it is this form of apprehension that both feeds and guards the communion of the church.

A whole set of matters of lived faithfulness has been brought up anew in the midst of this awakening. This has happened, though not in a way that raises the suspicion of some orthodoxy abandoned in the past that now requires reassertion. Rather, these matters have come to the fore again with a realization that traditions are rightly reexamined in light of Scripture and of God's judgment of the church through the working out in time of our condition. It will be useful now to restate some of the issues used by critics of Episcopalian and Anglican conservatives, and to attempt some distinguishing of the varying ways we must approach these matters given our particular outlooks. Not only are these in fact matters of contest, but they well illustrate the way that an emergent "communion" character of knowledge — "conservative" precisely in its communion-oriented historical constraints — will pursue its discernment. What we will later in this book identify precisely in terms of our communion's "conciliar" economy, represents the context in which these kinds of issues listed below must be addressed. They will need to be addressed on a global scale, because they are themselves diversely and passionately debated among the churches of the global communion; and they will need to be addressed according to the "virtues" of communion life that further the apprehension of the truth, that is, within the postures of mutual subjection we will argue for in coming chapters.

### Divorce

Let us first take the question of divorce. One of the concerns expressed with regard to conservatives on the matter is that there is a kind of hypocrisy at work in their midst, one that has led them to permit and perhaps embrace divorce and remarriage, in a way contrary to Scripture and "orthodox" Christian teaching, even while bristling at changes in same-sex practices. This charge can be assessed honestly by conservatives only within the context of the "continuities" given in our church's historical life and now within the awakened apprehension of our common life in communion, as each set is clarified, challenged, and judged within a scriptural framework. It is not entirely clear where this might lead, since it requires more than a perfunctory and immediate attempt. But we can make some initial comments on the matter from a conservative — communion — vantage point.

As to the primary scriptural demand, there has been a longstanding debate about exegesis here: the Old Testament permits divorce and remarriage under certain circumstances. Jesus calls this permission by "Moses" something based on a certain accession to human "hard-heartedness" (the text in Mark 10 is the classic one), something which he then states as ultimately contrary to God's creative will "from the beginning." Elsewhere, Jesus equates remarriage after divorce to a form of "adultery." The problem that exegetes have found in all this, however, is that a) Jesus gives an "exception" — Matt. 19:9/5:32 — for a wife's "sexual immorality" (the meaning is debated); and b) Moses' leniency (for "hard-heartedness") is not explicitly condemned or ruled out by Jesus, and may or may not still be an acceptable element of divine mercy in certain cases.

The historical continuities by which the church is bound, within this framework, have a certain kind of ramified focus. Thus, while divorce and remarriage has always been discouraged and usually forbidden outright in the Christian Church, this has never been universally so in either time or ecclesial geography, there being many permitted divorces and remarriages in the Middle Ages and (as well we know in Anglicanism) within Reformation/Protestant churches (not to mention Eastern Orthodoxy) — although always within strict bounds and with nothing like the *laissez-faire* attitude of the present society and American Episcopal Church in particular.

It is this history, bound up with not always universally accepted scriptural exegesis, that perhaps lies behind the differing attitudes conservatives have held with respect to divorce and remarriage, on the one hand, and same-sex partnerships on the other. The very fact that Scripture does not prohibit divorce and remarriage in an absolute way (as it does, say, adultery itself), and that the church universal has had a long history of varied and more nuanced interpretation and practice on the matter, distinguishes divorce and remarriage from homosexual behavior and same-sex blessings. For the teaching of Scripture and the church's reading of this teaching on the latter topic — homosexual physical expression — has been universally consistent and, as we know, consistently negative. (This is accepted by all historians and today by most biblical scholars.) It is, in this light, not an insignificant measure of our ecclesial apprehensions of the truth that the Anglican Communion — via Lambeth, the Anglican Consultative Council, the Archbishop of Canterbury, studies, commissions, resolutions, and individual synodical actions around the provinces — has, since the 1950s, variously accepted divorce and remarriage (of priests and others) as a matter in which a variety of practices within the communion would be tolerated. Yet it is also a fact that the communion has, by contrast, steadfastly refused to accept such a variety of practices and attitudes with respect to the acceptance and affirmation of homosexual physical expression. The contrast between how our larger church has responded to these two matters is telling.

But what conservatives — indeed not only they, but all of us — are being called to through the present moment as it is constituted precisely by the awareness of communion as our vocation, is a reflection on the way our attitudes and practices, in this case of divorce and remarriage, are part of other webs of continuity, often destructive and deforming of the gospel. Varying practices and limited permissions and the rest are not unimportant; but they cannot exhaust, or even come close to explicating, the full meaning of the ethical significance of the questions of marital and sexual practice. We are awakening now to the "fruit" of practices and the tendencies of permissions that indeed throw us back upon the molding powers of the scriptural witness to the larger human destiny and creative purposes of God. In this sense, the Rubicon of sexuality is a gift for a larger catalepsis.

The *communion* question on this matter, then, is perhaps less rightly posed in terms of "hypocrisy" or even "orthodox consistency" than it is in terms of "attention": what are we being asked to see in the midst of these changes, asked, that is, by God's own providential calling? And it would seem that we are indeed being asked to deepen and elevate our concern about the church's permission of divorce and remarriage. The number of divorced and remarried Christians and even clergy in America is, as some have noted, "shocking." If permission for all this were ever itself "permissible," we can surely say — we are awakened to this affirmation — that this permission has now gone too far, "too far" in terms of the negative social effects on children and families, and "too far" in terms of undermining the calling clearly laid out for men and women in their created and creative purposes by and for and with God.

Events alone have proved the "permission" to be a mistake in its extensive application. Bishops and diocesan commissions in America and around the communion should rethink their policies with respect to ordination of divorced (and divorced/remarried) persons, and bishops should rethink the circumstances in which they give permission for individuals to remarry. Clergy and lay leaders must pause and step back and reexamine their own teaching and example. How drastically this rethinking should be and on what timetable its force should be implemented is a matter, obviously, for careful discernment. Reversing policies of permission, of any kind, is always pastorally difficult and requires great prudence. But a conservative approach would rightly seek a reintroduction of discipline on a staged and gradual basis.

We need to stress, furthermore, that this call to reverse is probably necessary, quite apart from any final adjudication on the scriptural question of divorce and remarriage itself in absolute terms. That is, even if one thought that Scripture somehow allowed for divorce and remarriage under certain circumstances, it seems clear that such allowance in our day has been abused and needs at the least to be curtailed. This is a pertinent observation, if only to underline how the scriptural demand, from a more strictly conservative and communion perspective, is less one that is sown up in advance — in the kind of propositional form that authoritative or imagined communities often take them — but that asserts itself in renewed and renewing ways in the course of a historical apprehension of God's truth which the Scriptures, in a lively way, would sow within *us* as we pursue our vocation in communion. It is not so much that such an approach can make vanish the "clash of orthodoxies" that liberal and radically conservative commitments must engage on these questions; it is simply a matter of engaging another way altogether — if one, however, that seems to have less attraction to people of our day.

### Women's Ordination

On the matter of women's ordination, the pattern of a conservative approach will now appear more predictable. We are to ask questions regarding continuities, both entrenched and emerging, both limiting and gradually transforming, and all within the framework of the scriptural press that is apprehended within the structures and forms of communion life. In this case, Anglican conservatives in particular are left with varying illuminations. The scriptural framework of discernment and formation is, pragmatically and theologically, far less clear-cut with respect to women's ordination than is the case with same-sex relations, certainly, but even than is the case with divorce and remarriage — which, as we know, provides several pungent teachings of Jesus, and a few by Paul. The Anglican Communion's own practice and discernment have proven highly diverse around these scriptural realities with respect to women's ordination, and along different lines than simple assignments of "orthodox" systems of doctrinal enunciation. This is so especially among the younger churches, where the vast majority of provinces now ordain women. These practices and discernments, furthermore, have followed lines of communion-wide decision-making that, for all their bumps and lacunae, have nonetheless achieved a certain acceptance by the majority of the communion's members as legitimate, largely because the scriptural priority of Anglicanism's system of authority has not, in the minds of Anglicanism's councils, clearly prohibited women's ordination, and has even provided some evidence for its encouragement: the "icon" of "image" of Jesus is, according to Scripture, one borne by male and female Christian together, and cannot therefore preclude a woman's presidency at the Eucharist. (This is not, of course, accepted in the minds of certain minorities, both liberal and traditional in certain senses.)

The generally accepted legitimacy of the communion's manner for permitting or for not accepting the ordination of women in this or that province lies, however, in some tension with other historic continuities within Christian churches and through the binding (by hope at least) of Christian churches together. It is fair to say that a conservative approach that takes seriously these limiting ecumenical and historic continuities, but that also takes its place within the more flexible ordering of the specifically *Anglican* Communion, and finally that would be attuned to some "awakening" to the world's varying concerns about women's leadership roles, politically and ecclesially, would find itself reduced to a kind of humbled openness to the "not yet" of this apprehension — a place of modest freedom of conscience and dignity of diverse witness. And this has generally proved the case among Anglican conservatives (including many women conservatives, some ordained and some lay), not all of whom share the same practical commitments in their own ministry on this matter, but who have found a common space for respectful disagreement and cooperation together.

On a matter like this, conservative self-limitation in both claims and insistences, formed along the lines of "council in communion," appears irritating to those with more principled agendas and objections. By comparison, it is therefore important to note that conservatives are willing to make distinctions among matters of crucial discernment, and to apply critical tools of inquiry, ordering, prioritizing, and moral adjudication among doctrinal matters. Not all analogies and parallels are valid, scripturally, theologically, or historically, and it behooves the Christian — from this perspective — to exercise "reason" in clarifying the relationships between and the differences among issues like divorce, women's ordination, and same-sex partnerships. This willingness and obligation to distinguish properly ties conservative thinking with the kinds of creative inquiry identified variously with Patristic speculation, scholastic comparative investigation, and Enlightenment critical discipline — rather than with a single and integral body of dogmatic definition or "principled" commitment. And it is precisely a concern for the historical demands of varying continuities of witness and example, enmeshed in the scriptural net, that makes for such reflection and distinctions particularly expressive of communion life.

## Liturgy

Finally, the matter of Liturgy can be examined. Within the Anglican Communion, it would appear that the *Book of Common Prayer* and its revision would be an issue precisely of conservative concern, rather than of a strict and given orthodox complaint. That is, parsing most current revisions — and let us take the 1979 American Prayer Book as the main example — according to a variety of doctrinal standards does not, in fact, yield clear areas of transgression (or for that matter, lucid dogmatic expression), in large measure because most of the concerns enunciated through the application of versions of orthodox criteria rely mostly on arguments from silence and from formal arrangement.

For instance, one might worry about the dilution of penitential character in the newer revisions, or of the clear affirmation of sacrificial atonement in this or that eucharistic prayer. It is not that the worries are baseless — surely they are not! — but rather that they are difficult to mount into a compelling picture of error given that the revisions themselves articulate other scripturally-based assertions of some kind, in however bland or dispassionate a manner, that properly engage communal worship. (The scriptural base is a critical standard that can, at least in theory, be applied and tested; it can properly evaluate, often negatively, some of the more radical revisions and "alternatives" available in the Episcopal Church, although not, probably, the 1979 Prayer Book itself.) Indeed, so long as the liturgy is in fact scripturally-founded, arguments about its theological justification or lack thereof must rely on systemic standards of doctrinal proposition that do not, in fact, enjoy a common application in the church or churches at large, even as they live in communion. Indeed, the problem with theological exegesis of the liturgy is that, after having noted matters of bare conceptual articulation, one is forced to engage in a kind of rhetorical formalism, akin to aesthetic criticism, whereby the weight and significance of order, arrangement, and coordinated meaning among the phrases and parts of the prayers will be instrinsically contested.

By contrast, however, the kinds of objections to Prayer Book revision that take account of consistency with historic forms of prayer, formulary, and communal focus — precisely some of the matters that, historically, have organized the Anglican Communion around common formational practices — demand our attention in ways that go beyond contested orthodoxies. Here is where some critics have strong arguments in conservative eyes. The fact that the 1979 Prayer Book (not to mention more radical revisions or alternative liturgies) breaks lines of liturgical genealogy in stark ways, that it imposed upon the people's worship new doctrinal foci, that it complicated and multiplied prayers and eucharists, and so diluted "common" scriptural formation, dislocating liturgy from the Anglican Communion's practice as a whole — all this and more represents a serious disordering, some of it ongoing, of the "measure" of articulated belief and praise of God that has had serious consequences, especially in terms of the larger communion's capacity to engage coherently in the apprehensive vocation of catalepsis itself. The major question is raised of whether these negative consequences of revision have outweighed the gains in ecumenical coordination that, at least superficially, something like the American 1979 revision achieved. In retrospect, and given the turmoil engendered in the midst of the communion's and the ecumenical community's common life by the 2003 General Convention, the answer is clearly that the revision's evangelical task has been desperately foiled.

As with the matter of divorce and remarriage, however, the issue is how to live with the realities of an already re-formed common life. It is difficult — and not necessarily wise — simply to call for an abandonment of current liturgical life. Continuities and common ordering, such as communion requires and encourages, require some coherence between recent and historic lines of influence and adherence both. It is probable that a conservative approach to the matter would seek for some version of the historic Prayer Book's form — whether 1662, 1928 or another — to be recognized as authoritative in terms of communion-wide connection — "Common Prayer" — and that more recent revisions be given a permitted "alternative" status. But this should be done, in a sense, only within a conciliar discussion and coordinated set of decisions involving the communion as a whole.

## Conservatism and the Rubicon of Sexuality within the Anglican Communion

In light of these kinds of particular challenges as confronted with a conservative posture, the basis upon which sexuality itself has acted as a Rubicon of concern for conservatives is perhaps now more obvious. The "awakening" to the new web of Anglicanism's geographical and cultural continuities around the world has brought into inescapable view the fact that local worries over disciplinary and doctrinal changes with regard to same-sex partnerships represent a connective reality that goes far deeper and moves far more broadly than a particular communal orthodoxy. Here is where, among other realities, the "overlap" of ethical and scriptural teaching by diverse Christian communities becomes vitally important. The debate over sexuality has exploded within the secular and political realm independent of either ECUSA and Anglicanism itself; and the character and extent of the dispute have unveiled the roots of concern as reaching across cultures and denominations and even religions to the degree that the fundamental continuities of natural law and the scriptural disclosures of God's very purposes for humanity — the intersection between divine creation and human culture itself — have been placed in question. In other words, the present crisis has thrust conservatives against one of the most basic and historically integral realities their pragmatic modesties are driven to conserve. And it is just this that drives the conservative theological program of reflection and commitment to take a stand at this point, even as they must revisit and reclaim and perhaps reorder the breadth of continuities that move out from this created reality into current relational life (e.g. divorce and remarriage).

To make a stand at this point, while working responsibly within this breadth in ways noted above, is a theologically coherent procedure, however difficult it may seem and despite the criticisms of liberals and radicals. Theologians, after all, have long distinguished the two "orders" of creation and redemption. And while each must ultimately be coherent with the other — God's created and creative purposes in nature are finally "at one" with his purposes and means for nature's redemption — there is a kind of historical as well as conceptual distinction between the two that is both helpful to make and to allow to order the practical expectations of our commitments in the world. Here is where conservative theologians would perhaps attempt to explicate their fundamental resistance on this score.

The "creation of male and female" — for companionship and procreation — is bound to the natural purposes of the created order (and Paul affirms this explicitly in e.g. Romans 1), which witnesses to the sovereign goodness of God and to a basic means by which humanity is to live fully with God. This is the main and basic purpose (and thus created "icon" of God within the world) that same-sex behavior obscures, and it is this that Christian conservatives rightly now recognize as informing one of the basic continuities that bind their focus of the truth's apprehension within the world of ordered human relationships before God (a fundamental character of orthodoxy itself).

This created order is, furthermore, foundational to the understanding and embodiment of the shape of "redemption's order": the self-giving by the Father of the Son, in love, for the salvation of humankind. This latter reality is "figured" in the life and virtues of the married state (cf. Eph. 5:21ff.), and is grasped through the historical process by which men and women grow into the sanctified reality of marriage and chastity. The vocation to exclusive "indissolubility" of marriage, and celibacy outside of it, is tied to this order of redemption, in a similar way to which the "life of the Cross" and "prayer" and so on are tied to it. The vocation itself cannot be in question, from a conservative perspective; nor can be its ultimate calling and demand. But, as with all matters of transformation and sanctification, it is temporally imperfect in its fulfillment within our lives here and now; we grow into it, even as we are judged by it. The cautious approach to the historical embodiments of this process within churches that conservatives follow ultimately constitutes no more than the kinds of pastoral wisdom that, as we now realize, can never be freed from the critical constraints of perceived failures. Hence the need to reassess.

In some sense, the present crisis has thrust conservatives to the very threshold whereon the work of apprehension — at least on this matter — finds its goal, whereon grasping merges into the fullness of being grasped. The male/female/marriage reality within creation's order is the basis upon which the male/female/marriage/indissolubility life of Christian discipleship is built and pursued within the temporal order of redemption. Although there is, within both orders, much latitude for mercy, the frontier has been reached from which it is now clear that there is no room for the denial of the created forms by and in which mercy is sought and received; there is no room for them simply to be contradicted or rendered of an optional character. For to do the latter is to obscure the very redemptive calling that is given by God in Christ, which the exclusive and self-giving form of marriage — now tied to the Incarnate form of Christ — is molded by God to represent.

From a conservative point of view, we have reached an epochal moment. And how we have reached it is significant: borne down by the weight and constraints of peoples, whose ties to us — in creation and in Christ's communion! — we have somehow misunderstood or simply ignored before now; pressed by the cries of martyrs and saints, whose form we had been accustomed for too long to miss. *Their bodies,* from Africa and Asia and Latin America, and from within the corners of American churches too — not the liberal or radical principles embodied in an elite class of scribes and agitators — represent the ballast, the drag, and the momentum of history itself. To this we bow, as to the Author of time.

It is important to reemphasize that Christian conservatism is not a doctrinal party, in itself. It is a practical stance, oriented towards discernment and decision-making in time, not a statement of the truth. And this practical cast does not represent "all there is"; in William Witt's phrase, it is engaged with penultimates, though for the sake of what is ultimate.[11] It is concerned with maintaining the practice of receiving and ordering a collective and ecclesial space for such receipt — the receipt of One who is the

11. See the unpublished paper by William Witt, "Reflections on non-theological interpretations of General Convention and a theological alternative." Witt is not satisfied with the "conservative-liberal" dichotomy as a useful template for understanding what happened at ECUSA's General Convention in 2003, although his concerns lie chiefly with the way the terms have been applied to reduce the debate to a more limited politico-cultural struggle, rather than illumine its more theological concerns. With this I whole-heartedly agree; although it is unlikely that Witt would feel wholly comfortable with my own typology.

gift itself, the One whom we cannot give to ourselves or conjure up for ourselves, the One whom rising up we cannot "bring down from heaven," and whom descending we cannot "bring up from the dead" (cf. Rom. 10:6f.), but who can only give himself.

Jesus Christ is not a liberal, a conservative, or a radical conservative. He is neither a principle nor a system of propositions. He is neither orthodox nor heretical. He is not the Scriptures themselves but has fulfilled them all in himself (Rom. 10:4). He is the Body. For he alone has founded the communion and embodied the authority through which we might know and praise God; and he did not so much "order" its relatedness to God according to a measure, as measure all by his own being (cf. Job 38:5ff.).

Yet in his work of "giving gifts," he has "led a host of captives" (Eph. 4:8) and moved forward "with the children God had given" him (Heb. 2:13), bringing "many to glory" (Heb. 2:10). This freeing and leading, this pioneering and herding and gathering — of Scriptures, of principles, of passions and thoughts (2 Cor. 10:5), of created persons — is the basis for the continuities of life and constraint of love and meaning that set the current of our catalepsis in the truth and inform the dynamics of discerned and directed "life in communion."

> For his sake I have suffered the loss of all things . . . that I may know him and the power of his resurrection, and may share his sufferings, becoming like him in his death, that if possible I may attain the resurrection of the dead. Not that I have already obtained this or am already perfect; but I press on to make it my own, because Christ Jesus has made me his own. Brethren, I do not consider that I have made it my own; but one thing I do, forgetting what lies behind and straining forward to what lies ahead, I press on toward the goal for the prize of the upward call of God in Christ Jesus. Let those of us who are mature be thus minded; and if in anything you are otherwise minded, God will reveal that also to you. Only let us hold true to what we have attained. (Phil. 3:8, 10-16)

# CHAPTER FOUR

# The Scriptural Community:
# Authority in Anglicanism

*Ephraim Radner*

## Introduction: Authority, Ethos, and Anglican Scripturalism

We have said something, in the last chapter, about the "conservative" character that in fact informs Anglicanism's approach to religious truth, and that this approach itself is peculiar to a life lived "in communion." We also spoke of the dynamic character of this kind of conservatism, even as it lives and apprehends God within a context of constraint and historical connectivity. In the present chapter, we hope to explore more fully how this kind of conservative and cataleptic approach to the truth has actually exerted itself authoritatively within Anglicanism. This in turn will helpfully ground a further discussion in the chapter that follows on the constraints to diversity that properly constitute communion life. We have already indicated the limited usefulness, in the present era of the churches, of the category of "orthodoxy." But that was not to question either the reality of God's truth or its actual apprehension, nor to undermine the practice of authoritative structures governing Christian life within given communities and in a way that is somehow coherent with this truth. But how, in fact, can a "communion" live under "authority" if it is to remain open to the historical realities that beset necessarily the church's temporal apprehension of God? To understand this properly is one of the great challenges, and potential gifts, that Anglicanism can offer the larger church.

To characterize authority for a community, one must first understand the organs of reception, the framework by which individuals and groups "hear and obey" the authoritative norms by which they live. Indeed, actual "authorities" — whether they be persons, ideals, or documented standards — achieve identifiable focus only within the parameters of these organs of reception, and ought not to be identified apart from them.[1] Along these lines, Anglicans have often spoken in terms of an "ethos" that shapes and limits their common life, as opposed to a defined system of "authority" or "doctrine" that explicitly constrains it. This is a helpful and also misleading way of speaking. It is helpful in pointing to the fundamental force and reality of communal attitudes of particular authorities as they in fact order the church's life; but it is misleading if the appeal to "ethos" is used to dissolve the reality within Anglicanism of a constraining authority altogether. Furthermore, it is often logically difficult to ground authority in ethos or in communal organs of reception in an exact manner, and hence Anglicans tend to work around the edges of the challenge, and, as we are seeing today, in controverted situations to ignore the challenge altogether in favor simply of alternative modes of authoritative appeal which fail to convince precisely because their articulation tends to float free of the "ethos."

Despite, or because of, the purported "vagueness" of an Anglican framework of authority, the experienced and increasing reality of diversity in both teaching and practice within and among Anglican churches has both seized upon and suffered from this longstanding inexactitude, giving rise to a host of competing arguments for "particular standards of authority." These arguments have boiled down to several main commitments. All maintain a reference to Scripture, but the latter's actual force in controverted discussions has been weak. The more substantive disagreements are from within the following positions:

1. To take the United States as a political example: while the Constitution represents a final authority of appeal, in fact very few people know it or refer to it. Representatives of the people do, under particular circumstances, and those circumstances themselves mark the parameters in which the Constitution is articulated and applied. But what orders the representatives and their circumstances of hearing, especially in relationship with the "people"? Without arguing the point, we can see why some would place the Declaration of Independence on an authoritative par with the Constitution, insofar as it may define the limiting and informing character of the community's encultured expectations or values, as it selects representatives and the circumstances that elicit and constrain appeals to the Constitution. "Constitutional" governments, from Africa to Asia, vary in the nature of their authority, despite having a common structure and set of appeals, in large measure because there is enormous variation in the organs of reception from culture to culture.

- Anglicanism has no constraining authority besides the "Creeds";[2]
- None besides the *Book of Common Prayer* (interpreted in full or thin terms);[3]
- The normative authority of the several "Formularies" together;[4]
- In every case, "Canon Law" as the proper adjudicator of the above, defined within particular local synods.

Thus, whatever one's views on the matter, the practical struggle over authority has moved into the realm of the legislative, and probably the proposal with the most potential for political and perhaps clarifying influence within Anglicanism as a whole, has been the initiated project out of Lambeth 1998 to rationalize and make coherent among themselves the canonical systems of the communion's constituent members.[5]

The press for canonical uniformity is, however, more a reactive response to a situation of growing unease within the communion than the expression of a positive dynamic actually driving the communion. In the past, the seeds of conflict between the kinds of positions noted above have

2. This represents the views of progressives within the Communion, especially in North America, who argue that beyond the creedal affirmations and the scriptural base to which they refer — variously understood — much (all?) falls into the category of *adiaphora;* this might even include the shape and duties of the threefold ministry (and here radical evangelicals in, for instance, the Diocese of Sydney overlap pragmatically with radical revisionists, in the manner expected from the typology of our previous chapter). We deal with this position later in our chapter on conciliarism.

3. This represents the more moderate position of most North American Anglicans, and undergirds hopes for "comprehension" through the BCP's wide set of references as well as the assumption that Prayer Book revision represents the appropriate place in which to further theological reform. Again, see some of the theological and pragmatic pitfalls this position encounters in our preceding chapter.

4. This, finally, is the more properly self-styled "orthodox" position, embodied in something like the Prayer Book Society, which appeals to a strict set of purportedly "classic" Anglican "standards" — Creeds, BCP, Ordinal, and Articles of Religion.

5. Cf. the paper of Norman Doe on "Canon Law and Communion," presented to the Anglican Primates in March of 2001 (available through the Anglican Consultative Council), and the basis for Doe's rich work in support of the Commission that produced the Windsor Report in 2004. Doe had urged a kind of Communion "common law," based on foundational and overlapping commonalities in the canon law of various Anglican provinces. There is reason to doubt the Communion's ability to further this project legislatively any time soon; however the Windsor Report's recommendations on something like an "Anglican Covenant" overlap somewhat with this perspective.

been historically contained by functional "structures" of authority — the respectful collegial oversight of bishops bound to patterns of counsel and to *de facto* commonalities of formulary — and it is just these structures that today appear unsteady. The Inter-Anglican Theological and Doctrinal Commission's so-called "Virginia Report" on the "communion" of the church (see Chapter 7 below), for all of its careful examination of theologically substantive concepts like Trinity and *koinonia,* actually made its public mark by suggesting new and wider adjudicatory structures for the communion, thereby furthering the sense that ecclesial "politics" should remain the arena in which "authority" finds its legs.[6] And in light of these trajectories, taken in the midst of very serious and developing conflicts around the communion over teaching on sexuality in particular, the notion of "Anglican authority" might perhaps best be sifted from ecclesial debris when the dust settles over the next decade, and not before.

Short of such futuristic retrospectives, the purpose of this chapter is to uncover a deeper source to this increasingly manifest problem of locating authority within Anglican churches. The problem itself, after all, is also one increasingly afflicting most church traditions, even ones founded more explicitly on historical doctrinal definitions, as the reality of a resolutely pluralistic context for religious life envelops almost all Christian bodies, even around the world (see our concluding chapter). What will be argued here first, is that this originating problem actually lies in a peculiar stance that Anglicanism has taken with respect to Scripture and community; that is, it can be found in the historic Anglican refusal to inhibit the "first-order" character of scriptural language and substance, a refusal that derives from what can be called the "encultured" (and hence, in a deep way, "communion-informed") base of Anglicans' various appeals to authoritative entities or documents. From this, we can see that the odd disappearance of Scripture's claims in present Anglican discussions (despite appeals made by conservatives especially to its supreme authority) is probably attributable to the disarray of Anglicanism's "second-order" structures (those noted above).[7] In-

---

6. The report, commissioned by Lambeth 1988, was published in 1997 (London: Anglican Consultative Council). Chapters 3 and 6 raise the "structural" issues which caught people's attention.

7. Cf. arguments in R. R. Reno's *In the Ruins of the Church* (Grand Rapids: Brazos Press, 2002), chapters 5 and 9. In these chapters, Reno contrasts the increasing inability of the "standards" *qua* functional norms to maintain the more fundamental (to Anglicanism) practice of the "reiterated" hearing of Scripture embodied in the Daily Office.

deed, the original relationship of Scripture and Standard was one wherein the latter's role was to protect the former's unfettered hearing. The dynamic of evolution in rapidly emerging modernity, however, with its overturning of the "corporate" character of scriptural formation, has been to reverse these roles and purposes: Scripture has more and more been applied primarily to buttress the authority of the Standards, however they may be identified by various Anglican groups. Unlike other churches, Anglicans have traditionally refused to demand anything other than Scripture as the ostensive framework for their primary claims (a claim that consciously here flies in the face of much contemporary popular, if unexamined, wisdom about the supposed "three-legged stool" of Anglicanism's appeal to Tradition and Reason in addition to Scripture). In any case, the problems inherent in such broad scriptural "fundamentalism" when it is corporately — as opposed to individually — embraced are those with which we live today.[8]

## The Form of the Eighteenth-Century Anglican "Ethos": The Religious Society

A useful way of examining this whole matter is to take a kind of typical comparative approach. We can first look at the question of Anglican "authority" in terms of the eighteenth-century alternatives of ethos which, in a critical way, bear some connection with contemporary realities: that is, in response to the growth of religious pluralism within the British nation, a pluralism which, after all, so bedevils our efforts at grasping the true character of Christian communion. From there we can move backwards to locate a more general set of informing Anglican commitments about the role of Scripture and community that, according to this argument, continue to be embodied in the movement outside of England into America and the evolving Anglican Communion.

The reality of religious pluralism in England was determined amid the violence of the Civil War and subsequent Commonwealth in the mid-

8. For a pugnacious discussion of the conceptual ambiguities in speaking about "Scripture, Reason, and Tradition" within the context of contemporary Anglicanism (in contrast to its more "classic" sixteenth- and seventeenth-century texts), cf. Christopher Seitz, *Word Without End: The Old Testament as Abiding Theological Witness* (Grand Rapids: Eerdmans, 1998), chapter 8, "Biblical Authority in the Late Twentieth Century: The Baltimore Declaration, Scripture-Reason-Tradition and the Canonical Approach."

seventeenth century. Its intractability and social challenge, while resisted in many ways at the time of the Restoration, were inescapable; and by the early eighteenth century it had become the primary motive behind ecclesiastical politics and the theology that grew up around such discussions. There was a time when every English schoolboy — and certainly every student of divinity — knew about the Bangorian Controversy. The fact that this episode is no longer a standard part of Anglican self-understanding, however, does not subvert its status as an exemplar of the religious age: the bishop of Bangor, Benjamin Hoadly, had argued in a sermon that the "Kingdom of Christ" was a purely "spiritual" reality and hence was not logically (or morally) subject to a political establishment. Hoadly's vision, impregnated as it was with overt Lockean sentiments, was designed to open up a social space in England for most religious sects and denominations ("toleration"), and to question the Anglican claim that ecclesial structures (including and especially forms of worship) themselves formed an essential part of the gospel. The ensuing controversy grew so heated, and came to engulf the passions of the church's political parties so voraciously, that the synodical center of the Church of England, its "Convocation," was simply dissolved — "prorogued" — indefinitely; indeed, it failed to meet again for almost another 150 years.[9]

The practical result of this studious avoidance of decision-making was that religious pluralism became ensconced as the "new fact" of British society by the 1720s, its legally protected status, of course, requiring another century to work itself out. And in line with Locke's own explicit theological vision, the center of gravity for understanding Christianity began to shift from communal conformity into the realm of "private" belief, the standard of which was, to use the technical phrase of the day (so pilloried by someone like William Law), "sincerity of conscience."

Amid the growing and increasingly recognized marketplace of religious choices, the individual's religious identity demanded new criteria, beyond the authority of hierarchy and nation, indeed beyond even the imprimatur simply of Protestant claims to scriptural origins, by which to judge the internal commitments by which religious values were now seen to be determined. These criteria fell within the category of what today we would call "authenticity" of Christian character, and what in the eighteenth century were qualified as "marks of genuineness."

9. See the discussion of this episode as a "typical" form of Anglican "counsel" in our Conclusion below.

It is here that we can disengage some of the peculiar elements that pressed Anglicanism and its "evangelical" reform movement (what became Methodism) in different directions: how do we know and judge what is "genuine" Christianity, or a "genuine Christian"? While a complicated question, we can at least answer it broadly in the following manner. The search for the "authentic" in the face of religious privatization had for some time — indeed as a recurrent dynamic within the church's history but with a special purpose since the Reformation — followed the logic of "primitivism": that which could be tied most closely to the apostolic and early church was to be most valued. In the debate among competing sects in the sixteenth century, this form of argument had gained a new edge with the evolution of historical research, and by the mid-seventeenth century in England it had triumphed as the standard form of documentary science. Now thrown to the individual, the quest for the "original" Christianity in the eighteenth century had become a national passion, for many something almost at one with religious faith itself.

On a broader level, primitivism came to fuel a variety of what could be called "renewal" movements designed to refocus the lives, not only of individuals in their private decision-making, but in their association with the church or churches themselves. Chief among these renewal movements were the so-called Religious Societies that began to spring up around London and elsewhere in the country beginning in the late 1600's. Just here emerge some useful contrasts between conforming Anglicanism and the nascent Methodist movement, ones worth noting because, although so much attention has been paid to Wesley's adaptation of the Religious Society, Anglicans have tended to ignore the illuminative value for their own tradition of the original structures that Wesley, as it were, inherited and transformed.[10] And the choice between Wesley's "method" and Anglicanism's social orientation represents a continuing one today on a large scale between Anglican "federation" and Anglican "communion."

The form of the Religious Society was that of a weekly gathering of parish laymen for the purpose of prayer and mutual edification. Its origin is usually associated with Anthony Horneck, a German émigré to England

10. The literature on the Religious Societies has grown over the years. For an overview, see J. Walsh, C. Haydon, and S. Taylor, eds., *The Church of England c. 1689–c. 1833* (Cambridge: Cambridge University Press, 1993), esp. chapter 5 ("The Church, the societies and the moral revolution of 1688" by John Spurr) and chapter 7 ("The origins and ideals of the SPCK 1699-1716," by Craig Rose).

who became an Anglican minister and who, in 1678, organized such a group in London for which he wrote a set of "Rules" that became fundamental to the many societies that later spread through the church. The religious motive behind these societies was explicated by Horneck in a number of sermons and books, including a work entitled "The Happy Ascetick" (1681).[11] Horneck conceived of his small groups as the seed or leaven of witness by which the larger church and world would be converted to a deeper Christian discipleship. This hope was, in turn, based on his reading of the conversionary history of the early church (particularly through the eyes of the highly popular primitivist historian William Cave). As Horneck explained, the Roman Empire was converted through the testimony of small societies of "holiness" — the early Christians that is — whose pneumatic existence exhibited the embodied form of the Crucified Jesus in the pagan culture's midst.

However much Horneck's Lutheran background may have influenced his stress upon the Cross, his theological outlook apparently hit upon an Anglican enthusiasm (if there is such a thing), for not only did his societies proliferate but the shape of their life, as Horneck described it, followed a pattern bound to appeal to the established church.[12] While the overall criterion of membership was an individual "resolution" to pursue "a holy and serious life" (Rule 1), the way this was to be enacted was decidedly familiar: only those "confirmed by a bishop" could be members; only ordained ministers could lead the group; only prayers from the Prayer Book could be used; only "psalms" could be sung; personal discussions of "practical divinity" or of "spiritual concerns" were neither required nor to be freely pursued except with the direction of the minister; and a large part of the society's efforts involved the regular collection of dues and contributions to be used for preaching missions and almsgiving among "the poor." Finally, Horneck appended a set of "special" rules, which included the relational elements of the Sermon on the Mount, the discipline of self-examination, daily prayer, obedience, and commitment to the Church of

11. *The Happy Ascetick: or, The Best Exercise, To which is added a Letter to a Person of Quality, Concerning the Holy Lives of the Primitive Christians* (London: Henry Mortlock, 1681).

12. Horneck's "Rules" were published as a Preface to his *Several Sermons upon the Fifth Chapter of St. Matthew; Being Part of Christ's Sermon on the Mount*, 2 vols. (London, 1717), pp. viiiff. They are reproduced in David Lowes Watson, *The Early Methodist Class Meeting: Its Origin and Significance* (Nashville: Discipleship Resources, 1987), pp. 188f.

England (Rule 17) — all things that, in his other writings, Horneck associates with the apostolic imitation of Christ's own life.

It should be said that subsequent societies, whose origins were quite independent of Horneck's personal legacy, tended to cohere in vision with this general outlook: that is, they all exhibited an intentional renewal of "primitive apostolic" holiness of life that was tied to the "form" of the crucified Christ in such a way that its manifestation might work for the "world"'s conversion. Further, this renewal's formative vehicle proved to be the instruments of the established church itself, in whose patterns of relationship "holiness" would be embodied. Finally, we should note that while the explicit theological rationale disappeared, many of the practical forms of this "society" devotion entered into the mainstream of Anglican evangelical spirituality, in part through the nineteenth-century evolution of the Religious Society itself into the missionary movement of the Church of England through organs like the Church Missionary Society (CMS). (This is worth noting because specifically *Anglican* evangelicalism moved in a direction somewhat different from the original branching out of the Religious Society Movement that marked the birth of Methodism, and this difference informs the emergence of the Anglican "Communion" itself.)

It is worth simply contrasting Horneck's vision with Wesley's more mature use of the Classes and Bands. One way to state this contrast is to describe Horneck's societies as a kind of communally *formative* primitivism, while Wesley increasingly saw his societies more explicitly as the instruments of *conversionary* primitivism. And in this sense Wesley's instincts were far more in tune with the religious thrust of evolving pluralism, for he tied primitive holiness more to the individual's conscience than to the individual's community, and saw the latter more as a vehicle for this conversion and transformation than as the object of the holy, and even less (in the Puritan sense) as an *ecclesiolum* of the holy. Not that the formative character of the religious society was not somehow basic for Wesley as for his contemporaries. But because Wesley's understanding of "Genuine Christianity," with its emphasis upon the experiential contours of justification and sanctification, found its articulation as an internal phenomenon, the communal character of the society was identified less by its ostensive practices — common prayer, study, discussion, almsgiving, and relational accountability — than by the *nota* of its conversionary functions: preaching that leads to justification, commitment, and the effectiveness of individual encouragement and growth. "Authentic" Christianity, as Wesley described it, found its demonstration in the internal legitimation of the era's critical religious categories: the "assurance" felt by a "sincere conscience."[13]

The formal "standards" for this genuineness, as Wesley saw it, were of course scriptural, just as with all the religious societies; indeed, they were soon explicitly "Wesleyan" as well. But our purpose now is to bring into view the "ethos," and not the bare standards themselves. For as the religious societies went, so arguably went the churches that finally embraced them. While the Classes and Bands of Methodism finally moved in the unambiguous direction of conversionary devotion and the ecclesial structures that facilitated this, renewal primitivism that remained within the Church of England eventually fell back firmly upon the standards that the High Church movement had been culling from its documentary mining of the Early Church over many years, that is to say, the particular "forms" of communal life deemed "apostolic." In William Beveridge's enumerations (common with many others'), these included the "Apostolic Deposit" of Scripture (and enshrined in the Book of Common Prayer and in the Articles of Religion); the "fellowship" or "communion" of established ecclesial life; the Lord's Supper as the "highest act of religion"; and finally regular corporate public prayer according to the Book of Common Prayer.[14]

And while it is true that the "conversionary" ethos of the Methodists initially had a far greater missionary success than the "conforming" religious societies, "formative primitivism" had its own outward impetus, enacted by the missionary societies like the Society for the Propagation of the Gospel (S.P.G.), which sought to "propagate the gospel" precisely by multiplying and supporting the formal and apostolically "genuine" standards articulated by people like Beveridge.

13. Note, for instance, Wesley's 1753 "A Plain Account of Genuine Christianity," reprinted in Albert C. Outler, ed., *John Wesley* (New York: Oxford University Press, 1964), pp. 181-96. We should also be aware that, in our own post-Emersonian American context, Horneck and Wesley will seem to have far more in common than in distinction, given their sense, for instance, of the essential Christian need for a regulated and formative "society" at all.

14. Cf. his sermon (102) on "The Exemplary Holiness of the Primitive Christians," found in his *Theological Works* (Oxford: John Henry Parker, 1844), vol. 4, pp. 441ff. Cf. Robert D. Cornwall, "The Search for the Primitive Church: The Use of Early Church Fathers in the High Church Anglican Tradition, 1680-1745," in *Anglican and Episcopal History* 59:3 (September 1990), 303-29.

The crucial element of distinction was not, in the end, missionary desire in any case, but the location of apostolic authenticity: for conforming Anglicans it lay in the usage of the Prayer Book and in the dynamics of that "fellowship" or "communion" that lived within the Prayerbook's molding parameters. In the eyes of eighteenth-century Anglican theorists, the Prayer Book's framework — and its effective imposition on society was part of its own character — in itself worked the gears of apostolic formation, and the society of the larger Church acted as the very arena wherein "holy living" was necessarily embodied through the virtues and crucible demanded by the very process of "conformity."

Finally, if this sketch of the matter is accurate, it seems to cohere with a consistent Anglican "ethos" that stretches from the sixteenth century through much of the twentieth century. It is this ethos that defines the "organs of obedience" and that thereby points to the character of authoritative witness and ministry that has in fact marked the Episcopal Church, until recently, and that is now under such assault worldwide. We can now attempt to define it more broadly.

## Cranmer's Founding Ethos of Formative Scripturalism

If we turn to what is widely acknowledged to be one of the main pillars of the Anglican ethos, the Book of Common Prayer, we find that its theological rationale as articulated by Cranmer was fundamentally explicated in terms of the corporate formative powers so clearly presupposed still by the eighteenth-century renewal groups of the religious societies. Cranmer, however, describes that power in a particular and important way as the force of specifically *scriptural* immersion by a people. Indeed, this represents the sixteenth-century value of the "primitive," if you will, in contrast to the more institutional elements identified by seventeenth- and eighteenth-century Anglican divines. Nonetheless, we can see the continuity of interest here.

Right at the opening of the 1549 BCP's Preface, Cranmer seeks to display the scriptural basis and goal of his revision in the practice of the early church: "the common prayers in the Churche," he writes, have their "firste orginall and grounde," as far as their purpose is concerned, displayed in the practice of the "auncient fathers." It was they, Cranmer goes on to explain, who first "so ordered the matter that all the whole Bible (or the greatest parte thereof) should be read over once in the year," by both clergy and people. Indeed, throughout the Preface and the essay "Of Ceremonies," the "auncient fathers," the "olde fathers," and "antyquitye" are used as groundings for the specifically scriptural (not doctrinal) revisions the new Prayer Book attempts.

This appeal to *antiquity,* stated so forthrightly by Cranmer, was not, however, a simple desire to "return to the sources" in the way that later primitivists, and certainly that modern liturgical scholars, have sought to govern their researches. The authority of "antiquity," for Cranmer, in fact lay elsewhere. He appeals to the "olde fathers," not for liturgical forms or even for doctrinal substance within the liturgy, but only because the early church (in Cranmer's mind) offers a faithful model of scriptural exposition within the "divine service" of clergy and people. We could call the authority of antiquity in this case a matter of "pragmatic exemplarism," the historically proven virtue of scriptural conformance. This is a far cry from "antiquarianism," because Cranmer was not actually interested in the forms of public prayer from the early church. Nor does he appeal to the past, liturgically, as to a theological "tradition" which bears the weight of authority because of some intrinsic continuity it holds with apostolic truth. If the past deserved to be followed, it was only because the past had read the Scriptures, presented them in whole to the people, and practiced their formative powers in an ordered and effective manner. If Anglicanism has a take on "sanctity," it lies in this discernment of formal historical providence.

Such an authority is hardly insignificant for Cranmer. The fact that scriptural prayer has actually been enacted in the past is a gift from God to be seized in the present, and utilized through the continuous submission of the church to its best achievements. Thus, *antiquity* exercises authority in liturgical matters through the church's present willingness to engage its continuous forms of faithfulness. (This view is articulated formally in Article 34 of the later Thirty-Nine Articles of Religion, "Of the Traditions of the Church," one of the most useful summaries of a classic Anglican view of the relationship between Scripture and Tradition.) What Cranmer calls *order* essentially orients the church's common prayer towards the achieved examples of its past, and asserts an intrinsic conservatism in revision from the start. In theory, after all, *any* form of prayer that built up the people of the church in scriptural knowledge and practice would be acceptable as a liturgical framework for the Christian church. In practice, however, the achievement of scriptural upbuilding made accessible through continued forms of prayer actually demands embrace out of a humble trust in its reiteration.

In "Of Ceremonies" especially, the dependence of "order" on "antiquity's" achieved scriptural formation is clearly spelled out: one is to revise only those rites that "confounde and darken" the clarity of scriptural edification; but other than this, one "oughte rather to have reverence" for past ceremonies. Why? For "theyr antyquitye," whose reiteration, in contrast to all "innovacions and newefangelnesse," necessarily promotes "unitie and concorde." Cranmer uses the phrases "decent ordre" or "quyete dyscyplyne" repeatedly throughout these expositions of liturgical revision, and they refer to far more than the virtues and benefits of political submission within a hierarchical society. "Order" allows for the reception of the past's examples; and these examples grant the pragmatic leverage needed to fulfill the church's mandate to build up her people in scriptural truth.

Informing all of Cranmer's commitment to the elements of Scripture, antiquity, and order in liturgical life is the final purpose of "edification," a word whose cognates and semantic relatives run through the Preface and "Of Ceremonies." For some, this has seemed to mark out Cranmer's over-intellectualized Reformation culture, where "right doctrine" was made the key to salvation. Our own modern term "formation," however, gives a better hint at this purpose's meaning for Cranmer, and we can yet better grasp its fuller sense by perceiving the flow of imagery in something like Ephesians 4:12-16. Here we find a concatenation of words like "building up," "growing into," "maturing," "knowing," "believing together," "measure of fulness," all applied to the process by which the church, through its mutually accountable life together in ministry and teaching, comes to resemble the image of Christ. A glance at Cranmer's homily on Scripture shows how he imbues the reading of Scripture in general with just these effective virtues. (Cf. the wonderful Collect, for Proper 28 in ECUSA's current Prayer Book, for an example of this essentially and salvifically "formative" understanding of Scripture.) Applied to the liturgical realm of priest and people conjoined, this power of reading and hearing the Word constitutes the central act of "divine service" or "liturgy" for Cranmer, an event whose formative and corporate shape is given in the received ordering of Scripture's public reiteration.

While there is no question, then, that Cranmer's reformation placed Scripture as the supreme "authority" for the church, how this Scripture was to be received or heard was peculiar, especially in comparison with other well-known Reformation leaders. Cranmer is adamantly opposed to viewing Scripture primarily as a source of right doctrine, and therefore as the object of human reasoning and interpretation; rather Scripture is to act as the practical "organizer of life" for the whole people, and its meaning is accessible only to the "virtuous" who submit to the corporate demands of the church's (and nation's) "body." His early "Preface to the Bible," a defense of the 1540 vernacular translation promoted by Henry VIII, provides in this case a kind of hermeneutic mirror to his later liturgical explications in the Prayer Book prefaces: the Bible is for "all people" as the sole trustworthy guide for their common "edification" for salvation; it provides for the "complete" ordering of life in "all things," and scriptural "abuse" is conversely tied to scriptural applications that induce "disorder" within the church and commonwealth; the right understanding of Scripture is given only for and to the formation of "pure morals," and its distortion is most readily provoked through its subjection to the demands of "speculative reason." The "purest" imposition of scriptural "authority," therefore, is an ordered process whereby the people are exposed to the "whole" Scriptures in a regular and socially interconnected way, such that the Bible's content saturates their common hearing, and from this, their common life. In Cranmer's terms, this would mark the fulfillment of the Holy Spirit's particular vocation within the church.

Outside these parameters of scriptural practice, the "reformed" Cranmer exhibited an astonishing looseness of concern with the details of patristic testimony, dogmatic systems, and even the theological bases for ecclesiastical and sacramental forms. The latter — including the vaunted Anglican commitments to episcopacy and a particular shape to the "Holy Communion" — had "authoritative" value for a mixture of reasons (mostly social order and the efficacy of "edifying" exposition and historical experience) that only *indirectly* derived from Scripture. Indeed, Cranmer's personal subordination of the actual form of the "historic episcopacy" to the needs of social policy is notorious, and when the late-seventeenth-century bishop Gilbert Burnet published (for his own Whig purposes) until-then unseen records demonstrating Cranmer's willingness, under certain circumstances, even to jettison the episcopacy altogether, it caused a sensation.[15]

---

15. Cranmer's remarks, recorded in the course of a royal Commission's conversations, can be found in the volume of "Records and Original Papers" in Burnet's *The History of the Reformation of the Church of England* (1714).

## "Scripture-in-Communion" as a Conciliar Reality: The Evolution of the Anglican Communion

This looseness, however, was not the same as voiding the notion of the "authoritative" itself. Rather, it tended to solidify its center within the corporate practices of the "scriptural liturgy," and enhance — "authoritatively," in a secondary sense — those elements of common life that supported, regularized, and protected these practices. And while Cranmer himself hardly constitutes the *fons sapientiae* of the Anglican tradition, the framework he bequeathed to the Church of England in fact remained fairly firm, and provided the basis for subsequent theological articulations of "authority" for the church in just such a way that the eighteenth-century religious societies fell almost imperceptibly within their ordering reach.

What became a rather more pedestrian form of authoritative "standard" or formulary, viz. the Thirty-Nine Articles (whose demanded subscription by Anglican clergy has, around the world, been gradually relaxed or wholly abandoned), was in any case an outworking of this more basic authoritative ethos of "formative scripturalism." Unlike most other Protestant "confessions," the Articles adopt a simple and creedal narrative approach to the doctrine of God, ending with an exposition of the "sufficiency" of Scripture for the explication of the "faith," and then moving on to a short list of controverted dogmatic questions (following a mild, though largely Protestant slant on these matters). The bulk of the remaining articles, however, are devoted to church order and social relations. These reflect a strong Augustinian ecclesiology, especially in their emphasis upon the realities of the *corpus permixtum* of the visible Body of Christ, and of the entailed demand for the virtues of corporate order within this historical object of tension between sin and grace.

To this degree, the Articles stand in complete coherence with the organs of formation and reception that Cranmer had so carefully outlined: a people corporately formed by the whole Scripture, whose doctrinal identity was to be circumscribed by protections against dogmatic interpretation and detail (generally thought to be Roman Catholic vices, and later attached to forms of Puritanism). And the Elizabethan church which edited the original Articles from Cranmer's hand did so with a quite deliberate view to founding Cranmer's formative vision upon theological rationales, like Augustine's, that explained "antiquity, order, and edification" in terms of the pressures exerted by the call to national evangelical reconciliation within the realm of fallen individual passions. Elizabeth's Archbishop Whitgift, in particular, provided the theological tools for this argument in his defenses of the Prayer Book and ministerial order of the Church of England against the growing Puritan movement.[16]

What came to be called "conformity" in this context was therefore far more than a political program, but a broad theological argument about the nature of the Christian Church's authoritative witness within a "communion of the scripturally-molded," whose contours lay in the practices of a people's common worship and order rather than in the definitions of an institution's or an individual's confession; and in the virtues of a person's scripturally-infused social relationships ("duties") rather than in the dogmatic integrity of a person's discourse. The relationship between "conservatism" and "communion" is here most evident; and it is founded upon a notion of corporate scriptural formation that is essential to the New Testament itself. But the paradox to which this later gave rise — that individual conscience is provided latitude precisely in its strict subjection to the boundaries of the ordered corporate hearing (and praying) of Scripture — is one that remains as puzzling to contemporary individualists as it was to sixteenth- and seventeenth-century dogmatists and to eighteenth-century pilgrims of the "sincere."

It has been rightly recognized that this character of authority, as given scripturally in "communion and conformity," is a very "catholic" one, both in a Western and Eastern sense, and as opposed to many Protestant approaches. For it sees Scripture's interpretation as finding its authoritative expression only as it is discerned and articulated within the unity of the Body of Christ, and enabled through the virtues of communion itself — *sola scriptura* as the joining of Word and Body of Christ. And once this "catholic" element is recognized (as even many contemporary Anglican evangelicals are increasingly willing to admit), some of the contemporary and popularly knotty arguments within Anglicanism itself over the authority of human "tradition" and "reason" are eased. Certainly, the nineteenth-century Tractarians (like Isaac Williams) who lifted the "threefold cord" of "Scripture, Tradition, and Reason" to a new level of explana-

---

16. This take on the matter follows the splendid argument of Peter Lake in this. Cf. his *Anglicans and Puritans: Presbyterian and Conformist Thought from Whitgift to Hooker* (London: Unwin Hyman, 1988).

tory power understood Hooker, their primary source here, aright when they tied the latter two elements intrinsically to both Scripture's popular reception and the community within which it is received. "Tradition" in this light is properly understood as the ordered way that Scripture is heard and "Reason" is identified with the *communal* apprehension of the natural law coherent with Scripture.[17] Here is where the "conservatism" of Anglicanism, as described in the previous chapter, finds its particular dynamic.

The thoroughgoing character of this Anglican reliance upon the formative expression of authority as "Scripture-in-communion," however, also makes its catholicism distinct from Roman and Eastern traditions precisely in its formal self-limitations. The late-seventeenth- and early-eighteenth-century "High Church" program, for instance, more and more identified ecclesial authority with the marks of the episcopacy, the structures of the Holy Communion, and the explicit contours of the Prayer Book. This identification proved a kind of overstatement of particulars in comparison with the "ethos" of Anglican authority that had, by contrast, generally granted primary weight to the communal virtues which these ecclesial elements *historically* deployed *(de facto* rather than *de jure divino)* for the sake both of fulfilling the formative power of Scripture and also embodying its truths in its true object (the Body of Christ). Notions of "primitive" authority like Beveridge's, then, could reasonably be viewed — and many later Evangelicals did so view them — as a deforming exaggeration.[18]

Of all the treatments of this matter, amongst the best is the seventeenth-century theologian Herbert Thorndike's nuanced under-

---

17. Williams, in his discussion of the "providential" character of the *Book of Common Prayer* in *Tract 86,* actually replaces "reason" in this triad with "the Sacraments," a revealing move that implicitly ties forms of prayer with a collective wisdom, whose "nature" is divinely governed by providence. The 1981 "Elucidation" of the Anglican–Roman Catholic International Commission's Report on Authority tries valiantly (par. 2) to express this essential and hierarchical connection between Scripture and Tradition and Reason, constrained (oddly enough) by its inability to draw clearly the historical implications of its own *koinonia* ecclesiology for scriptural authority.

18. Although the dictum of the seventeenth-century Anglican apologist Chillingworth to the effect that "the Bible and the Bible alone is the religion of Protestants" evoked the Tractarians' ire, its application to Anglicanism is credible if it is understood within the context of the "formative communion" whose stable "catholic" structures are in fact demanded by Scripture's purpose. Anglo-Catholic hostility towards liberal Protestantism was so great, however, that they latched onto the distortions of High Church primitivism without properly grasping the deeper scriptural sources of its initial impetus.

standing of the church. It probably constitutes the furthest one can and ought to push the "catholic" character of Anglican authority.[19] Thorndike's creative work as a pre-Restoration High Church Royalist proved, more than any other Anglican thinker's, the most profound detailing of the commitments already laid in Cranmer's era that viewed the church as the historically effective (and historically accountable and responsible) *culture* of scriptural formation. His masterful exposition of the nature of Christian authority within the reality of human history, wrung from the personal tragedy of Civil War and ecclesial self-destruction, was governed by a sensitivity to the weight of social history's providential demands upon the Christian vocation. This acuity with regard to historical constraint, which included a sophisticated account of the cultural and thereby conservative character of religious knowledge, is what, in turn, allowed him to maintain the validation of "traditional forms" even while acknowledging their secondary status as servants to the Word's destiny to give birth to and mature a "new people" in Christ Jesus.

It is not surprising that Thorndike proved the primary exponent of the so-called Vincentian Canon as the authoritative template of ecclesial self-exposition. This summary of the parameters for the church's discriminating test in controverted matters — *quod ubique, quod semper, quod ab omnibus creditum est* ("what has been believed everywhere, always, and by all")[20] — was more expressive than constructive of a number of Anglican attitudes towards the authoritative constraints upon Scripture's interpretative rule. It included appeals to the "primitive" church of the Fathers (later expressly of the "first four centuries"), the "apostolic deposit" of the "undivided church," the respect due to what was coherent with and sustaining of these elements including later Western standards of orthodox scriptural and doctrinal exposition and liturgical practice, and finally the appeal to the corporate articulations of these various elements in historic ecclesial and catholic council. While Thorndike himself provided a sophisticated set of arguments for drawing together these already embedded Anglican sentiments under the Vincentian Canon's ordering, he never

---

19. The key text is Book I of Part I of his *Epilogue to the Tragedy of the Church of England* (1659), reprinted in Vol. 2 of Thorndike's *Theological Works* (Oxford: John Henry Parker, 1845). Long consigned to the limited lineage of Tractarian forbears, Thorndike has emerged more recently as a great synthesizer of Anglican theological concerns, on a par with Hooker and even his better in terms of systematic clarity and theoretical creativity.

20. Defined by Vincent of Lérins in his *Commonitorium* II.3.

claimed to be suggesting some new framework of authority, only to be identifying a healthy way of "being the Christian church" that was already established in the church's historical nature. Later Tractarian theologians brought into relief the various elements noted above in explicit ways, and it could be argued that something like the famous "Chicago-Lambeth Quadrilateral" is itself but an ecumenically-oriented tool for articulating Thorndike's basic point.

It is worth mentioning Thorndike, furthermore, less because of his influence (which was slight) than because of the explanatory force of his ecclesiology for experienced Anglicanism, particularly as it took form in a context independent of the particular struggles of England, viz. the American colonies and the nascent United States. The odd theological amalgam that characterized the self-understanding of eighteenth-century Episcopalians[21] is matched only by the ease with which the founding conventions of the Episcopal Church could move from jettisoning creedal articles (and whole creeds themselves!) to restoring their full canonical force in ways that were to enhance their popular authority in comparison with the past.[22] The pragmatic demand was strong, of course, that the young church accede to the strictures of England's hierarchy on these matters if it was to receive permission to have its own bishops consecrated in Britain. But there was more to the topsy-turvy swings back to "uniformity in Doctrine and Discipline" with the Church of England than the savvy politics of Latitudinarianism.

For what finally asserted itself through all the machinations of denominational self-construction in North America was the underlying drive to "conformity," in the Anglican sense, that finally came to rest upon the undergirding character and shape of the Prayer Book's "scriptural wor-

21. Cf. the recommended 1804 "reading list" and "library" for ordinands and clergy, which includes a potpourri of Restoration High Church writers, Revolutionary Latitudinarians, Patristic scholars and historians, Primitivists (of all stripes), Hutchinsonians, Protestant biblical commentators, and rationalists.

22. The shape of the *Proposed Book of Common Prayer,* an emended version of the 1662 English book edited by William White and William Smith, included the excision of the Athanasian and Nicene Creeds (for both moral and doctrinal reasons), the removal from the Apostles' Creed of the article on Christ's Descent into Hell, reference to baptism as "regeneration" and to ministers as "priests." All of these were restored *in toto* (except the Athanasian Creed) along with some new language regarding ordination vows, upon the objections of Canterbury (not to mention the clamorings of many American Anglicans).

ship." The rationalist master formulator and politician of the Episcopal Church's origins, William White (later a bishop from Philadelphia), was at first no great proponent of doctrinal standards nor of subservience to British ecclesial attitudes (though he later worked hard to reestablish a revised form of the Thirty-Nine Articles for ECUSA[23]). Nonetheless, his framing descriptions of Anglican Christianity in America were given in decidedly "conformist" tones: a church defined by the "ancient habits" and "stated ordinances" that render a church closest to the "form of the religion of the Scriptures."[24] It was an explanatory vessel into whose hold the practices of the Prayer Book naturally fell, and the doctrinally minimalist face of corporate scriptural formation was smoothly assumed by the life of the newly birthed Anglican "communion."

The reality of this "communion" character, already intrinsic to the Church of England's identification with Scripture's social formation through conforming worship, took on a concrete political relief: the new Anglican church in America owed its being to and maintained its integrity through its dependence upon corporate accord with the British church, its hierarchy, and the forms of its communal prayer. What was to become the official ground to the "Anglican Communion" that the Lambeth Conferences would enunciate in the later nineteenth and earlier twentieth centuries, was therefore actually enacted before the fact in the mechanisms by which the Episcopal Church was founded — adherence in "uniformity" to England's "Doctrine and Discipline," bound by a cohesive episcopate, embodied in a set form of "common prayer," and open to national variation in matters "inessential" and non-"contradicting" of the "Word of God," in accordance with the demands of local "civil constitutions."[25]

In a way that far exceeded the Church of England's own self-norming, ECUSA thereby adopted a "conciliar" approach to its self-formation, not merely through the structures of its representative "con-

23. The Articles were indeed restored to the Prayer Book in 1801, edited with an eye mainly to the changed civil structures of America; their subscription, however, was never made mandatory by canon.

24. From the opening Preface and closing chapter of *The Case of the Episcopal Churches in the United States Considered* (1782), reprinted in Robert W. Prichard, ed., *Readings from the History of the Episcopal Church* (Wilton, Conn.: Morehouse-Barlow, 1986), pp. 61, 79.

25. These matters, contained in the Acts, Resolutions, and convention correspondence with the Archbishop of Canterbury, are detailed in the *Journals* of the first Conventions (ed. William Stevens Perry [Claremont, NH, 1874]).

vention," but more fundamentally through its accepted limitation by "counsel" (and even permission) with another national church. As a result, no set of "formularies" in themselves, apart from Scripture, could hold legal explanatory force for the faith of ECUSA, and Scripture's authority came to bear only in coherence with the common practices and counsel of some "larger" Church.[26] The Church of England can rely upon a canonically established pattern of appeal to certain doctrinal authorities.[27] But ECUSA's only "legal" explicated parameters are found in the "Preamble" to its Constitution and focus, by contrast, less on documented standards, than on the church's "constituent" membership in the larger Church, both "one, holy, apostolic, and catholic" and defined by the "communion" of other Anglican churches.

The search for documented definitions of these standards, however, has stymied many. The only reference to the "Book of Common Prayer" in this constitutional context is apparently to a generic version ideally shared within the communion itself, and only insofar as it enunciates something called the "historic Faith and Order." The "vows" of the ordained in ECUSA require a written affirmation that Scripture is to be identified with "the Word of God," that it "contains all things necessary for salvation," and that the ordinand will "conform to the doctrine, discipline, and worship of the Episcopal Church." What exactly explicates these elements is left unclear, especially when (as in the case of the consecration of bishops) the "guarding of the faith, unity, and discipline of the Church" is something stated in a context in which "the Church" itself seems to be equated with an entity "throughout the world" whose "heritage" far exceeds ECUSA's own canonical structures.[28]

It is also sociologically odd that, within the self-conscious denominational pluralism of America, ECUSA did not respond to the normal pressures of sectarian exactitude by clarifying its internal standards, but continued instead to exist within a system whose coherence still presupposed

26. This is precisely one of the legal issues now brought to the roiling surface of the division over same-sex blessings in ECUSA. But the theological point is more substantive. See below, Chapter 9, and its discussion of "conciliarity."

27. Cf. the Anglican-Methodist Covenant, paragraphs 104f. Even here, however, the canons refer to Creeds and "councils" and the "teaching of the Fathers" only insofar as they are "agreeable to the Scriptures," a traditionally loose order of appeal. The "formularies" of the Prayer Book and Ordinal, however, are explicitly noted.

28. See the 1979 BCP, pp. 513 and 517f.

the corporate force of normative "conformity" tied to the culture of an alien politics. Furthermore, as the Anglican Communion has evolved, numerically exploding in membership after the middle of the twentieth century, Anglican self-identity has drifted in this same direction as ECUSA's foundational conciliarism. As the Lambeth Conferences progressively outlined the basis for admission to the communion, the standards of the formularies were gradually allowed to fall away as necessary conditions (already, the Articles were dropped at Lambeth 1888), leaving in their place something like ECUSA's dependence upon "Prayer Book" testimony to "historic faith and order," which is practically embodied and adjudicated in episcopal conciliarism (the latter of which was formally articulated finally at Lambeth 1988). These developments have not been happily received by all, including for example American "autonomists" and non-Western "confessionalists." But the developments are nonetheless real.

From one perspective one can see this evolution as part of the consistent Anglican refusal to erect as legislatively normative anything beyond a formative scripturalism whose framework remains grounded in the somewhat fluid reality of conciliar consensus, still embodied primarily in episcopal collegiality. And to this degree, the Communion's own life can be understood as a continued (if often undeliberated, until the Windsor Report of 2004) groping after something like Thorndike's Vincentian Canon. But from another perspective, there is a growing awareness that perhaps the present circumstances of both local and global social fragmentation cannot support either the time or even the theological presuppositions required for this groping. Confusion over Prayer Book revision within various national churches, widening disagreements over the place and even value of normative scriptural applications among and within various national churches, and the political dynamics that are more and more pitting local and wider conciliar accountabilities against each other are all rendering the very practice of formative corporate scripturalism something pragmatically and conceptually incoherent for many Anglicans.

But it is incoherent largely because of a cultural drift that has little capacity to value the corporate continuities and formative embrace of Christian ecclesial life itself, understood in terms of the historically tethered apprehension of the conciliar authority of "scripture-in-communion." And this drift, furthermore, is one whose direction has clearly moved along a path in some tension with the emergent desires for communion that have brought together both geographically dispersed and often dynamic national churches, whose sense of scriptural dedication clearly yearns for a coherent formative context in which the Word of God can bring unity. The "authority" at work within Anglicanism, on this account, is oddly being mitigated by the forces of autonomous pluralism even as its power is being embodied in a vast expansion of ecclesial Christian life that is without historic precedents. It is a strange tension. But it is exactly the challenge of this tension, and its resolution within the church's communion life, that we now turn to examine in the next chapter.

# CHAPTER FIVE

# Diversity and Integrity:
# The Challenges of Life Together

*Philip Turner*

> *"Love and Truth go before your face."*
>
> Psalm 89:14b

> *"For too long Anglicans have appeared willing to evade responsible theological reflection and dialogue by acquiescing automatically and immediately in the coexistence of incompatible views, opinions, and policies."*
>
> Inter-Anglican Theological
> and Doctrinal Commission

## Introduction

The current tension between the reach for the "authority" of "Scripture-in-communion" and the pluralistic impulse towards local autonomy represents an overarching dynamic within the global church that is Anglicanism. More particularly, this tension takes the form of a division over responses to "diversity." The above quotation from the report of the Inter-Anglican Theological and Doctrinal Commission, *For the Sake of the Kingdom,* juxtaposes two of the most prominent options now before the Anglican Communion with respect to the reality of "diverse" ecclesial commitments within it or of diverse theological commitments within individual members of it. Confronted as they are by fearfully divisive issues, Anglicans are faced with the option of "responsible theological reflection and dialogue" on the one hand; and acquiescence "in the coexistence of incompatible views, opinions, and policies" on the other.[1] One can see these options at work in relation to a series of issues that have appeared in recent years, and for which we have sketched some typically "conservative" responses in Chapter Three. Most immediately, one thinks of the ordination of women, the blessing of gay unions, and the ordination of non-abstaining homosexual persons. To this list can be added other points of contention. These include lay presidency at the Eucharist and replacement of use in public worship of the Trinitarian name (Father, Son, and Holy Spirit) with identifiers denoting divine functions (e.g., Creator, Redeemer, Sanctifier).

It is dangerous to generalize overmuch about reactions to these issues in the various provinces of the Anglican Communion. From the point of view of one who is a member of The Episcopal Church U.S.A. (ECUSA), it can truthfully be said, however, that the first option, "responsible theological reflection and dialogue," takes place only rarely and with little effect. What parades as reflection and dialogue on the whole amounts to no more than impassioned repetition, within a politically controlled space, of hardened positions. Absent a means to carry on successful theological debate, the second option, acquiescence "in the coexistence of incompatible views, opinions, and policies" (known in ECUSA as "local option"), presents itself as the politically expedient method of dealing with the conflicts these issues have produced. It is sad but true to say that the first option has been avoided because, as a church, ECUSA no longer has the means or the will to carry on "responsible theological reflection and dialogue." It is also sad but true to say that the second option has been chosen in large measure not only because ECUSA lacks the will and means to achieve theological agreement, but also because a strategy that tolerates contradictory positions and practices, even on matters regarded as essential to a faithful witness to Christ, seems a necessary means to hold together a fast unraveling denomination.

The problem is that the adversaries in these ecclesiastical battles believe that their position is an aspect of the gospel itself and, as such, in the end, not open to compromise. As a result tolerance in respect to these mat-

---

1. *For the Sake of the Kingdom* (London: Anglican Consultative Council, 1986), para. 97, p. 60.

ters is in fact but a temporary strategy and not a perdurable conviction.[2] One suspects as well that when these issues are placed in the context of the Anglican Communion as a whole it will appear, as it has in ECUSA, that "responsible theological reflection and dialogue" will prove difficult; and that acquiescence "in the coexistence of incompatible views, opinions and policies" will present itself as a tempting option. One suspects also that mutual toleration of this sort will prove itself a short-lived expedient.

In respect to these options, adoption of the second strategy will not only prove futile but in the end will change the nature of Anglicanism in a way that destroys it as a communion of churches. To be specific, adoption of the second strategy will issue by default in a federation rather than a communion. It is this statement that presents the subject of this essay. If one wishes to preserve a communion of churches, what degree of diversity is compatible with ecclesial integrity? This question is not only important to Anglicans, but to all Christian denominations. Within a pluralistic society, the question is in fact unavoidable.

For Anglicans, a version of this question was posed as long ago as 1948 when a committee of bishops (chaired by Archbishop Carrington of Québec) assembled for the Lambeth Conference asked, "Is Anglicanism based on a sufficiently coherent form of authority to form the nucleus of a worldwide fellowship of churches, or does its comprehensiveness conceal internal divisions which may cause its disruption?"[3] These very pressing questions are generated by an even more fundamental one; namely, how, in the midst of the changes and chances of history, does the One, Holy, Catholic, and Apostolic Church both speak meaningfully to its time and place and yet remain faithful to the original witness of the Apostles? Fidelity to the apostolic witness poses the question of integrity, and faithful witness within particular times and places poses the question of tolerable diversity.

It will prove helpful to provide at the outset a summary statement of the answer we propose to give to this question. I shall do so in a series of

---

2. See *Journal of the General Convention, 2000*. In an action directly contrary to the advice of the Lambeth Conference of Bishops, the General Convention of ECUSA held in 2000 mandated that in the future all dioceses of the Episcopal Church open the ordination process to women. (See e.g., Resolution III.4 of the Lambeth Conference of Bishops, 1998.) This action on the part of the General Convention effectively did away with a "conscience clause" that had been in effect since General Convention sanctioned the ordination of women in 1976.

3. *The Lambeth Conference 1948* (London: SPCK, 1948), p. 84.

propositions, some negative and others positive. In the argument that follows, I shall seek to establish each of these propositions, but not in the order they appear below. Rather they will appear from time to time in various orders; and, in so doing, provide the warp and woof of a textured argument that will unfold rather slowly.

Negatively, we hope to establish five propositions:

1. ecclesial integrity and tolerable diversity cannot be maintained simply by citing scriptural "proofs";
2. ecclesial integrity and tolerable diversity cannot be maintained simply by citing creedal or confessional statements;
3. ecclesial integrity and tolerable diversity cannot be maintained simply by reference to political or legal authority, Episcopal, canonical, or otherwise;
4. ecclesial integrity and tolerable diversity cannot be maintained simply by referring to historical or social developments;
5. ecclesial integrity and tolerable diversity cannot be maintained simply by reference to any or all of the above in combination.

Positively, we hope to establish that ecclesial integrity and tolerable diversity can be maintained only if the presence of the Holy Spirit keeps the following five factors in a dynamic and mutually correcting relationship one to another. Under the guidance of the Holy Spirit:

1. disputes affecting ecclesial integrity and tolerable diversity take place in the midst of a scripturally formed people who hear the whole of the Bible in particular historical circumstances and in the midst of an ordered fellowship of worship and prayer;
2. disputes affecting ecclesial integrity and tolerable diversity are addressed within a community whose life is rooted in a shared will to unity and shaped by Christ's cross;
3. disputes affecting ecclesial integrity and tolerable diversity are carried out by means of a protracted, free, and open theological debate in which mutual correction is both expected and welcomed;
4. disputes affecting ecclesial integrity and tolerable diversity are addressed by political authorities in a cohesive manner that inhibits changes in practice until wide agreement about "novelties" has been reached;

5. disputes affecting ecclesial integrity and tolerable diversity are carried out within a wider "conciliar economy" that places limits upon the "autonomy" of any given parish, diocese, or province within the Anglican Communion.

## Anglican Ethos, Diversity and Integrity

The task, of course, remains to defend this normative proposal. In this enterprise, it is perhaps best to begin by noting that, for Anglicans, there is a formal way in which to address the issues of integrity and diversity. The way is one that has developed rather slowly over time and, to date, has stood the test of time. Within authoritative constraint of "Scripture-in-communion" as described in the last chapter, this way recognizes only that diversity that corresponds to the witness of Holy Scripture as apprehended in the common life and worship of the church. As we have argued, such apprehension is aided by (although not founded upon) the creeds, the *Book of Common Prayer,* the "Ordinal," and, in a looser sense, the Thirty-nine Articles, the first four ecumenical councils, and (in an even looser sense) the writings of early fathers of the church.[4] Traditionally, Anglicans have sought both ecclesial integrity and tolerable diversity within these parameters.

There is a substantial tradition among Anglicans that holds that, within these parameters, substantial diversity is tolerable. There is substantial agreement as well that ecclesial integrity is to be found within the circumference marked by these boundary stones. Thus, generally speaking, Anglicans agree that if the need arises to establish or defend doctrine and practice one must first show that the doctrine or practice in question accords with Holy Scripture. It is at this point, however, that a difficulty arises. The problem is that doctrine and practice cannot always be read off the Holy Scriptures in a way that compels necessary conclusions. The boundaries they set for determining faithful doctrine and practice are in large measure porous rather than fixed and easily identifiable. One must interpret scrip-

4. For a helpful and interesting discussion of the authority of these sources for Anglican theology see Henry Chadwick, "Tradition, Fathers, and Councils" in *The Study of Anglicanism,* ed. Stephen Sykes and John Booty (London: SPCK, 1988), pp. 91-105. See also Norman Doe, *Canon Law in the Anglican Communion* (Oxford: Clarendon Press, 1998), pp. 197-200, 378.

ture to arrive at doctrinal formulations and faithful practice. In this interpretive enterprise, the creeds, forms of worship, confessions, councils, and the writings of trusted authorities are necessary points of reference. Indeed, by reference to them one can in some instances, with more or less certainty, rule out some options and establish others. Nevertheless, citation of Holy Scripture and its standard interpretations is generally a sign of contestation; and, in numerous instances, appears unable to resolve the struggles in the midst of which citation is made. There is often some gap, be it large or small, between the Holy Scriptures and the way in which they are to be understood in relation to particular times and places. In short, reference to Holy Scripture and its subsequent interpretations cannot always resolve the tension between acceptable diversity and ecclesial integrity. The gap between original witness and present circumstance can in part be bridged by reference to the way in which this witness has been grasped and expressed previously; but the gap can be bridged only in part.

The next question is then how the gap is to be bridged in a satisfactory manner. Most Christians agree that the presence of the Holy Spirit in the heart of the believer and the common life of the church is utterly necessary if diversity and ecclesial integrity are to be satisfactorily combined.[5] Nevertheless, more needs to be said for the simple reason that both the Holy Spirit and the gospel message itself are mediated to both individuals and to the church in certain ways. In times of conflict, these means of reception themselves become matters of dispute; and, given the fact that we live in a time of conflict, little headway can be made in respect to the issue of diversity and integrity apart from some resolution of the conflict over these means.

Contrary to much recent Anglican thought, our contention is that the most godly and, in the end, most adequate way to bridge this gap is, in the first instance, neither by the exercise of ecclesial authority, nor by the rationalization of canon law, nor by reference to creeds, confessions and/or formularies, nor by the invocation of rather vague notions like "core doctrine."[6]

5. Only rarely do Anglicans go on to draw an important implication from this belief; namely, if agreement cannot be reached about what constitutes ecclesial integrity and tolerable diversity, the absence of the Holy Spirit ought to be assumed. For a well-argued defense of this conclusion see Ephraim Radner, *The End of the Church: A Pneumatology of Christian Division in the West* (Grand Rapids: Eerdmans, 1998).

6. An example of the first of these inadequate strategies is the recent suggestion of the Lambeth Conference of Bishops to give more authority in settling contested issues to the

To be sure, save for the notion of "core doctrine" (whose equivalents, "fundamentals" and "essentials," have proven themselves again and again impossibly vague and unstable),[7] these options all play a necessary role in forming the mind of the church. None of them, however, function properly if they are not rooted in a foundational practice. This way is one in which acceptable diversity and ecclesial integrity are maintained, in the first instance and most basically, by common participation in an ordered fellowship of prayer and worship. In this ordered fellowship, the public and reiterative reading of Holy Scripture entire (or almost so) provides the foundation of all else; namely, common prayer, eucharistic celebration, communal instruction, common practice, ecclesial integrity and tolerable diversity.[8] It is of basic importance to note that the practice of hearing the scriptures over time in the midst of common life, worship, and order constitutes an attending condition that renders a strategy of "responsible theological debate and dialogue" an effective means of preserving ecclesial integrity while allowing for tolerable diversity.

---

Primates of the Anglican Communion. See, e.g., *The Truth Shall Make You Free* (the report of the Lambeth Conference of Bishops, 1998), Resolutions III.6a-c. An example of the second option is a paper by Prof. Norman Doe presented to the March 2001 meeting of the Primates suggesting that rationalization of canon law throughout the communion is the way to deal with diversity. (See also Doe, *Canon Law in the Anglican Communion*, pp. 274-82). The third strategy is illustrated by a chapter in *To Mend the Net* entitled "The Formularies' Limits of Diversity." Here a case is made for the authority of formularies such as the Ordinal and the Articles of Religion in settling contested matters. (Drexel Gomez and Maurice Sinclair, eds., *To Mend the Net: Anglican Faith and Order for Renewed Mission* [Carrollton, Tex.: The Ekklesia Society, 2001], pp. 93-105). The decision of the Ecclesiastical Court in the trial of Bishop Walter Righter for heresy provides an example of the final strategy. The court found against the plaintiffs because it judged that the defendant, in ordaining non-abstaining homosexuals had not violated "core doctrine." (See R. R. Reno, "An Analysis of the Righter Decision," *Pro Ecclesia* 5, no. 4 [Fall, 1997]: 392-96.)

7. The notion of core doctrine may be taken as analogous to others like "fundamentals" or "essentials." Bishop Stephen Sykes has shown with remarkable clarity how difficult these ideas are to employ in any controlled and helpful manner. He points out that there is no agreement about what the fundamentals are, that the basis of their authority in an undivided church is difficult to sustain, and that they have proven themselves again and again ineffective as a means of overcoming ecclesial division. See Stephen Sykes, "The Fundamentals of Christianity" in *The Study of Anglicanism*, ed. Stephen Sykes and John Booty (London: SPCK, 1988), p. 242. See also Stephen Sykes, *The Integrity of Anglicanism* (London: Mowbray, 1978), pp. 11-14.

8. See Chapter Four above.

For a number of reasons, a grasp of and commitment to the central place in Christian formation of what the previous essay has called "scriptural immersion by a people" (as opposed to prior constraint by "a defined system of 'authority' or 'doctrine' or the sovereignty of unconstrained individual conscience) have, in parts of the Anglican Communion, been steadily eroding for some time now.[9] Erosion of commitment to this communal practice has, not surprisingly, been accompanied precisely by a loss of ecclesial integrity and a proliferation of intolerable diversity.[10] Central to our argument is the belief that, apart from increased awareness of the importance of and participation in "scriptural immersion by a people" within ordered forms of prayer and worship, the gap between Holy Scripture and present circumstance cannot be adequately closed. This belief leads to the further conclusion that disputes over tolerable diversity and ecclesial integrity are finally settled by the presence of a common mind among a people formed by scriptural immersion. Apart from such immersion and agreement, no satisfactory solution can be found to the presenting problem of this essay. To put the matter another way, apart from common allegiance to and renewal of this central practice, Anglicanism will find itself unable to bridge the gap between Holy Scripture and circumstance in a way that promotes unity and peace. In this case, Anglicanism will most certainly cease to be a communion. It will either divide or devolve into a federation, by which we mean a group of churches that are linked for practical reasons, but not necessarily by fellowship or communion in the gospel. Indeed, federally linked churches (as opposed to churches in communion one with another) might be more than willing to acquiesce "automatically and immediately in the coexistence of incompatible views, opinions, and policies" that reflect irreconcilable differences in respect to both beliefs and practices implied by the Christian gospel.

Again, as argued previously, Thomas Cranmer is the source of the complex of practices we have identified as most supportive of ecclesial integrity and tolerable diversity. This notion, namely, that both the integrity and diversity of the church are rooted in Scripture as it is appropriated within a communion of saints who, over time, conform to certain prac-

9. For a description of this erosion and a suggestion as to how it might be reversed see Philip Turner, *The Anglican Digest* (Advent 2002).

10. See e.g. R. R. Reno, *In the Ruins of the Church: Sustaining Faith in an Age of Diminished Christianity* (Grand Rapids: Brazos, 2002), pp. 83-96, 149-64.

tices and forms of worship is to be found in most forms of Catholic Christianity. It is not unique to Anglicanism. It is, however, a notion that demands great faith in the power of the Holy Spirit to preserve both integrity and tolerable diversity within a framework that is not overly defined either by formularies, laws, or political structures. Consequently, the temptation constantly arises to pin down the precise nature of integrity and the precise limits of diversity by elevating the importance of one or another of these ways of limiting the possible signification of Holy Scripture.

One can see these temptations rise to the fore among both Catholics and Evangelicals alike, especially in times of conflict. Anglican history is filled with examples of attempts to locate ecclesial integrity and tolerable diversity by reference to the Articles of Religion, or the Creed, or the authority of the episcopacy, or, latterly, identifiable forms of religious and/or social experience. We wish to make no universal claims about the way in which Anglicans seek to preserve ecclesial integrity and identify the limits of diversity. We only note a strand of thought and practice that has had lasting effects upon Anglicans throughout their history; and that has produced a particular ethos — one that eschews overly defined theological statement, overly centralized forms of Episcopal authority, and extensive codes of canon law as "front line" means of addressing issues of integrity and diversity.

## Anglican Ethos and the Birth of a Communion

One can see the formative power of this strand rather clearly if one surveys the origin and growth of what we now call the Anglican Communion. At the inception of the Episcopal Church (and so perhaps the conception of the Anglican Communion), William White, who became bishop in Philadelphia, wrote, in *The Case of the Episcopal Churches in the United States Considered*, that the Episcopal Church is defined by "ancient habits" and "stated ordinance" that render a church closest to the "form of the religion of the Scriptures." The first General Convention of the Episcopal Church, in its various acts and resolutions, went on to bind itself to the "Doctrine and Discipline" of the Church of England, to a cohesive episcopate, and a set form of common prayer. Its foundational documents permitted diversity only in respect to "inessential" matters, and these were defined as ones that contradicted neither the "Word of God" nor the demands of local "civil constitutions."[11]

In this self-definition, one sees the same reticence in respect to doctrinal definition, ecclesial governance, and canon law noted previously. Nevertheless, this peculiarly American formulation added a new emphasis. R. R. Reno, C. Seitz, P. Turner and P. Zahl have termed this new element a "Conciliar Economy."[12] As was the case of the Church of England, the foundation of this new church lay in "ancient habits" and "stated ordinances" that its authors believed rested upon and placed it "closest to" the Holy Scriptures and the early church. The Holy Scriptures, however, were not to be appropriated in ways that ran contrary to the "Doctrine and Discipline" of the Church of England. Thus, the Episcopal Church, like the Church of England, centered its life in the ordered reading of Scripture in the context of ancient forms of worship that were to be overseen by a unified episcopate. However, this scripturally formed and prayerfully ordered life was to cohere with the common practice and beliefs of another church whose common life was rooted in the same sort of scriptural formation.[13]

Here at the inception of what was to become the Anglican Communion one sees a conciliar principle imbedded. From this small beginning grew the conciliar economy that came to characterize what became the Anglican Communion. As the Anglican Communion grew, conformity to the Doctrine and Discipline of the Church of England was transformed into "uniformity with the 'Primitive Church'" of the first four centuries as explicated in the *Book of Common Prayer* shared throughout the globe. With a proliferation of versions of the *Book of Common Prayer* came yet another shift; this time to a fellowship of churches bound by communion with the Archbishop of Canterbury. The conciliar constraint once located

11. Reno, *In the Ruins of the Church.* For the original actions, resolutions, and correspondence see *Journals* of the first conventions (Claremont, N.H., 1874).

12. See "An Open Opinion on the Authority of General Convention." This statement can be viewed on the Web site of *The Living Church* (http://www.livingchurch.org).

13. It is well to note, however, that the American arrangement of a convention of the whole was different from the separate but interacting institutions of the Church of England. The English institutions served to make decisions based on consensus; but, because of their greater degree of separation, they necessarily went through a more gradual process than their American counterpart to reach their goal. The American arrangement brought about more immediate results, but at a cost. The cost is decisions reached in haste by a body that is dominated by its own internal dynamics, and that has no ongoing accountability to a constituency.

in the Doctrine and Discipline of the Church of England has become a constraint located in a communion of autonomous churches whose fellowship is represented and furthered by the Archbishop of Canterbury, and by the Lambeth Conference of Bishops that he has authority to "gather."

Despite variations in the *Book of Common Prayer,* this communion of churches manifests the same basis in the primacy of Holy Scripture appropriated in common worship and informed by ancient forms of prayer, the Creeds, the councils of the undivided church, and, to a lesser extent, the Articles of Religion and the writings of the church fathers. The polity of this communion can be said to be conciliar in two ways. (1) Each church, in its appropriation of Holy Scripture, is bound to and constrained by others in a wider communion. (2) Each church and the communion as a whole are ordered by a number of different and interlocking councils, each with its own structure, canonical status and range of competence.[14] One function, indeed the primary function, of these councils is "to uphold the Christian faith of the Apostles of Jesus as given in Scripture."[15] As such, it is their responsibility "to discern where that teaching is being compromised by the actions and decisions of a few."[16]

To bring this particular part of our argument to a close, it can be said that, for Anglicans, ecclesial integrity and tolerable diversity are kept in faithful balance by maintenance of a particular sort of ethos that is defined by a distinguishing set of practices rather than by reference to a teaching authority, or the promulgations of an ecumenical council, or by a confession. That ethos is grounded in the reiterative reading of Holy Scripture within the context of a common form of worship. To be sure, faithful reception of Holy Scripture necessarily involves reference to the *Book of Common Prayer,* creeds, theological formularies, codes of law, and ecclesial office, but none of these "authorities" provide a point of reference that precedes or supplants Holy Scripture.[17] Further, none of them can func-

---

14. For a recent description of the interlocking councils that define Anglican polity and canon law see Doe, *Canon Law in the Anglican Communion,* esp. pp. 43-126, 339-82.

15. "An Open Opinion on the Authority of General Convention," 8.

16. "An Open Opinion on the Authority of General Convention," 8.

17. Bishop Gore thought he could stave off the effects of biblical criticism by elevating the status of the creeds. Thus, a reference more primary than scripture itself was elevated to a position of supreme importance. Bishop Gore failed to notice that the creeds can be subject to the same critical analysis as can be the books of the Bible. He thus failed to secure a

tion properly apart from the witness of Holy Scripture upon which they depend for their legitimacy. Finally, we note that, within the conciliar economy described above, the way in which Holy Scripture is received in each church is constrained by its reception in others.

## Doctrine Embedded in Practice

The central importance for Anglicanism of communal hearing of Holy Scripture is a position well established by Stephen Sykes, sometime Regius Professor of Theology at Cambridge University and former Bishop of Ely.[18] He has made the point in a forceful manner by insisting that, in addressing these issues, Anglicans, despite assertions to the contrary, in fact do have specific doctrines that are properly used to aid and guide the interpretation of Holy Scripture. As Bishop Sykes has pointed out, these doctrines are contained within the pages of the *Book of Common Prayer,* the Ordinal, and in canon law. Within this complex, their most fulsome presence is to be found in the liturgical forms located in the various books of common prayer.[19]

To be sure, the doctrinal content of the *Book of Common Prayer* (in its various guises) does not appear in the form of a confession like that of Augsburg or Westminster. Neither does it appear in a conciliar document like that of Trent or Vatican II. Rather, the doctrinal content Anglicans share is imbedded primarily in liturgical practices the purpose of which is to form the character of a communion of believers. Its liturgical and formational setting means that the doctrinal content of Anglicanism is, as it were, scattered through a complex of practices rather than focused in a specifically theological document. Scattered though doctrinal content may be, however, it is simply impossible to say, after reading through any of the books of common prayer with which we are familiar, that Anglicans do

---

place for the defense of Christian belief that stood, as it were, above Holy Scripture as a means of protecting its essential content.

18. See Stephen Sykes, "Anglicanism and the Doctrine of the Church," in *Unashamed Anglicanism* (Nashville: Abingdon, 1995), pp. 116-18. In the same volume see also "Authority in the Church of England," p. 168, where he writes: "Giving the whole people of God access to the Scriptures through the interpretative medium of the liturgy was the fundamental catechetical act of empowering the people, taken in the sixteenth century."

19. See Sykes, *The Integrity of Anglicanism,* pp. 44-52.

not hold, among others, the doctrines of the Trinity, the two natures of Christ, Christ's atoning sacrifice, the resurrection of the dead, the life everlasting, the presence of the Holy Spirit in the church, the inspiration and primary authority of Holy Scripture, the effective character of the dominical sacraments, and the second Advent of Christ. Further, if one were to analyze the various litanies and pastoral offices in use within the communion, considerable additional doctrinal content would present itself — everything from statements about the various goods of marriage to others about the purposes of the state under God.

Anglicans throughout the world owe Bishop Sykes a considerable debt for exposing the bogus claim that Anglicanism is a form of Christianity that has a distinctive theological method (the interplay of Scripture, tradition, and reason) but no specific doctrinal content.[20] Sadly, however, the Anglican Communion as a whole has failed as yet to take up his challenge to make more explicit the largely implicit doctrinal content he has identified.[21] As a result many can harbor the earlier and mistaken view expressed so clearly by Maurice Wiles who wrote in a report on doctrine within the Church of England:

> What is important for the Christian community at large is not that it gets its beliefs absolutely clear and definite; it cannot hope to do that if they are really beliefs about God. It is rather that people within the community go on working at the intellectual problems, questioning, testing, developing, and seeking the practical application of the traditions that we have inherited from the past.[22]

20. Sykes, *The Integrity of Anglicanism*, pp. 61-75.

21. Sykes, *The Integrity of Anglicanism*, pp. 50-51. Bishop Sykes is right to contend that Anglicanism has doctrinal content and not simply theological method. Nevertheless, I question his location of this content primarily in the Doctrine of the Incarnation. I believe, rather, that it is the Doctrine of the Trinity that is most basic to Anglican belief and practice. Justifying this belief would, however, take an article, if not a book, in itself. Suffice it to say that I believe that prayer to the Father, through the Son, in the Spirit lies at the center of the doctrinal content of the *Book of Common Prayer*. It is for this reason that the most serious issue in respect to ecclesial integrity and tolerable diversity that faces the Anglican Communion does not concern women's ordination or the ethics of sex, but attempts to diminish or rid ECUSA's *Book of Common Prayer* of use of the Trinitarian name, Father, Son, and Holy Spirit.

22. Cited in Sykes, *The Integrity of Anglicanism*, p. 43. For Wiles's original essay see *Christian Believing* (London: Doctrine Commission of the Church of England, 1976), p. 130.

If taken at face value, this view (now pervasive within ECUSA) implies that the Anglican Communion is a society for theological investigation and debate rather than a part of the Body of Christ commissioned to proclaim a gospel with an identifiable content. To avoid this finally incoherent position, it is of vital importance to note, as has Bishop Sykes, that it is not incoherent to assert that Anglicanism has embedded in its practices and in its canon law identifiable doctrinal content, and yet that free and open theological debate in respect to both belief and practice is both permissible and desirable.[23]

The combination of free and open theological debate and identifiable theological content, however, raises at least two very thorny questions in respect to the issues of ecclesial integrity and tolerable diversity. The first, which by far is the easier to address, is what to do when clergy (who by solemn vow are committed to upholding the doctrine, discipline, and worship of the church of which they are a part) begin to use the pulpit to proclaim doctrinal novelties that represent personal opinion rather than the easily recognizable doctrinal content of the *Book of Common Prayer,* or when they make alterations, based on personal preference, in the forms of worship they are pledged by vow to use. The way in which Anglicans have chosen to address this problem is easy to state despite the fact that it is beginning to prove difficult to carry out. Anglicans hold that one of the primary reasons for having bishops is to provide the churches of the communion with an "ordinary" (or keeper of order) whose responsibility is to see that those charged by vow to uphold the doctrine, discipline, and worship of a given church within the Anglican Communion in fact comply with the vows they have taken. Bishops should be allowed considerable latitude in the way in which they fulfill this responsibility. However, if bishops on a fairly wide scale ignore this responsibility or fail to exercise it in an effective manner, then the common context within the worship of the church in which the Holy Scriptures are read, marked, learned, and inwardly digested, simply fragments. One can reasonably assume that such an eventuality will sooner rather than later be accompanied by a degree of diversity that proves itself intolerable because it obviously compromises ecclesial integrity.

The second (and far more difficult) issue arises when a province or diocese within the communion either adds practices or changes the doc-

23. Stephen Sykes, *The Integrity of Anglicanism,* p. 44.

trinal content of its practices in ways that do not cohere with those of the other provinces. When such an event occurs the question arises as to whether the novelty in question is an example of tolerable diversity or whether it compromises the integrity of Anglicanism as a communion of churches. At present, pre-eminent among these added or changed practices are the ordination of women, the ordination of non-abstaining homosexual persons, and the blessing of gay unions. The adversaries in these ecclesial battles all believe that they are fighting over the proper doctrinal content of the church of which they are a part. None of them hold that the argument in which they are involved is simply over theological method.

## Episcopal Authority, Free Debate, and Constancy of Practice within an Ecclesial Economy

How then are these circumstances to be addressed? Let it be said first of all that disputes of this nature about the practices of the provinces within the Anglican Communion are of importance to its health. Apart from such disputes, the various churches that make it up would fail to address the faith of the Apostles to their particular time and place. The issue is not whether these disputes should be allowed. The issue is how they are to be carried out in a way that preserves ecclesial integrity while allowing at the same time for tolerable diversity. We have argued that no solution is possible apart from a biblically immersed people joined together in common forms for prayer and worship. It is here, in the accepted belief and practice of the people, that a satisfactory resolution of these issues will finally be achieved. Nevertheless, a properly functioning polity vastly aids the necessary and proper communal process of sifting, receiving, or rejecting novelty. For Anglicans this polity is rooted in the sort of conciliar economy described above. The point we wish to make now, however, is that, within this economy, a cohesive episcopate and constancy of practice play as essential a role as does free and open debate.

In the midst of conflict, time can be viewed as a space for the presence of grace. Even from a purely secular point of view, space and time are necessary if thorny issues are to be satisfactorily addressed. Crucial to the provision of an ordered and peaceful space in time is a cohesive political authority that acts with slow deliberation and shows itself reluctant to change practice prior to fairly widespread communal agreement. Authors of *To Mend the Net*, a proposal as to how the Primates of the Anglican Communion might assume an "enhanced responsibility"[24] for its unity and health, made this comment in respect to the necessity of cohesive political authority. They said, "In the midst of passing on the faith, it is necessary for the church to use Holy Scripture and the Apostles' and Nicene Creeds to 'prove' doctrine and practice."[25] They then went on to make two additional statements. First, "that the process of 'proving' takes place in the midst of the baptized members of the Church as they are engaged in a regular round of expository preaching, eucharistic worship and prayer"; and second "that the unity of the Church, as it struggles to pass on the faith and practice of the Apostles, is expressed and maintained through the collegiality of its bishops."[26]

In making this statement, the authors of *To Mend the Net* align themselves with the conciliar economy that has until recently served as the foundation of the polity of the Anglican Communion. It is precisely this economy that is now being challenged by the Diocese of New Westminster and by the General Convention of the Episcopal Church. Both the action of the Diocese of New Westminster and the action of the General Convention of ECUSA run contrary to resolution I.10 of the 1998 Lambeth Conference of Bishops that states such action to be contrary to Holy Scripture. By saying that the practice of blessing gay unions is contrary to Holy Scripture, the bishops assembled at Lambeth by implication have expressed the view also that actions of this sort lie outside the circumference of tolerable diversity; and that they compromise ecclesial integrity. In taking this stand, they further have, by implication, distinguished the blessing of "gay unions" from the ordination of women. In this latter case, despite the very dubious way in which the first of these ordinations occurred within ECUSA,[27] no statement has been made to the effect that this practice runs contrary to Holy Scripture. Rather the bishops have recognized a serious

24. The charge for the Primates of the Anglican Communion to assume an "enhanced responsibility" was given in Resolution III.6. of the Lambeth Conference of Bishops held in 1998.

25. Gomez and Sinclair, *To Mend the Net*, p. 29.

26. Gomez and Sinclair, *To Mend the Net*, p. 29.

27. For a discussion of the disorderly way in which the ordination of women became a practice of ECUSA see Philip Turner, "Communion, Order and the Ordination of Women," *Pro Ecclesia*, Vol. II, No. 3 (Summer 1993): 275-84; "Episcopal Authority in a Divided Church," *Pro Ecclesia*, Vol. VIII, No. 1 (Winter 1999): 23-50.

disagreement and, because they have found no clear scriptural warrant to the contrary, have allowed for diversity of practice while at the same time urging that a process of reception be allowed to continue without hindrance throughout the communion.[28] The process of reception they recommend is meant to provide a space in time in which to test a practice that is indeed a novelty, but which reference to Scripture does not seem clearly to forbid. Indeed many hold that reference to Scripture provides positive warrant for the change.

Thus, in one case they have judged that Holy Scripture speaks against diversity of practice and have sought to prevent it. In another, they have judged (despite the fact that innovation has produced "impaired communion") that a period of testing should be allowed to determine if the diversity is indeed reconcilable with ecclesial integrity. In both cases, however, they have expressed how serious it is when bishops do not act in concert. In both cases they have also shown a cautious response to changes in practice. Nevertheless, it is important to note that in neither case have the bishops sought to inhibit "responsible theological debate and dialogue." Furthermore, in neither case have they been content when diversity appears to allow "incompatible views, opinions, and policies" simply to coexist. Rather, they have sought, with varying degrees of success, to create a space in time that will allow for the resolution of difference and the restoration of peace and unity.

Here are two examples of a cohesive episcopacy seeking to preserve a conciliar economy. However, claims to unfettered autonomy like those put forward by the Diocese of New Westminster and ECUSA are clearly subversive of both a conciliar economy and a cohesive episcopate. In anticipation of developments such as these, the Lambeth Conference of Bishops, in 1998, accorded an "enhanced responsibility" for the unity of the Anglican Communion to its Primates. It is through this "enhanced responsibility" that the bishops of the communion hope to preserve their collegiality and so inhibit the introduction of changes in practice that threaten division. Prior to their action, however, at least one province (the Anglican Church of Korea) had perceived the issue circumstances have now forced upon the bishops of the communion as a whole. In consequence, it wrote into the "Fundamental Declaration" upon which its constitution and canon law are based the condition that any proposed amendment to this declaration

---

28. *The Truth Shall Make You Free,* Res. III.4.

must be sent "to all the Metropolitans of the Anglican Communion and an assurance received from them that the proposed amendment is not contrary to the terms of the Communion between the Anglican Church of Korea and the Churches of which they are Metropolitans."[29]

The "Fundamental Declaration" of the Anglican Church of Korea gives constitutional expression to a crucial aspect of the ethos in which we believe Anglicans on the whole have sought to reconcile integrity and diversity. That is, Episcopal order and Synodical governance, while allowing for free and open debate in respect to disputed issues, are to be slow to change the practices of the various provinces of the communion. Change is to be undertaken only when there is extensive agreement that any diversity caused by a change in practice does not compromise the integrity of the communion into which that diversity seeks entrance. It is within such an ethos (one in which there is free debate combined with a cohesive Episcopal authority and a relative constancy of practice) that a scripturally formed people can find a space in time for the peaceful resolution of difference in respect to what must be held in common and the recognition of those things about which there may be tolerable diversity.

### Integrity, Diversity, and Virtue

This last remark prompts yet another question. How can a space in time indeed be one that leads to the peaceful resolution of differences? In respect to this question, we have mentioned already the importance of a cohesive episcopacy and constancy of practice. For episcopacy to remain cohesive and practice constant, however, a certain quality of life within the communion they order is required. In his "Preface" to the *Book of Common Prayer,* and in *Of Ceremonies,* Cranmer insists that the communal reading of Holy Scripture entire within the context of ordered worship leads to "edification" or "godliness." Both "godliness" and "edification" are terms that refer to a good deal more than right doctrine. They refer to an entire form of life in which belief and virtue are brought into correspondence. Our point is that ecclesial integrity and tolerable diversity cannot be main-

---

29. Cited by Norman Doe in *Canon Law in the Anglican Communion,* p. 26. For the statement of fundamentals see *The Constitution and Canons of the Anglican Church of Korea* (1992).

tained apart from the "godliness" of the scripturally informed people who must determine the boundaries of each. Apart from godliness, neither Episcopal authority, nor confessional adequacy, nor canonical provision, nor ancient forms of prayer can guarantee the peace of the church.[30]

In Resolution III.2e of the report of the Lambeth Conference of 1998, the bishops took note of the fact that the ordination of women had served to strain and impair communion among Anglicans, and in response they urged "courtesy, tolerance, mutual respect and prayer for one another" coupled with a "desire to know and be with one another" as necessary virtues and practices in circumstances where people felt tolerable diversity had been or might be exceeded. The list of virtues and practices they recommend are totally inadequate for maintaining the peace of the church, but they do indicate recognition that structures of authority and statements of belief are insufficient in and of themselves to guarantee a right relation between integrity and diversity. For this purpose, Thomas Cranmer suggested the virtues that comprise godliness rather than those that comprise civility in a pluralistic society. As will become clear in the exposition below, the virtues associated with godliness work in support of communion among Christians. The virtues we associate with civility, namely, "courtesy, tolerance, and mutual respect," are not designed to support communion but to help people who have fundamental disagreements coexist peacefully within a single polity. It is to the virtues associated with godliness rather than civility that one must turn to grasp the full nature of the ethos in which it is possible to preserve ecclesial integrity and foster tolerable diversity.

We may take the fourth chapter of Ephesians as a classical statement of the content of godliness. In describing the virtues and practices that serve the unity of the church, the author speaks not of "a desire to be with one another" but of "striving earnestly to maintain the unity of the Spirit in the bond of peace" (Eph. 4:3). He does not list the civil virtues of courtesy, tolerance and mutual respect but a series of virtues and practices that imitate the sacrificial life of Christ. These include humility, gentleness, patient endurance, kindness, compassion, forbearance, forgiveness and love (Eph. 4:2, 32). His point is that these virtues and practices both preserve and

---

30. For a more extended defense of the argument that follows see Philip Turner, "The 'Communion' of Anglicans after Lambeth '98: A Comment on the Nature of Communion and the State of the Church," *Anglican Theological Review,* Vol. 81, No. 2 (Spring 1999): 281-93.

make up the sort of ecclesial unity Christ's death was intended to procure. These are the virtues apart from which ecclesial integrity and tolerable diversity will come undone; and all the bishops, and the confessions, and all the canons in the world cannot, apart from them, put Christ's broken body back together again.

That this statement is true can be seen easily by asking a simple question.

When Christians find themselves in serious disagreement about the content of the gospel message or the form of life that bears witness to it, how are they to reach an agreement that does not amount to acquiescence "to the coexistence of incompatible views, opinions, and policies"? The previously mentioned virtues and practices are precisely those that allow for the truth spoken in love to be distinguished from false or inadequate representations of Christian faith and practice. All depends upon a prior attitude, namely "an earnest desire to maintain the unity of the Spirit in the bond of peace." This desire for unity and peace is manifest and made effective in the first instance through the sort of humility that makes room for mutual correction. Gentleness with one's opponents creates an atmosphere of trust. Patient endurance of the foibles of those with whom one disagrees allows for relations (even troubled ones) to continue over time. Kindness and compassion make it possible for one to see one's opponent in the best light. Forgiveness sustains relationships through the harms inevitably done. These virtues and practices, as the author of Ephesians makes clear, give the love of Christ very definite contours. They make love recognizable. Thus, it is finally charity in its many guises that creates the space in time in the midst of which Christians can find their unity in Christ. Prior to Christ's return, the peace of the church does not exist in a steady state. It constantly comes to be as Christians, in the power of the Spirit, deploy the marks and works of love.

## Conclusion

The argument we have put forward about the best way in which to preserve ecclesial integrity and promote tolerable diversity has unfolded slowly. The process has been slow because it is not possible to preserve the one and promote the other by simple reference to fixed and certain points. We speak of points of reference like episcopacy, creed, confession, or canon law. Were it possible to sort out the divisions that inevitably appear within the life of the church by direct invocation of any of these singly or in combination, one could write a much shorter response to the presenting question of this essay.

We do not wish to deny the importance of any of these points of reference. Each of these varying forms of authority play their part in maintaining the right relation between integrity and diversity, but none can function on its own apart from the communal practices and virtues that they serve and from which they are derived. Thus, we can say by way of summary that ecclesial integrity and tolerable diversity in many cases are not matters with a fixed and plainly recognizable identity. Rather, the first is preserved and the latter promoted when Christians in communion one with another are rooted in the common practice of hearing the Scriptures entire in an ordered manner and within ordered forms of common worship. When disputes arise which threaten their communion, cohesive Episcopal authority serves to preserve common practice while responsible, free, and open theological debate takes place concerning matters in dispute. During the course of this debate, the presence of godliness within the communion of Christians is essential for the successful resolution of conflict. Apart from godliness, interpretations of Holy Scripture fragment, forms of worship multiply along party lines, Episcopal cohesiveness disintegrates, Episcopal authority loses its effectiveness, and confessions become battle standards hoisted against people who are regarded as enemies.

If this analysis is correct, two conclusions follow. The first is that the debates that now rage concerning the ordination of women, the ordination of non-abstaining homosexual persons, the blessing of gay unions, lay presidency at the Eucharist, and the use of functional nouns to replace God's proper name are in fact debates that need to occur. They are absolutely necessary if the churches of the Anglican Communion wish to speak the gospel message to our times in a way that preserves ecclesial integrity and promotes tolerable diversity. The second is that the action of the Diocese of New Westminster and the action of ECUSA's General Convention — as well as many actions taken in reaction to them — represent direct attacks on the ecclesial economy that provides the conditions for preserving ecclesial integrity and promoting tolerable diversity.

The question of our day is how the Anglican Communion as a whole, its member churches individually, and its ecumenical partners will respond to the constitutional crisis brought on by the Diocese of New Westminster and ECUSA's General Convention. Many will look to the enhanced authority Lambeth has assigned to the meeting of Primates to resolve the difficulty. Others will take a more canonical approach and urge that the canon law of the various churches of the communion be brought into greater coherence. Others will look to Anglican formularies, and when they see variance from them declare themselves no longer in communion with the parties they view as heterodox. Others may seek to exclude the offending diocese or province from fellowship in the larger Anglican Communion. Some may bring ecumenical discussions to a halt. Some, though not all, of these strategies may prove of limited use. Nevertheless, none will succeed apart from a self-conscious attempt to renew and strengthen the particular ethos and economy we have sought to describe and defend. We believe that this ethos and this economy provide a way to preserve ecclesial integrity and promote tolerable diversity that, in the end, will prove more effective and more godly than the other remedies that will most certainly take the field. It is our belief that apart from this ecclesial economy, other remedies (Episcopal authority, canon law, confessions, etc.) will lose their moorings in the common life of the church and prove ineffective. Failure to abide within this economy and strengthen this ethos will compromise ecclesial integrity and produce intolerable diversity. Such a failure will be accompanied by increasing division and an inability to overcome conflict. The likely result will be a federation rather than a communion of churches and a further rupturing of ecumenical relations.

# CHAPTER SIX

# Episcopal Authority within a Communion of Churches

*Philip Turner*

One of the central elements of the conciliar economy that is peculiar to Anglicanism's development is the office of bishop. And we cannot properly address the challenges of our church's communion life without also focusing special attention on episcopal ministry within it. We will use as an outline for this discussion a specific set of questions. Some months before the Diocese of New Westminster made a decision to provide a rite for the blessing of gay unions, the bishops of the Anglican Church of Canada asked for a paper on the nature and function of Episcopal authority. They no doubt sensed that the division within the church over this issue would impact both their office and indeed the entire polity of the Anglican Church of Canada. In sending the request, they posed five questions that, if taken together, raise most of the basic issues connected with Episcopal governance and so also the nature and function of authority within a church. The five questions were:

- [Can there be] an exercise of authority that leads to the wholeness of the church?
- What does it mean to talk about authority in a pluralistic church?
- [What might constitute] an Anglican understanding of authority vis-à-vis the episcopate?
- [How ought one to understand] the role of bishops in relation to the three-legged stool of scripture, reason and tradition (with the fourth leg of experience as a concern as well)?

- [What is] the public ministry of bishops in society?[1]

By any standards, the list is a formidable one. Taken together, the items listed not only raise the most basic questions connected with Episcopal governance but also present what many believe to be the central crisis now facing those Christians who call themselves Anglicans. Might it be that the generally perceived crisis in Episcopal authority signals an even more profound one, namely, a loss of ecclesial identity so severe that it is increasingly difficult for the churches of the Anglican Communion to say with any degree of confidence that they are members of a communion of churches that are jointly members of the one, holy, catholic, and apostolic church?[2]

## Communion and Authority

To begin at the beginning, what is the relation between "an exercise of authority" and "the wholeness of the church"?[3] The first point to make is simply this — to the extent that authority functions legitimately, its very purpose is to procure "wholeness" or "the common good." Indeed, no other function is compatible with what both church and society have always understood authority to be. Nevertheless, it must be noted that the very presentation of such an issue implies a profound doubt as to whether authority and wholeness are compatible notions.

At some level, almost everyone now wonders if the juxtaposition of these two particular ideas constitutes something of an oxymoron. For many, if not most people, it most certainly does. Yves Simon, the Roman Catholic moral philosopher whose life's work focused on the issue of authority, wrote again and again about the rejection by our age of both au-

1. The original wording of the issues presented by the bishops does not include the words in brackets. We have added the material in brackets to interpret the issues the bishops presented.

2. It is important to note that this question has been posed not only about the Anglican Communion but also about the Lutheran church. See, e.g., William A. Norgren & William E. Rusch, *Implications of the Gospel* (Minneapolis: Augsburg, 1988).

3. For a more extended version of the following argument about the relation between authority and the common good see Philip Turner, "Authority in the Church; Excavations Among the Ruins," *First Things* 8 (December 1990): 25-31.

thority and true community.[4] In all his writings, he pointed to the pervasive individualism of contemporary Western society that works constantly to undermine both authority and community. Hannah Arendt made a very similar point about our post-Enlightenment age in her article "What Was Authority?"[5] As the title suggests, Arendt argued that authority in its classical sense (the sense in which in the West it has from the beginning been understood both within the church and the body politic) has all but disappeared in the modern age. According to Arendt, what we now call authority would be unrecognizable to Paul or Augustine, Plato or Cicero. It would be unrecognizable as well to Cranmer or Calvin.

That more classical notion is, however, alive and well in the Ordinal of all the books of common prayer with which I am familiar. What Anglican churches *say* in their formularies about authority and community health remains consistent with the classical tradition. Nevertheless, these formularies enshrine a view of authority and community health that, in the West, has become culturally strange — so much so that its presentation can bring out both division and considerable hostility. If what Simon, Arendt, and others say about authority in the modern and postmodern worlds is true, it is no wonder that Episcopal authority, along with all other forms, has become so problematic. Put simply, there is a disconnection between authority as it has been understood over the ages and the basic social facts of our time. To put the matter another way, it seems probable that bishops in England and North America (along with their counterparts in other denominations) have been given a job that in fact few if any really want them to do. At their consecrations as bishops, there was, in all likelihood, a false transmission of authority. The church through its formularies said one thing, but its members may actually have meant another.

Thus, it is necessary to ask what this classical and, to many, anachronistic view of the nature and function of authority is, and how, according to the classical view, the exercise of authority is related to community health. It must be said at the outset that authority is a complex rather than a simple notion. Its meaning is equivocal rather than univocal. It is, therefore, important to ask which sense of the word one is seeking to identify. In

---

4. See especially Yves Simon, *The Philosophy of Democratic Government* (Chicago: University of Chicago Press, 1951).

5. Hannah Arendt, "What Was Authority?" in *Authority,* ed. Carl Friedrich (Cambridge, Mass.: Harvard University Press, 1958), pp. 81-112.

the first instance, given the nature of the questions posed, it is what might be called the political sense of the word that is being sought. This sense can be found most easily by asking what, within the classical tradition, it might mean to say of someone, let us say a bishop or presbyter, a mayor or governor, that they *have authority* rather than saying simply that they *are an authority*. This more political sense of the word becomes clear by comparing it to terms used for other means of social control: in particular, *domination, manipulation,* and *persuasion.* Within the classical tradition, authority in its political sense is understood as a form of social control, or better a means to order the common life of a society, that lies between power (i.e. domination and manipulation) on the one hand and the non-executive authority of simple persuasion by example, rhetoric or competence on the other. To have authority is different from being a dictator who relies on force, and it is different from being a leader who relies simply on the ability to *persuade* others by charisma or eloquence to follow.

Why? For authority to be political authority and not a form of domination or manipulation, those who have it cannot bypass the liberty of those over whom they exercise it. They must in some sense govern with the assent of the governed. They must act on behalf of all. Conversely, to be *in authority* rather than to be simply *an authority,* those who are entrusted with it must have the right and obligation to require obedience from those who may not agree with particular decisions they make. To have political authority, one must enjoy more than the persuasive authority of a leader or expert. People with authority to govern have a right, even in cases of disagreement, to expect compliance with their *justifiable* commands, and to apply sanctions if compliance is not forthcoming. Incidentally, that is why in older ordinals, presbyters and deacons promised by solemn vow to obey their bishop, and the very fact that vows of obedience have been so muted in recent years indicates the extent to which the classical notion of authority is now only marginally operational. Indeed, people generally now prefer to speak of *leadership* rather than *authority* — a shift in usage that indicates their individualism — their willingness to respond to persuasion (which allows them to maintain a maximum degree of autonomy) but not to executive or political authority (whose *commands* they perceive to be contrary to that autonomy).

To continue with the main line of argument, according to the classical tradition, political authority, lying as it does between domination and persuasion, is a means of ordering social life that implies both the right to command and the liberty of those to whom commands may be issued. On first hearing, this statement may sound improbable or simply wrong-headed, but it can easily be shown that it is neither. Think of the relation between these two words — power and authority. They are linked but not identical and it is their difference that begins to reveal the very genuine links that exist between authority and liberty (and consequently healthy community).

What then is power? What is authority? How are they related? How are they different? As Max Weber pointed out long ago, power is nothing more than the ability to achieve purpose. Authority is somewhat different in that, as illustrated, say, by President Bush's inability to rally the nation behind the war in Iraq, those who have it do not always have the ability to achieve all they might desire. Nevertheless, if they *never* have the ability to get done what they propose to do, it would be stretching things a bit to say that they have authority.

So power and authority are not identical but they are related notions. How are they related? A few simple observations will reveal an answer. It is easy to imagine a situation in which someone has great power yet little or no authority. An obvious case is that of a tyrant or a bully. People who have power but not authority are known to everyone, and they make everyone justifiably nervous. What people fear is that the purposes those in power may pursue are not ones generally shared. What people fear is that their liberty will be infringed upon in ways that are both harmful and wrong.

Images of people who have power but not authority haunt the imagination. Images of people who have authority but not power are more difficult to come by. Indeed, it is probably the case that no such images exist because authority with no power at all is both a logical and practical impossibility. It appears to be the case that those with authority may on occasion lack sufficient power to achieve their purposes, but they cannot be altogether without power and still be said to have authority. This is so because political authority without power cannot enforce its commands, and without this ability, political authority simply ceases to be.

By way of example, we can think of Nelson Mandela during the time of his incarceration. His authority was necessarily connected with the power he had among his people. To be sure, his power was limited and could be exercised only indirectly, but it is undeniable that his power was real and that it was inseparably connected with the authority invested in him by the peoples of South Africa. Conversely, a total inability to use power, as perhaps would have been the case in the USSR or China, would have destroyed his authority or indicated that it had been withdrawn. If his authority had decreased, so would have his power. The reverse is also true.

The example helps show that though authority requires some degree of power to remain authority, power does not require authority to remain itself. It is this fact more than any other that, within the classical tradition, has served to define the nature and function of political authority. This sort of authority has been understood, both within the church and the body politic, as a way of making power responsible to a standard that is shared both by one who has authority and by those over whom authority is exercised. In short, authority is a way of investing power with moral and religious accountability. It is a way of ordering power within a community in such a way that the power of the community itself is augmented and directed to purposes acceptable to the community as a whole. Within the classical tradition, and in contradistinction to our own most immediate perceptions, authority does not separate ruler and subject; rather it links them in a common bond of fundamental belief and in a common form of life. Power disconnected from authority presupposes no such bond. Thus, in response to the question about an exercise of authority that leads to wholeness, the first thing to say is that, within the classical tradition, it is the very nature and function of authority, properly conceived and exercised, to lead to social health. Its very purpose is to allow a society to pursue purposes definitive of the life of the particular community in question.

It is this very point that is contained in the original meaning of the word *authority*. The English word derives from the Latin *auctor*. In Roman society, an *auctor* was one who, by virtue of a combination of qualities, was thought to stand closer to the foundational beliefs and ways of life of the Roman people than others. Consequently, it was the function of an *auctor* to protect and augment the Roman way, particularly in times of change or threat. Furthermore, in the classical tradition, the very notion of authority carries with it two attendant ideas that underline the close links between authority and community health. One is that there is a common set of beliefs and a common way of life, and the other is that there are people who have a particular set of virtues that allow them both to understand those beliefs and ways better than others and to protect and augment them in the midst of life's chances and changes. Noting these foundational beliefs, Hannah Arendt has made an observation that takes us to the heart of our own problem with authority.[6] We have a crisis of authority because our society no longer has widely shared beliefs and forms of life to which common reference can be made. Beliefs and ways of life, save in respect to certain minimal attitudes and practices without which social life could not successfully be carried on, are considered matters of private rather than public business. Further, because our notions of equality constantly seek to exclude discussion of the personal qualities of excellence that make one a fit person to govern, we increase the number of arguments over what ought to be done by those in authority and simultaneously narrow the range of personal qualities we believe make one fit to be entrusted with it. We seem less and less concerned that those we invest with authority embody a common ideal and more and more concerned that they succeed in the particular matters that touch our own interests.

At this point, an example from the American political scene might prove useful. American politics are now dominated by political action committees and, as their influence has increased, the ability of political parties to pursue consistent policies that have genuinely national goals has declined. What are now called "special interests" comprise the better part of the political landscape, and with their ascendancy have come a corresponding cynicism and political disengagement on the part of the general populace. It would be nice if one could say that things are different in the church, but that is not possible. Episcopal elections in America now turn on how the candidates stand on the issues, and behind each issue stand contending interest groups each pressing their particular cause. Seldom, if ever, does one hear questions asked about a candidate's grasp of Christian tradition, the depth of their life in Christ, or what might be called their wisdom in the Lord. The ability of a candidate to further what is common seems in no way to be a qualification for office. The important thing is their commitment to a particular set of interests. In short, the life of the Episcopal Church has been politicized all the way down, and the result of this process is erosion of the church's communion.

The process has also produced a subtle but profound change in the understanding of authority that informs the majority of those who now hold office in the Episcopal Church. Their focus has shifted from maintaining peace in the church to "prophetic witness." Of course, in a formal sense, there is no necessary conflict between "prophetic witness" and the

---

6. Arendt, "What Was Authority?"

peace of the church. The witness of Amos, Hosea, Jeremiah, and Isaiah was intended to call Israel to its ancient covenant roots and by so doing insure that *shalom* characterized the common life of the people. The prophets (and Jesus) spoke with authority because they spoke for YHWH who had all authority in earth and heaven and who, with mighty acts of power and words of truth, gave the common way of Israel as a light to the nations. The job of the prophet was to call the people back to a way of life from which they had strayed — a way of life definitive of community health.

Prophetic witness now carries a different connotation. No matter by what denials it is accompanied, the phrase generally calls to mind partisanship — dedication to a particular set of interests. The range of matters included in the Christian way narrows down in the contemporary ecclesial mind. Bishops, deans, and rectors, more frequently than one would like to think, see themselves as advocates not for the people of God but for some segment of that body.

Tracing recent debates within the Episcopal Church over the role of its presiding bishop can make the same point. Indeed, innumerable examples can be brought forward to show that authority seems to be understood and exercised in a different way than in the past. It is no doubt the case that matters are less extreme in Canada and England. They certainly are less extreme in Africa. Nevertheless, no less a figure than Bishop John Taylor wrote after the suicide of Professor Bennet (who killed himself because of distress over the state of the Church of England) that his death signaled a profound crisis in the Church of England — namely both the politicizing and the atomization of the English House of Bishops. As an English friend once said, "Things really are the same in England and Canada as they are in America. It's only that what happens in the Commonwealth is muted like the English weather while what happens in America takes place under the full glare of the Enlightenment sun." It does indeed appear that the Episcopal Church has more severe symptoms than do the other churches of the Anglican Communion; but distressing as it is to say so the same disease seems to be slowly eating its way throughout the body as a whole.

## Authority and Pluralism

These observations lead quite naturally to the second of the bishops' questions, namely, "what does it mean to talk about authority in a pluralistic society?" The answer to this question depends upon what is meant by pluralistic. If one means a society in which there are divisions over how to interpret and live out a common set of beliefs and practices, then the right answer to the bishops' question is that the meaning of authority in its classical sense derives from the fact that the passing on of tradition is always an agonistic process that involves disagreement and struggle. Authority exists, in part, to insure that social transitions do not divide people in an irretrievable sense or alienate them from the beliefs and ways of life that have provided identity through the ages. Indeed, it exists to augment that which is common by successfully guiding a people through these inevitable struggles and disagreements.

If, like Alasdair McIntyre, one understands tradition itself to be, in one sense of the word, pluralistic, then one can say that speaking of authority in a pluralistic church means what it has always meant — maintaining and augmenting the common traditions of the church in the midst of a struggle over their meaning and implications.[7] That is, in fact, the way the term is used here, and it is the way presupposed in the ordinals found in the various Anglican books of common prayer. Nevertheless, the present absence of the attendant notions that necessarily accompany the classical idea, namely, assumptions about the existence both of a common set of beliefs and practices and of personal qualities generally believed to make some more qualified to hold authority than others, makes this way of speaking less and less intelligible to the average person. In the absence of these preconditions for the normal functioning of authority in its classical sense, there has arisen another view of what having authority is and how it ought to be exercised. Elsewhere, I have called this novelty "the new authority."[8] The new authority rests not upon the presence of shared beliefs and practices but upon their absence. Within modern and postmodern cultures, this new way of having authority depends upon the very absence of shared beliefs and practices; and it functions not to further what is common but to insure a social order within which people, who regard one another as strangers and potential enemies, can follow differing beliefs and ways of life without in the process doing unacceptable harm one to another. The peace it seeks to foster is the avoidance

7. See, e.g., Alasdair McIntyre, *After Virtue* (Notre Dame, Ind.: University of Notre Dame Press, 1981).

8. See Turner, "Authority in the Church; Excavations Among the Ruins."

of conflict between contradictory aims rather than common though conflicted pursuit of shared goals.

In short, the new authority is justified not by what is common but by irreconcilable differences in what people believe and the ways in which they choose to live their lives. The new authority therefore functions not by producing consensus within a common, but nonetheless dispute-driven, tradition but by seeking to guarantee the *rights* of people who are strangers one to another — people whose lives are informed by different traditions. These guarantees are insured by creating buffer zones between people who are not civic friends or brothers and sisters in the Lord but adversaries with differing interests. These interests are protected (supposedly) by fair procedures, which are designed not to augment common beliefs and ways of life but to insure that individuals are able to make their own choices about these matters. The new authority exists, in short, to see that *the rights of individuals* are protected and to lay down and enforce the fair procedures that are designed to guarantee their protection.

The presuppositions and so also the justifications that lie behind the new authority are completely different from those that lie behind the classical idea and so also the idea that informs the various Anglican books of common prayer. And if the justification of authority has changed so also have the qualifications thought necessary for its possession. No longer is it necessary for those in authority to stand close to a common tradition or exhibit a range of virtues prized by all. What is necessary is to have the skills of a manager of conflict and the expertise of a technician. The job is to manage conflict in ways that allow people with various desires and "life plans" to coexist. The new authority functions, at least in theory, to insure that a plurality of beliefs and practices, indeed a plurality of traditions, are allowed to coexist and that the devotees of these various ways of life are not excluded from participating in and benefiting from the goods of social life.

"Inclusivity," which in the context of the new authority is interpreted as the amalgamation of people with vastly differing beliefs and ways of life, becomes not only the method but also the end of the exercise of authority. In theory, that is the way the new authority works. In practice, things are often quite different in that those who inhabit the postmodern world of plural world views and who are invested with authority fail again and again to act in impartial ways. Instead, they seek power as a means to pursue a particular set of interests and to use their authority to further those interests. Authority that is supposed to practice fairness in fact, more often than not, becomes a stalking horse for an interest group. If the truth be told, in the social world most people now inhabit, it is power rather than authority that is sought and, once power is attained, those who have it all too frequently exercise it behind a façade of fairness that thinly veils the well-defined purposes of one or another interest group.

Having made this observation, it is important to say that, no matter what one may think of the new authority, its appearance was brought about in the first instance by the inability of the Western church to manage in a peaceful manner its disputes over the interpretation of its traditions. Jeffery Stout has pointed out that this novel view of authority was articulated as a means of promoting toleration during the wars of religion that followed the Reformation.[9] Most will agree that its benefits to the body politic have been enormous. If one looks, for example, at the sacred canopy that covers Islamic societies in our own day, they probably breathe a sigh of relief that John Locke left the legacy of toleration he did. Few want to return to the iron fit between church and state that it was both Hooker's and Cranmer's purpose to strengthen. Most people like the free air of political and religious toleration in the public square where as much liberty as is feasible within an open national polity is given to every group and ideology to purvey its wares no matter how detestable they may be.

When attention is turned to the interior life of the church, however, the pluralism of modern democratic societies exhibits a more menacing face. It is corrosive of the very idea of a church, if one understands the church to be a *body* or *communion.* Indeed, it seems impossible to hold such notions and at the same time support the modern form of pluralism as proper for the internal life of the church. What is necessary for a modern democracy is in fact fatal for the *koinonia* of the church.

To say these things about the new authority and the sort of pluralism that accompanies it does not mean for one minute that each and every voice in the church ought not to be heard. To say these things does not mean either that anyone should be excluded from the fellowship of the church for reasons that have nothing to do with the gospel message or the common life of the church. Saying these things does not mean either that authority always acts charitably, wisely and justly or that those who hold authority in the church are above criticism. These assertions do not mean

9. See Jeffery Stout, *Ethics After Babel* (Boston: Beacon Press, 1988).

either that disobedience to those in authority is never a proper course of action.

They do mean, however, that if it is assumed that truth itself is plural or, more likely, that truth, though single, simply lies beyond reach, then one denies that Christ is *the* way, *the* truth and *the* life. He becomes simply *a* way, *a* truth and *a* life. It is not surprising, therefore, that the uniqueness of Christ and the question of universal or limited salvation are issues that have appeared concurrently with the crisis of authority which the Canadian bishops have so clearly perceived. Buried beneath the moral issues that now divide the church and the crisis of authority those divisions have surfaced, lies a more profound question — the content of the Christian gospel itself. What view of authority will be brought to the debates about Christian doctrine that inevitably accompany our more immediate ones over sex and gender issues? The most pressing issues now before the churches in fact concern the great mysteries of Christian believing, and it is highly likely that the view of authority the churches adopt will be directly related to their views on these more fundamental matters. Those who see an adequate understanding of truth to be beyond human grasp will tend toward what I have called the new authority. They will understand their job as keeping peace between people whose view of truth makes them strangers one to another, and as supporting those who they believe are in some way excluded from the church's institutional life. Those who believe truth both to be one and graspable, will perforce lean toward the more classical view. They will see themselves as charged with defending and promoting essential Christian mysteries and ways of life in the midst of forces that work to compromise both.

It would be inappropriate for an American to comment on how the balance between these two views now stands in the Anglican Church of Canada, but it would not be inappropriate to describe how matters stand south of the border. The real upshot of the Righter trial, which recently took place within the Episcopal Church, does not concern homosexuality but doctrine.[10] It is most easily read as indicating the predominance of the new authority within ECUSA. This statement is true for the simple reason

10. Bishop Walter Righter was recently tried for heresy by an ecclesiastical court set up under the canons of the Episcopal Church. The occasion for the charges or "presentment" was his ordination of a homosexual man known to be living with a partner. Bishop Righter was acquitted on the grounds that his action did not violate the "core doctrine" of the Episcopal Church.

that the notion of "core doctrine" used to justify the court's decision seems on the face of it to mean two things — one is that heresy is now a notion that cannot be brought into play; and the other is that moral matters are in no way matters of doctrine.[11] "Core doctrine," as used by the jury in the Righter trial, refers only to the bare outline of the apostolic preaching as sketched by C. H. Dodd in 1935.[12] Gone is the full scope of the biblical witness that once was thought to establish *doctrine*. Further, according to the panel of bishops who gave the judgment, even the thin reed of "core doctrine" must be interpreted within its "contemporary context." In all cases of conflict between "core doctrine" and the "contemporary context" it appears to be the "contemporary context" that wins out. In short, doctrine is gone and in its place there has appeared a Babel of theological opinion, none of which is privileged unless those who support a particular theological fashion are in power. If they are, they inevitably find themselves under pressure to use their position to insure that only those who share their theological views are allowed in an effective way into the councils of the church. In this way, no need arises to speak of "the doctrine of the church." Those in power need only refer to the presently fashionable theology that serves to justify the interests of people who have like minds to themselves.

## Summary and Initial Conclusions

If, for a moment, we stand back from this analysis and take the long view, what do we see? The most obvious thing is two views of authority. One, the new authority, dominates present-day social and political life and intrudes itself more and more into the life of the churches. The other, what has here been called the classical view, appears less and less an effective operational idea in either church or society. It more and more resembles an antique notion comparable to Cranmer's English — beautiful but barely intelligible to the modern ear. It is, in all probability, the new authority that in fact informs the actual charge given to its bishops by the church at their consecration as bishops rather than authority in its classical sense — the sense

11. See R. R. Reno, "An Analysis of the Righter Decision," *Pro Ecclesia* No. 3 (Summer 1996): 271-81.

12. See C. H. Dodd, *The Apostolic Preaching and Its Development* (New York: Harper and Row, 1935).

that informs the charge written down in the *Book of Common Prayer.* So there is a clash between doctrine and practice and it is this clash that helps explain why the job of Anglican bishops is so very difficult. They increasingly labor under two very different job descriptions, and inevitably they are torn apart by the tension that exists between them. If the bishop in question is of a more conservative nature, this tension will be acute because of an attachment to an idea that has less and less social support. In fact, such bishops may well find themselves simply at a loss as to what to do. They know what their job is supposed to be but find themselves, because of a lack of extensive support, unable really to do it. If, on the other hand, the bishop in question is of a more liberal inclination, he or she will find that the tension between these two points of view produces a good bit of frustration because what such bishops perceive as necessary reforms keep getting delayed by what, on the part of their more conservative colleagues, often appears simply as a benighted reluctance to change — a pastoral insensitivity that seems unwilling to take account of the real circumstances in which people live.

It is indeed possible to hold to a classical view of authority and at the same time exhibit pastoral sensitivity, but that is an argument that will have to wait another occasion. Of more immediate concern is a very disturbing implication of this analysis of the clash between these two views of authority. If it is the case that the new authority is ill suited to the common life *(koinonia)* of the church as it is presented in Holy Scripture, and if it is the case also that present social ideas and practices render the more classical notion less and less intelligible, then the issue of authority in the church, be it Episcopal or other, cannot be addressed from the top down. No amount of self-study and reflection will make things any better. Or, to put the matter another way, the Anglican houses of bishops in England and North America cannot of themselves solve the crisis in authority that so haunts their deliberations, and so constantly renders the exercise of Episcopal office ineffective. The fact of the matter is that the crisis of authority that they have perceived is tied to a more fundamental issue — namely, a deformation in the everyday lives of the congregations that make up the dioceses in which bishops are supposed to exercise the authority entrusted to them at their consecration.

And what exactly is the authority given? In a nutshell, it is to take the steps necessary to ensure that the witness, teaching, and common life of the church remain faithful to the apostolic witness. To put the matter another way, the authority given is to be used to ensure the fidelity and unity of the church as a whole. The question of course is this: How many people now think that anyone has the right and the responsibility to undertake such an enterprise? The correct answer to this question is "very few," and if this is so then the renewal of authority in the church must await a renewal of the church as church. This renewal will have to be of a particular sort. It will have to be one that does not focus on the self and its particular spiritual needs (as does our present craze for spirituality, spiritual direction, and religious experience) but rather on new life *in the body of Christ.* It will have to be a renewal of a catholic nature — one that recognizes that we grow in Christ through incorporation into a communion of believers who profess one Lord, one Faith and one Baptism and who follow one way rather than many. That way is none other than the way of the Cross, and we learn that way from one another in the communion of Christ. In such a church, and only in such a church, will authority once more have a context in which it can function in its classical sense. Barring such a development, the churches will exist in a context in which only the new authority can operate. In this environment, the churches will continue to struggle on but their communion will steadily erode as their factionalism increases.

The point can be made in another way — one that provides a nice point of entry into the next question, namely the relation between authority and Episcopacy. Max Weber argued that authority is born from a charismatic individual who, by the force of his personality and vision, can impose his will on others. This authority is then "routinized" by succeeding generations and finally bureaucratized by their successors. If he were right, then the answer to the issue of authority in the church could be solved by finding a charismatic primate or by the emergence of a prophet. Such a search may well be taking place, here and there. But Weber was not right! The presence of authority in its classical political sense presupposes, no matter what the personality of those invested with it, a common way of life and a common set of beliefs. People follow charismatic leaders because they see in them true champions of their way of life. Sad to say, what has just been said is as true of Hitler as it is of Churchill. But no matter! The point is that authority in its classical sense emerges out of *communion* rather than *magnetism.* This suggests that the first order of business for bishops of the church at the present time remains what it has always properly been; namely, the nurture and protection of the *koinonia* of the church. The difficulty is that there seems less and less possibility for that task to be undertaken.

## A Possible Misunderstanding

To this point, an attempt has been made to provide an analysis of some of the factors that, in our place and time and within the Anglican Communion, make the work of a bishop both difficult, frustrating, and, in respect to the way in which the Ordinal describes the office, impossible. In making this argument with such strength, it may well be the case that a false impression has been created, namely, that one view of authority, the new one, inevitably brings factionalism in its wake and that the more classical view is always accompanied by peace and harmony.

In fact, this is not the intent of the argument. Until Christ comes again, factionalism will remain a part of the life of the church. What Paul called *party spirit* will be present in both church and society until God is all in all and the "peace which passes understanding" characterizes the life of the entire creation. The claim made here is not that one view of authority produces factionalism and the other does not. It is rather that these two views carry with them very different assessments of this factionalism and very different views of the role of authority in relation to it. One, the new authority, sees factionalism as written into the nature of things. Truth (or its perception) is, according to this view, pluralistic in a non-pejorative sense. Accordingly, it views the function of authority to be provision of guarantees that allow each faction to have its place so that each can pursue the truth as they see it. The other (what I have called the classical view) sees factionalism as the result of a profound human flaw, and divisions over the nature of truth as indicative of this very flaw. Accordingly, the classical view understands the role of authority to be, in part, provision of help in overcoming factionalism when it appears; and, in the midst of a dispute-driven tradition, encouragement of that unity which God has in mind for the consummation of all things in Christ Jesus.[13]

13. In the classical tradition, authority is thought also to have a positive function that is based on human plenitude rather than deficiency. This positive function is to call forth the full complexity of human giftedness and take measures to see that these various gifts are co-ordinated and exercised in ways that lead to a common good. I hope to explicate this more positive function of political authority in a work now in progress and tentatively entitled *Unity, Order, and Dissent: Ethics within the Body of Christ.* For the best extant presentation of the positive function of authority see Simon, *The Philosophy of Democratic Government.*

## Authority and the Office of Bishop

How might these considerations apply to the office of bishop? In particular, how in answer to the query of the Canadian House of Bishops might *an Anglican understanding of authority vis-à-vis the Episcopate* be described? Honesty compels any scholar to admit from the outset that there is no such thing as *an Anglican understanding of authority vis-à-vis the Episcopate.* During the course of their history, Anglicans have believed that the link between authority and Episcopacy is a necessary aspect of the very being of the church (e.g., Kenneth Kirk), that the link is ancient and effective but not necessary (e.g., Thomas Cranmer), or that the link represents an aspect of the church still in need of reform (e.g., various Puritans who nonetheless remained members of the Church of England). History simply does not yield *an Anglican understanding* of this matter, but it does yield *a continuity of practice* that cries out for an adequate justification. That is, even though Anglicans have articulated a variety of views about the relation between authority and Episcopacy, they have nonetheless, *as a matter of practice,* maintained the link throughout their history. Particularly in light of the recent objections of the Evangelical Lutheran Church in America to that part of the Lambeth Quadrilateral[14] that insists upon the link between authority in the church and the Historic Episcopate as a necessary condition for the unity of the churches and the mutual recognition of ministries, Anglicans owe both themselves and their ecumenical partners a more adequate explanation of this practice than they have given to date. They need to make clear what they believe this relationship to be both for the sake of the unity of the church and for the faithful exercise of the office they obviously hold to be so important.

From what has been said to this point, one possible direction in which the argument might proceed is easy to anticipate. One might hold that authority in the church ought to be understood, in its political sense, as a means of augmenting common beliefs and practices in the midst of the inevitable conflicts that characterize social life in all its forms. Because it is political authority rather than raw power on the one hand or personal magnetism on the other that is being spoken of, for such authority to re-

14. For a variety of comments on the importance of the Lambeth Quadrilateral for the ecumenical relations of the Anglican Communion see J. R. Wright, *The Lambeth Quadrilateral at One Hundred.*

main (in the good sense of the word) political, it must be able to issue commands that both require obedience and lie within what might be called *a circle of permissibility* circumscribed by beliefs and ways of life that are commonly recognized as authoritative. This much has been said already. But now a new point must be entered. Because there must be those in authority who are able to issue commands and impose sanctions if those commands are not obeyed, authority in its political sense can be accorded only to persons and never to "things" like books, traditions, confessions, ceremonies, constitutions or even legal codes. This is the case for the simple reason that books, traditions, ceremonies, confessions, etc., cannot issue commands. Rather they require interpretation and application, and only human agents can carry out these activities.

Having said this, one must go on to say that if one speaks of the authority of Scripture or tradition or reason or, yes, even experience one is using the word in a different sense than the one to which we have to this point been referring. Scripture, tradition, reason, and experience have authority, but in a different sense. They do not issue commands and they do not impose sanctions. Rather, they are points of reference to which, within the churches, those invested with authority and those under authority may or must make reference to justify the course of action they recommend, mandate, or follow. They have authority in the sense that they are necessary or common points of reference for determining the way people who share a common life ought to move through time. They do not have authority, however, in a political sense. Their authority is one that provides authorization for those with authority and those under authority but their authority is not one that can make a political decision and issue a command. This observation has important implications for more recent Anglican discussion of authority in the church.[15] At a minimum, it implies that the Anglican notion of *dispersed authority* first articulated at the Lambeth Conference as a means of distinguishing Anglicans from Roman Catholics needs more than a little clarification. When speaking of dispersed authority, the Lambeth document makes no distinctions between the various uses and senses of the word. In so doing, it runs together a variety of meanings that are in no way *identical*. Consequently, the notion of

---

15. For a history of Anglican statements about the nature and function of authority see Drexel Gomez and Maurice W. Sinclair, eds., *To Mend the Net: Anglican Faith and Order for Renewed Mission* (Carrollton, Tex.: The Ekklesia Soceity, 2001), pp. 73-90.

*dispersed authority,* as now it is articulated, does more to muddle the issue of authority in the church than clarify it.

The point of importance at the moment, however, is not the Lambeth Conference. It is rather that authority, in the political sense of the word, is properly invested only in people; and the question is why insist (a) that, within the church, the people who have authority be placed in an office called the Episcopate and (b) that those who hold that office be ordained to it only by those who are linked by their own ordination to the original apostles of Jesus? With this question the argument moves from a discussion of the nature and function of authority to a discussion of polity and office. Whether set out in a constitution and legal code or simply a matter of customary practice, authority within all forms of social life is generally located in and circumscribed by a system of offices and rules of operation that define the range within which those invested with authority may properly assume responsibility and issue commands. In short, only in the case of God does authority appear with an unlimited range of responsibility. Only the authority of God is without circumscription. Absolute monarchy may be a notion of which we can conceive, but it is practically impossible for an actual example of such unlimited jurisdiction to exist. Indeed, it is the function of a form of governance or a polity to demarcate or circumscribe the arena within which those with authority are to carry out their task. Thus, if the function of authority is to confine the use of power within a range of action that is considered legitimate, the function of a polity is to confine the range of operation of those invested with authority even further.

The examples of this fact that lie closest to hand are the various struggles between church and state that have occurred, still occur, and will always occur. The issue has never been and never will be over whether authority should be present within either church or state, but over the limits of the operation of authority within and between both. The disputes that accompany this conflict have had both theological and political dimensions. That is, people have argued (and fought) over whether the office, the authority of those who occupy office, and the range of their jurisdiction come directly from God or whether all of these are matters which God allows human wisdom (or foolishness) to determine. There have been and there remain significant differences of opinion over these matters, and they continue to plague our increasingly feeble attempts to unite the churches. As stated at the outset, there certainly have been differences of opinion among Anglicans about this issue, and these differences have not utterly disappeared.

In respect to these matters, no attempt will be made here to argue the case either way. The argument will begin not with this ancient and still unresolved dispute but from the point at which the Anglican Communion on the whole now finds itself. At the present moment, the defining document in respect to these matters is the Lima Document on Baptism, Eucharist, and Ministry that made a distinction between the Apostolic Succession and the Historic Episcopate.[16] Prior to this document, Anglicans as a general rule tended to run these two things together. The Lima Document, however, insists that many churches stand in the tradition of the Apostles and so in the Apostolic Succession. Some churches, however, retain the Historic Episcopate both as an effective means of maintaining this succession and as an effective expression of it.

On the whole, neither Roman Catholic nor Orthodox Christians are happy with this distinction, but the churches of the Anglican Communion have tended to accept it; and it is this acceptance that has, more than anything, allowed them to make such progress in their relations with the Lutheran churches. It appears, therefore, that, as a communion, Anglicans now have a working position that is not far from that of Thomas Cranmer, namely, that Episcopal polity is an ancient and effective means to order the life of the church and so is, where possible, to be kept; but that, in a strict sense, Episcopal polity is not necessary for the church to remain faithful to the witness of the apostles. To put the matter another way, the working position of the Anglican Communion seems at the moment to be that the Historic Episcopate is not a matter of the gospel. On the whole, Anglicans are prepared to say that they recognize the apostolic faith in other churches, and so enjoy with them a communion in the gospel.

Nevertheless, by continuing to insist that adoption of the Historic Episcopate, along with the Scriptures, the Dominical Sacraments and the Historic Creeds, is necessary for full communion and the mutual recognition of ministries, Anglicans make the Historic Episcopate something more than an *adiaphoron*. This move locates the working position of the Anglican Communion on the Historic Episcopate in a never-never land that lies between a Gospel truth on the one hand and a matter of indifference on the other. The

---

16. World Council of Churches, *Baptism, Eucharist, and Ministry* (Geneva: WCC Publications, 1990).

question, of course, is whether or not Anglicans can give an account of themselves that makes some sense of this rather murky and confusing position. Can Anglicans make plausible a position that refuses to make the link between authority and Episcopacy a matter of the gospel but, nonetheless, insists on its retention as a necessary condition for the unity of the churches?

Anglicans owe their ecumenical partners greater clarity on this matter than they have provided to date. Nevertheless, the issue will become moot if they do not also give attention to becoming more self-conscious than now they are about the way in which the office of bishop both furthers the ability of those in authority to protect and promote common belief and practice and (at the same time) circumscribes the limits beyond which it is illegitimate for those in authority to extend their reach. The current battle set off by the action of the Diocese of New Westminster (and latterly by the governing body of ECUSA) has made clear that, among Anglicans, the way in which the office of bishop is related to political authority has become a matter of dispute: and, for this reason, the polity that gives coherence and order to the Anglican Communion as a whole has been shaken, perhaps even shattered. An adequate grasp of the relation between authority and office thus seems a matter that Anglicans (and no doubt others) avoid at their own peril.

## Authority and the Three-Legged Stool
## or, Perhaps Better, the Four-Legged Bench

Attention must now be given to the fourth question posed by the Canadian bishops. What indeed is the relation between authority on the one hand and Scripture, tradition, reason, and, some would add, experience on the other? This is a question of particular importance if one seeks to maintain what has here been called the classical view of authority. According to this view, authority functions to further a common set of beliefs and practices amidst the stresses and changes of history. As already stated, it is obfuscating to speak of the authority of Scripture in the same way one speaks of the authority of a bishop or governor. When people speak in this way they do not mean that Scripture can give orders but that it is a necessary point of reference if one wishes to "prove" or test either the adequacy of the church's preaching, teaching, and example or the faithfulness of those invested with authority.

Through the ages Scripture has been a necessary source to which those in authority and those under authority must refer to justify either its exercise or an objection to that exercise. Until recently, Scripture has not been considered either first among equals or simply one point of reference among others (say tradition or, more recently, experience). It has been the primary and sufficient source for testing the stewardship of those who have been given authority and office within the churches, be that authority used to safeguard the unity of the church, or protect its teaching and sanctity. It has also been the primary and sufficient source for those in authority to show that their exercise of office has in fact been in God's name.

In recent years other legitimating points of reference for the exercise of authority in the church have been added and used in ways Richard Hooker would neither recognize nor approve. For Hooker, doctrine was to be established on the basis of Scripture. Reason was thought to yield moral truths open to all people of good will. These truths were in no way thought to be opposed to the witness of Scripture. Rather, they were simply "republished" by its authors. For its part, tradition was a minor matter, referring as it did to those aspects of the life of the church that had a venerable history and were not to be changed unless shown to be contrary to the witness of Scripture or contrary to the light of universal human reason. Experience, our current favorite source of moral and religious knowledge, was not a category Hooker would have separated from reason. This separation is, in fact, a product of the romantic movement. Experience, as something independent of these other sources of moral and religious knowledge, is a category Hooker would have had trouble even recognizing.

Thus, the reference to Hooker's three-legged stool that is currently so popular with Anglicans is both anachronistic and misleading. When they refer to its various legs as having a certain independence one from another, when they assign them more or less equal weight or, when they appeal to one or another of them over against Scripture, they show that they have engaged in a form of argument he would have rejected out of hand. A statement like this, of course, has nothing to do with whether or not Hooker was right and we wrong. Times have changed and present understandings of what constitutes an adequate argument have changed with them. At present, Scripture, tradition, reason, and yes, even experience are all considered forms of tradition to which reference can be made when trying to justify a particular set of views about the teaching and practice of the church. At present, these sources of moral and religious knowledge are separable one from another in ways Hooker's intellectual universe did not comprehend.

It is this difference, however, that presents the bishops of the Anglican Communion and its ordinary members with a problem that is far more severe than the one Hooker faced. In response to Roman Catholic criticism of the English Reformation, Hooker had to establish the authority of Scripture in matters of doctrine, and insist that doctrine could not be established apart from it. Against the Puritans, on the other hand, he had to establish that Scripture could not be used to assess all aspects of the life of the church. He had to show that there was a place for both reason and tradition.

Present circumstances are both different and more difficult. There are virtually no agreements about the range of operation or the relative authority of these various sources of moral and religious knowledge. It is true that Scripture, tradition, reason, and experience are incessantly referred to as people seek to justify either authority's exercise or their objections to it, but the references are without effect. They are without effect because there are no agreements about their relative weight or their interpretation. If there is a conflict between experience or modern learning on the one hand and the received interpretation of Scripture or the traditional teaching of the church on the other, which takes precedence and on what basis? These are questions to which no common answer has been found and, as a result, conflicts never seem to be settled. Indeed, it is now difficult even to have a reasonable discussion. The various parties in the contemporary church either square off like contending armies or pass like ships in the night.

The bishops of the church are caught right in the middle of it all — charged to guard the unity, teaching, and sanctity of the church but lacking agreed-upon sources of Christian knowledge and practice to which they can refer and make appeal as they seek to carry out their office. As a result, they are inevitably seen by those who may disagree with their decisions and commands as the tool of one or another faction in the church. Indeed, they may be. But perhaps they are not. Perhaps they simply lack the resources to show that they have decided in a way that lies within the circle drawn by the beliefs and practices the members of the church share with them and with one another.

Once more, it appears that the crisis of authority now present in all the churches is tied to a more fundamental rupture in the *koinonia* of the church — a rupture whose presenting symptoms are an inability to agree about the basic sources and content of that communion. How shall the Scriptures be interpreted and what weight should be assigned past interpretations? How shall modern learning and our own experience be weighed and interpreted? These are issues about which the churches do not agree. Is it any wonder that the bishops of the Anglican Communion, along with those in authority in many other churches, find it difficult to give a satisfactory account of their stewardship of the office to which they have been ordained? Given the way in which the members of the Anglican churches in England and North America prize their autonomy and given their lack of a common frame of reference for determining the *koinon* or common good that gives identity to the *koinonia* or communion of the church the bishops are supposed to guard and promote, one must conclude that at their consecration as bishops there was in fact a false transmission of authority. The bishops in fact were not given authority to do what the church in its Ordinal says it charges them to do.

If the analysis just completed is in broad outline correct, one must conclude that the crisis of authority that the bishops of the Anglican Communion are facing cannot be resolved from the top down. Authority in its classic sense can function only if the *koinonia* of the church is reconstituted. How that might be done and what the role of the Episcopacy in that reconstitution might be are subjects that go far beyond the range of issues listed by the Canadian bishops. The only consolation that can be offered at this point is to say that identification of the problem is the first and necessary step toward its solution. There are many things to be said about what is required for such a renewal of the life of the church and what is required of bishops if that renewal is to take place; but, on this occasion, in respect to the role of a bishop, it is possible to mention only a few. The first thing the bishops can do is call a spade a spade and point out to the church the true circumstances in which it exists. The time has come to be done with the self-congratulatory apologetic to which Anglicans are addicted, and to call for both a searching review of their common life (or lack thereof) and an attitude of repentance. The churches of the Anglican Communion, particularly those in England and North America, can renew their common life only after a long period of self-examination and repentance. Only from a stance of profound sorrow and humility can Anglicans live as a faithful communion of saints who stand in the tradition of the apostles, prophets, and martyrs.

The bishops of the Anglican Communion can call its member churches to themselves, but they can do some other things as well. They can, for example, call for the very hard theological work that must be done before Anglicans (and other Christian churches) can once more have a fruitful discussion of their differences. They can help focus the church's attention on the importance of reaching agreement on what they think about the various sources of religious and moral knowledge. They can as well call for and model the sort of practices that make for peace during times of stress and confusion. They can model these practices in their own deliberations one with another, and they can seek in their own persons those virtues that support the things that make for peace and truth. They can model in their individual and corporate lives the virtues and practices that properly belong to the office of bishop. That is, they can model the virtues and practices that protect and further unity, guard and promote Christian teaching and practice, and exemplify those qualities characteristic of a holy life. They can, in short, gather to themselves a form of authority that is related to political authority but different from it. This form might be called the *exemplary authority* of persons who embody in their lives the common beliefs and ways of life that Christians through the ages have recognized as imitating Christ. They can in this way begin to reestablish the political authority of bishops and the common good of the church by providing the church as a whole a model of that life in Christ to which all Christians are called.

## The Social Witness of Bishops

These remarks about the reconstitution of a common life and the relation of that life to the office of a bishop and the practices that define it lead directly to the last of the questions posed by the Canadian bishops — the one which concerns the social witness of the Episcopal office. By now it should be easy to anticipate the basic point that must be made, namely, that the witness a bishop, as bishop, is called upon to make is inseparable from the one which the church itself is called upon to make. This is a fairly simple statement but its implications are not. The implications can be displayed most easily by the following four examples relevant to this central point. They all concern recent attempts by Anglican bishops to make a social witness. One was both right and successful, another neither successful nor right, another was neither successful nor unsuccessful but certainly both right and appropriate, and yet another was unsuccessful but certainly right and appropriate.

First, the effort that was both successful and right. Though many may not know its details, most are aware of the witness made by Bishop Desmond Tutu. His opposition to racial segregation, which combined a remarkable combination of compassion, truth telling, and mercy called the peoples of South Africa to the highest standards of human behavior and the churches of South Africa to the highest standards of Christian conduct. In making the witness he did, Bishop Tutu spoke both for the church and the nation. If you will, he spoke and acted from within a communion and for this reason both instantiated and furthered a common purpose.

What, then, of the effort that was neither successful nor right? When allied forces were poised to invade Kuwait, Edmond Browning, Presiding Bishop of the Episcopal Church, went to see three men, all of whom are Episcopalians. The three men were George Bush, President; James Baker, Secretary of State; and Colin Powell, Chairman of the Joint Chiefs of Staff. The Presiding Bishop went to urge these men to stop the invasion and use more peaceful means to settle the conflict. Now it may be that the Presiding Bishop was right — that there were other means to resolve the conflict and that an invasion was premature. The problem, however, is not the wisdom of Bishop Browning's views. The problem is that he expressed these views as the Presiding Bishop of the Episcopal Church, and in so doing failed to speak for the church. He spoke in fact from no clear Christian warrant concerning a matter about which Christians might rightly differ. It is not surprising; therefore, that many felt and still feel his effort to change policy went beyond his authority as a bishop of the church.

It is instructive to compare Bishop Browning's response to the war in the Middle East to Archbishop Runcie's response to England's invasion of the Falklands. The Archbishop recognized, in a way that Bishop Browning did not, that there was no clear Christian warrant either for or against the war. He therefore refused to bless either the Prime Minister (an act for which, I am told, she never forgave him) or her opponents. Instead he said that the war "would not fail to find support among Christian people of good will." In short, recognizing that there were no clear Christian warrants either way, he allowed room for conscience on both sides of the issue; and so allowed space for debate both within the church and the nation about the morality of the war. His social witness was to make moral room for a political argument that needed to take place.

Finally, one can learn a great deal from the example of Bishop Bell of Chichester. During the Second World War, he spoke out against the saturation bombing of Cologne and Dresden. In doing so he called both the church and the nation to a standard of morality shared by the people, namely, that in war it is wrong to make direct attacks on innocent civilians. This attempt, in a time of duress, to recall the British people to a moral standard that had been a part of their tradition for several centuries failed but, nonetheless, it was an act born out of a common tradition and carried out in support of a common tradition. In rejecting the bishop's admonitions, so also those responsible for the conduct of the war rejected a tradition that lay close to the heart of both their moral and political identity. Sad to say, it was probably this act, which was in fact appropriate to the office of bishop, that cost this particular bishop the See of Canterbury.

Of what does this little bit of history serve to remind one? The most obvious reminder is that when bishops speak to society as bishops, the authority vested in them allows them to speak only for the church. That is, their charge from the church in respect to a social witness is to speak those things that Christians as Christians have to say to the powers that be. Most of the time, the right social witness will resemble the one made by Lord Runcie at the time of the Falklands war. Most of the time, particular political judgments have no direct Christian authorization, and to think that they do produces only an unhealthy fanaticism. Consequently, most of the time the social witness of bishops ought to be directed to the provision of moral warrant for preserving the public space necessary for civil discourse — for genuine political debate and struggle.

Such a stance is implied by the very nature of the authority with which a bishop is vested. It is not a limitless authority to say what is on a particular bishop's mind. It is a limited authority instituted to guard and further the *koinon* — the common thing that defines the identity of God's people. This means, and this point is of the utmost importance, that, when speaking as a bishop of the church, those who occupy such an office, out of fidelity to that office, must remain silent about their private views on many political and social issues of enormous import. The authority bestowed upon them gives them no right to speak these things in the name of the church. This form of ascesis will always prove painful, and certainly discerning the difference between private opinion and the implications of the church's common tradition will stretch one's mind, spirit and moral resources to their limits. This exercise will prove particularly difficult when one lives in circumstances like those encountered by Bishops Bell and Tutu.

This assertion will, to quote Kierkegaard out of context, certainly seem to most people both "too little and too much." To the extent that they care about their particular political and social views, the social ministry this argument grants to bishops will seem "too little." Surely, they will think, more must be done. They will feel that bishops cannot remain silent. On the other hand, to the extent they see the fearsome conflict that will arise if bishops indeed speak the word that Christians as Christians have to speak to the powers that be, then what is being asked will seem "too much." Having seen what Bishops Bell and Tutu had to live through in order to speak both to and for the church, they will wonder if they can stand before the dark forces their truthful speech will most certainly set loose. These difficulties will most certainly call forth the cry that what is asked of a bishop in respect to a social witness is either too much or too little. Nevertheless, if the sort of ascesis that has been suggested is indeed practiced, it will render the voice of bishops powerful. They will speak not for themselves but for the church, and their voice or voices will thunder if not in their own time then certainly in the age to come.

This treatment of the Canadian bishops' final question is extraordinarily brief. There is much, much more to say, but the point from which all the others flow has been made. In making it, yet another aspect of the office of bishop that, in our time, places such enormous burdens upon its occupants has been uncovered. No one can remove those burdens but they can be made lighter if the church as a whole learns to pray once more for its own health and for those in authority within it. The point once more is that the solution to the problem of Episcopal authority that is so widely experienced lies beyond the power of the Episcopal office to solve on its own. The problem of authority in the church is properly one for the church as a whole. The part bishops can play in providing a solution is quite limited but it is real, and it is to call the church to itself and, through their own lives and the faithful exercise of their office, to cultivate those qualities that promote the unity of the church, the sanctity of the church, and the faithfulness of its witness, and to do these things in communion with their fellow bishops. Bishops are not only in some real, if limited, sense responsible for the church's communion. They are themselves derivative of and embedded within communion's vital character and mission. They are also accountable to it.

# PART III

# QUESTIONS OF COMMUNION

CHAPTER SEVEN

# The Virginia Report:
# How Firm a Foundation?

*Philip Turner*

## Introduction

The question of communion is at the center of this volume's concern. We can see it implicated in all the matters we have been addressing thus far: the church's catholic character, the apprehension of God's truth, scriptural formation, authority, and the ordering of our common life. Yet, as a particular concern, the specific nature of ecclesial communion itself is a relatively recent topic of discussion for Anglicans, and has only rarely been the subject of careful examination.

The breakup of the British Empire brought to the fore a host of questions about the relations, past, present, and future, between the Church of England and the various churches to which the efforts of her various missionary societies gave birth. The ecclesial questions presented by the close of the colonial period affected more than Anglicans, however. All the churches have been presented with similar questions, and have sought in a variety of ways to address them. For Anglicans, the issues have centered in their quest for identity as a communion rather than a federation of churches. That is, amidst the plurality of national identities characteristic of the postcolonial era, Anglicans have sought a unity of belief and practice rooted in mutual subjection rather than in looser, more contingent, and voluntary connections or in a transnational form of ecclesial governance. In pursuit of this goal, Anglicans have turned to various "instruments of unity," chief among them being the Archbishop of Canterbury, the Lambeth Conference of Bishops, and the Meeting of the Primates.[1] In an attempt to define the nature of the communion that unites them, both the Lambeth Conference of Bishops and the Meeting of the Primates have turned to various commissions to prepare position papers that set out the issues before the communion and make suggestions about how best to address them. Perhaps the most basic of these remains a document prepared by the Inter-Anglican Theological and Doctrinal Commission of the Anglican Communion at the request of the 1988 Lambeth Conference of Bishops. The study is entitled the Virginia Report (hereinafter TVR).[2] As an important, influential, and focused treatment, in practical terms, of Anglicanism's communion character, I will use it as the lens through which to address the matter in this chapter, and through this discussion, prepare the ground for the crucial treatment of communion provided by the Windsor Report in the two chapters that follow.

TVR is foundational to recent attempts by Anglicans to understand themselves as a church that transcends national boundaries. It is consequently a document of fundamental importance both to Anglicans and to their ecumenical partners. My purpose is to give a critical assessment of how firm a foundation this report provides for a communion rather than a federation of churches. This assessment will focus on the one hand on its treatment of communion, its concepts of discernment, reception, subsidiarity, and interdependence; and on the other its recommendations concerning what it terms "the instruments of unity." Any assessment with this broad an area of concern necessarily begins from a point of view; and it will prove helpful for any ensuing discussion to place the starting point of this analysis plainly on the table. Of the convictions at the base of this argument four seem of particular importance. One has to do with what we believe to be a peculiar gift the Anglican Communion has to offer to the divided church, another with a view of the status of the church within the Christian narrative of redemption, another with the stance from which Christians should view their divisions and conflicts, and yet another with

1. The Archbishop of Canterbury serves as an effective point of unity for the Communion as a whole — membership in the Communion being defined as a province in communion with one who holds that See. The Lambeth Conference of Bishops is a meeting of all bishops in the Communion that assembles once every ten years. The Meeting of the Primates is a yearly gathering of all the Archbishops of the Communion.

2. See the Virginia Report, available online at http://anglicancommunion.org/lambeth/reports/report1.html.

the place we assign (or should assign) our disputes within the divided life of the Western church.[3]

First, does the Anglican Communion have a distinctive gift to offer the divided church? We believe it does, and that gift has to do with the way in which the church maintains both the apostolic faith and unity in the midst of historical change. *Parodosis,* the handing on of the faith and life of the church, is always a conflicted process. Alasdair MacIntyre is at least partially right to define "tradition" as an extended argument. He is certainly right to maintain that a tradition is sustained and extended by its own internal arguments and conflicts.[4] Conflict, in short, has both a positive and a negative face.[5]

It would not be difficult to show that this conflicted process is in some way present in all eras of the church's history, and one could write a fascinating history of the various ways in which the conflict has been addressed. However, if one looks at the present, it is fair to say that the following strategies are now dominant. The Roman Catholic Church seeks to overcome the ravages of time with (a) the notion of the "development of doctrine"; (b) the Petrine Office as the authoritative judge of what constitutes true development; and (c) a strongly centralized administration with the legal means to enforce the decisions of central authority. The Orthodox Churches of the East deploy a more static view of tradition along with the requirement of an ecumenical council of bishops to resolve disputed issues. Since the likelihood of such an ecumenical council seems at best remote, and since the writings of the Eastern Fathers have become almost a

3. Having spent ten years as a member of the Church of Uganda, I am more than aware that the churches of Latin America, Africa, and Asia do not see themselves any longer as part of the Western Church. However, they exist as an outcome of the missionary movement of the Western churches and thus are, in many ways, heir to their traditions about how to handle internal disputes about the adequacy of truth and practice.

4. See Alasdair MacIntyre, *After Virtue: A Study in Moral Theory* (Notre Dame, Ind: University of Notre Dame Press, 1981), p. 242.

5. At certain points, the authors of TVR suggest they may hold a similar view. See especially TVR 1.9, 3.11. For a far clearer statement of this view of tradition, one that illustrates its coherence with the views of respected Anglicans, see Lord Runcie's opening address to the Lambeth Conference of 1988 entitled "The Nature of the Unity We Seek," contained in *The Truth Shall Make You Free: The Lambeth Conference 1988, The Reports, Resolutions, & Pastoral Letters from the Bishops* (London: Church Publishing House, 1988), pp. 15, 101-05. See also *The Eames Commission: The Official Reports* (Toronto: The Anglican Book Center, 1994), p. 17; and TVR 1.8, 9.

second canon, their strategy amounts to a practical denial of the significance of historical change. The magisterial churches of the continental Reformation have relied upon confessions of faith to preserve the apostolic faith in the midst of the flux of history. The more evangelical churches which spun out of both the English and the continental Reformations have come to rely on agreed-upon, but non-creedal, readings of the Bible to stay the tide of change.

In the course of the history of the Church of England, and latterly the Anglican Communion, each of these strategies has made an appearance; but none has managed to establish itself as what might be called "the Anglican way." What does seem in place, however, is an agreement that in the midst of the conflicted process of passing on the faith, it is necessary for the church to use Holy Scripture and the Apostles' and Nicene Creeds to "prove" doctrine and practice, that the process of "proving" takes place in the midst of the baptized members of the church as they are engaged in a regular round of Bible reading, eucharistic worship, and prayer; and that the unity of the church as it struggles to pass on the faith and practice of the apostles is expressed and maintained through the collegiality of its bishops. Here we have a dynamic process that does not suffer from the unsupportable pretensions of the papacy, the diffuse inertia of Orthodoxy, or the narrowing fixity of either confessionalism or the unofficial but nonetheless normative readings of Scripture associated with evangelical Protestantism. Its effectiveness depends, however, on more than asserting the importance of Holy Scripture, the Creeds, the Dominical Sacraments, and the Historic Episcopate in dynamic interrelation. It depends upon both the presence of the Spirit within the church, and the actual exercise of collegiality on the part of the bishops. It is the last of these that has most obviously been thrown into question by the ordination of women, the ordination of non-abstaining homosexual persons, and the blessing of homosexual unions. In short, these actions, in varying degrees and in differing ways, have compromised both Anglican polity and its potential contribution to the way in which faithfulness and unity are to be maintained in the midst of the vicissitudes of history.

The second conviction is that the nature and calling of the church can be understood rightly only if placed within the scope of the entire scriptural account of God's relation to his creation. That narrative displays God as the source and end of all things, Israel as God's chosen people through whom the divided nations are to be unified in the knowledge and love of

God, Jesus as God's anointed son whose sacrificial death is the reconciling act that fulfills God's intentions for all things, and the church as Christ's body in which, through the presence of the Holy Spirit, Jew and Gentile together become the place within the creation where God's purpose to unify all things becomes visible. According to this narrative, unity is in no way an incidental consideration. It is God's chief business, and it is the chief business of the church.

The central importance of unity to the nature and calling of the church poses a basic issue, namely, the relation between the truth about God in Christ and the unity of the church. The Chicago/Lambeth Quadrilateral constitutes an Anglican attempt to address this question and, indeed, so does TVR. This vexed question, the relation between truth and unity, will be addressed in the body of this paper. It is enough to say for the present, based upon what can fairly be called the "plain sense" of Scripture, that we simply presuppose that each and every Christian is under an obligation to "make every effort to maintain the unity of the Spirit in the bond of peace" (Eph. 4:3). Any rejoicing in or acceptance of our divisions can only be read either as a failure to get the point of what God is "up to" in and through Christ and the church or a deliberate rejection of his providential purposes. Our second conviction, in short, is that, in the midst of the inevitable divisions that appear in the process of handing over the faith and practice of the apostles, the godly attitude is one which leads us to "make every effort" to overcome our divisions. To put it another way, in times of greatest stress, "patience" as well as love and truthfulness, is a power of soul necessary not only for the peace of the church but also for the truthfulness of its witness (Eph. 4:2).

What of the third conviction? It is related to an aspect of the biblical narrative as yet not mentioned. Indeed, omission of this aspect of the Bible's account of God's relation to the world is all too common, and the results of the omission are, as Douglas Farrow has recently pointed out, disastrous.[6] We speak of the doctrines of the Ascension and of Christ's coming again to judge the world. That Christ was not only raised but also ascended means that, in respect to his body the church, he is both present and absent. He is present in that the members of his body, the church, are

---

6. For the gist of the argument that follows see Douglas Farrow, *Ascension and Ecclesia: On the Significance of the Doctrine of the Ascension for Ecclesiology and Christian Cosmology* (Grand Rapids: Eerdmans, 1999).

joined to him not immediately but through the Spirit. He is absent, however, in that he has ascended to the Father; and even though the members of his body are seated with him "in the heavenlies" (Eph. 2:6), that seating is only in the Spirit which serves as a guarantee of their place with Christ and a share in the blessings which are his (Eph. 1:3, 13-14). It is this gap between Christ as present through the Spirit and yet absent, when coupled with a belief that he will return in judgment, that opens the possibility within the Christian narrative of infidelity — the possibility that the church as the body of Christ, in the manner of Israel, might, during the period of waiting for God to accomplish his purposes, prove disobedient and so find itself bereft of the Spirit which links it with its head. Indeed, it is the presence in the narrative of the Ascension and Christ's coming again in judgment (which Matthew reminds us begins with the household of God) that calls into question the essentialist and triumphal views of the church which seem to come to the fore whenever the story is ended simply with the resurrection and the gift of the Spirit.

It is the possibility of infidelity which sets the stage for the third conviction, namely, that when divisions within the church become intractable, as they seem now to be, it is mandatory that we think of the presence of the Spirit first of all as a call for the recognition of infidelity, for repentance, and for amendment of life.[7] Thus, we assume that the godly stance for entering the struggle in which the Anglican Communion (along with other churches) is now engaged is not one wherein an individual or group assumes the role of a self-designated "faithful remnant," but one characterized not only by eagerness for unity, love, and patience, but also by humility of mind (*tapeinophrosunē*; Eph. 4:2).

This comment leads to a fourth conviction, namely, that the intractable divisions that are beginning to appear within the Anglican Communion are best understood as continuing manifestations of the divisions within the Western Church. Though it is uncomfortable to admit it, the proclivity of the Western Church either to divide and subdivide or to make ever-stronger moves toward one form or another of bureaucratic centralism continues into the present. The reactions within Anglicanism seem to imitate in microcosm these more macrocosmic trends. Both trends seem

7. For a thorough exposition of repentance as the mode of the Spirit's presence in the Church in the midst of division see Ephraim Radner, *The End of the Church: A Pneumatology of Christian Division in the West* (Grand Rapids: Eerdmans, 1998).

to exacerbate rather than heal the strife within the churches, and this reason alone should cause us to ask if we are addressing our divisions in a godly manner or whether we need to find a better way.

The fourth conviction is then that we do need to find a better way and, as the third conviction suggests, that way is the way of penitence and suffering rather than the way of political strategies designed to insure the continued existence of a given party within our family feud. In saying this, we do not mean to say that political strategies have no place within the struggles that now so divide the communion, for they do. Indeed, the deployment and assessment of godly and appropriate political strategies is a matter of great importance. Nevertheless, these strategies in the end can neither guarantee the truth of the church's witness nor the unity of its life. They can at best buy time and perhaps create space for the appearance of that unity of the Spirit in the bond of peace for which our Lord bids us strive. These necessary, and one might say tactical, strategies are in fact but part of a larger one made necessary by the conflicted nature of *parodosis* and the duty of the church to maintain its own fidelity and unity during the conflict. I shall call this larger strategy a *strategy of time*.[8]

## *Koinonia*

These four convictions provide the context for the following analysis of TVR. At certain points, it will prove necessary to be critical of the report, but the first and most basic thing to say is that it represents a very positive step in the struggles of the Anglican Communion to assure its fidelity and unity in the midst of an extraordinarily stressful period of history. In particular, its strategy of building upon the emphasis Lambeth '88 placed upon *koinonia* and its particular suggestions about ways in which to strengthen "the instruments of unity" indicate a promising way forward. Thus, any critical comments that follow are intended not to cast doubts upon the adequacy of the report, but to strengthen its essential soundness.

There are a number of ways to describe the church.[9] Because the pres-

---

8. See below, the concluding chapter of Ephraim Radner.

9. For a catalog of the numerous images deployed in the writings of the New Testament see Paul Minear, *Images of the Church in the New Testament* (London: Lutterworth Press, 1960).

ent interest in ecclesiology is so closely linked to ecclesiastical divisions, choice of the notion of *koinonia* as the primary means of displaying the nature and calling of the church may fairly be judged, with exceptions, a promising one. Along with the "body of Christ," it is a conception that allows one to probe the nature and importance of unity within the church as well as, perhaps even better than, most others. It is as well a notion that links the internal discussion of unity with current ecumenical conversation.[10] The question, of course, is how adequately TVR presents and deploys this way of construing the church's life.

One certainly cannot accuse TVR of trimming the theological significance of communion. The authors of the report begin with the charge of Lambeth '88 that there be "further exploration of the meaning and nature of communion with particular reference to the doctrine of the Trinity, the unity and order of the Church, and the community of humanity."[11] They begin, in short, with the assumption that *koinonia* or *communion* is a way of construing the entire Christian mystery. The construal runs as follows. Communion is to be understood first of all as a property of the life of God "whose inner personal and relational nature is communion."[12] It is this mystery of the divine life that calls the church (and through the witness of the church all humankind) "to communion in visible form."[13] The sort of communion that imitates the life of God is a form of diversity within unity that is held together by mutual self-giving and receiving love. This kind of love is most clearly manifest in the love of the Father for the Son and the Son for the Father, but it is also to be seen in the love Christ has for us and the love we show toward Christ (and so his Father) and one another. In a paraphrase of Lambeth '88 the authors of TVR write as follows:

> The love with which the Father loves Jesus is the love with which Jesus loves us. On the night before he died Jesus prayed (John 17) that all who follow him should be drawn into that love and unity which exists between the Father and the Son. Thus our unity with one another is grounded in the life of love, unity and communion of the Godhead. The

10. See, e.g., *Anglican–Roman Catholic International Commission: The Final Report* (London: SPCK, 1982); and Alan Falconer, ed., *Faith and Order in Moshi: The 1996 Commission Meeting* (Geneva: WCC Publications, 1998).

11. *The Truth Shall Make You Free,* Resolution 18, p. 216.

12. TVR 1.11.

13. TVR 1.11.

eternal, mutual self-giving and receiving love of the three persons of the Trinity is the source and ground of our communion, our fellowship with God and one another. Through the power of the Holy Spirit we are drawn into a divine fellowship of love and unity. Further, it is because the Holy Trinity is a unique unity of purpose, and at the same time a diversity of ways of being and function, that the church is called to express diversity in its own life, a diversity held together in God's unity and love.[14]

Much is contained in this brief paragraph, but it would not be inaccurate to say that the communion God intends for the church (and along with it the entire creation) is brought about by the operation of the communion that characterizes the triune life of God, viz., the Father sends the Son who in obedience to the Father lives, suffers, dies, and rises. Through the Son we receive the Holy Spirit who draws us into Christ's life and so also into the life of the Father. Communion, understood as mutual giving and receiving love, is thus used to display the inner life of God, the relation between God and his incarnate Son, the relation between the Son, the Spirit, and the church, relations within the church, and finally the divinely appointed destiny of humankind.

Quite a lot of theological luggage has been placed upon a single cart, and one might well wonder at the wisdom of such a move. It is one, however, that is common enough at this particular moment. Indeed, the authors of TVR, in the use they make of the doctrine of the Trinity, join such distinguished theological company as Leonardo Boff, Catherine LaCugna, Colin Gunton, Jürgen Moltmann, Jean Tillard, John Zizioulas and Miroslav Volf — all of whom have employed the doctrine in similar, though not identical, ways.[15]

---

14. TVR 1.11, 2.9. See also *The Truth Shall Make You Free,* p. 130.

15. Indeed, the tracing of parallels between the life of God, the life of the Church and the intentions of God for human society has appeared at all points on the present theological spectrum. See, e.g., Leonardo Boff, *Trinity and Society* (Maryknoll, N.Y.: Orbis, 1988); Catherine LaCugna, *God for Us: The Trinity and Christian Life* (San Francisco: HarperSanFrancisco, 1991); Colin Gunton and Daniel Hardy, eds., *On Being the Church: Essays on the Christian Community* (Edinburgh: T&T Clark, 1989); Jürgen Moltmann, *The Trinity and the Kingdom: The Doctrine of God* (San Francisco: Harper and Row, 1981); J.-M.-R. Tillard, O.P., *Church of Churches: The Ecclesiology of Communion* (Collegeville, Minn.: The Liturgical Press, 1992); Miroslav Volf, *After Our Likeness: The Church as the Image of the Trinity* (Grand Rapids: Eerdmans, 1998); John Zizioulas, *Being as Communion: Studies in Personhood and the Church* (Crestwood, N.Y.: St. Vladimir's Seminary Press, 1985).

One can only celebrate this rediscovery of the doctrine of the Trinity, but it has not come without its own particular set of problems. The most significant of these appears not only in the work of the authors mentioned above, but also in TVR. The chief problem is that the parallel drawn by these authors and by TVR between the inner life of God and the shape of ecclesial and social life has, with the noted exception of Colin Gunton, been insufficiently modified by a refraction through the lens of the Fall and the Passion and Cross of Christ. As a result, communion is too frequently depicted apart both from the conflicts in the midst of which it appears and the deep root of these conflicts. As a consequence, the unsteady, punctual, and partial nature of communion within the church is vastly understated and, concurrently, the possibilities for communion both within the church and within human society in general are grossly overstated.

It is certainly true, as TVR insists, that "the climax of the Son's revelation of the Father occurs in the passion, death and resurrection of Jesus."[16] It is also the case that the report is fully aware of the conflicts that so bedevil the life of the church and the life of the nations of the earth. The conflicts within both church and society, however, are laid first at the feet of the forces of social change and cultural difference that characterize the modern world rather than within the "hearts" of those persons actually involved in these conflicts.[17] The forces said "to make unity and interdependence particularly difficult" are listed as "developments in the political, scientific, economic and psychological spheres" that have brought the disintegration of traditional cultures, values and social structures and unprecedented threats to the environment."[18] Also mentioned is a clash between "nineteenth- and twentieth-century notions of progress, economic growth, and the free market economy" along with "the omnipotence of scientific method and technology, and competitive individualism" on the one hand and "cultural, personal, and social identity which honors the integrity and value of cultural roots" on the other.[19] These factors do not exhaust the list of extenuating circumstances supplied by the report's authors,[20] but they do convey with sufficient clarity the fact that the major

16. TVR 2.8.
17. TVR 1.2-9.
18. TVR 1.3.
19. TVR 1.4.
20. See, e.g., TVR 3.3, which mentions differences in perspective between church parties and differing views which stem not only from cultural differences but also from differ-

impediments to communion are seen as cultural, historical, and technical. The forces aligned against communion are, in short, external to the agents involved. They act upon them, and breed differences in points of view.

The point to note is that the root of division is not linked to a specifically theological cause. It is no wonder, therefore, that the major suggestions of the report for dealing with division within the church do not involve the theologically based virtues of suffering, forbearance, forgiveness, and truth telling. Rather, they involve a range of virtues and institutional mechanisms of a more secular nature that serve for the promotion of the virtues of democratic pluralism; namely, mutual respect, understanding, and tolerance. Communion comes not from the sort of reconciliation that is born of suffering, forbearance, forgiveness and truthfulness but from insight that comes when we learn to see the world as others see it.

However, suppose one were to give a theological rather than a sociological account of the divisions between and within the churches. Suppose one were to speak of the presence of sin, understood as idolatry, infidelity, pride, sloth, and so forth as the root cause of these divisions; and suppose one were to attribute their intractability to the absence rather than the presence of the Holy Spirit. Suppose one were to attribute our interminable wrangling to the presence of God in anger and judgment, and so give a reading of our present history that mirrors the reading the prophets of Israel gave of the history of the divided kingdom.

A brief reading of the Letter to the Ephesians serves to make clear the problem with TVR and how it might be strengthened. How is the issue of truth and unity within the church presented in this letter?[21] The central point of the letter is one the authors of TVR most certainly share, namely, that the great purpose of God in history is to unite the peoples of the earth through the reconciling sacrifice of Christ (Eph. 1:9-10; 2:13-22). This purpose has been God's from the beginning, but it has now been made known through Christ to the church. Further, it is through the ministry of the Apostle Paul and the life of the churches that resulted from his preaching

---

ences in approach to biblical interpretation and difference in philosophical thought and scientific theory. Note, however, that these differences are cast in a mutually enriching role and the "cure" for their divisive potential is said to be dialogue and tolerance.

21. For a treatment of this letter that gives a more extended account of the argument I hope to make see Philip Turner, "The 'Communion' of Anglicans after Lambeth '88: A Comment on the Nature of Communion and the State of the Church," *Anglican Theological Review* 81:2 (Spring 1999): 281-93.

that the purposes of God are to become visible within the creation with such clarity and force that all people will see what God's plan for his creation is. Indeed, even the heavenly powers, the powers that ruled over the peoples of the earth until the coming of Christ, are to see through the visible unity of the church that they no longer have power to rule, divide, and destroy (Eph. 3:9-10). The calling of the church is to manifest the unity God intends for all peoples and, as one might expect, its nature is described accordingly. That nature is to be a new humankind or *Adam,* a single body that has many members but one head (Christ), fellow citizens of a single commonwealth, members of a single household of which God is the Father, and the temple of the Lord, the place where, through the Spirit, God is present on earth (Eph. 2:15-22; 4:11-16).

Given this high calling and given this exemplary nature, it is not surprising that the author of this letter's final exhortation begins by urging the saints to whom he writes to live a life "worthy" of the unity to which they have been called (Eph. 4:1). In spelling out the sort of life that is worthy of God's calling, he in fact not only urges a particular form of behavior, he also gives specific content to the sort of unity God has in mind. It is a unity of persons, each of whom has a particular gift to offer within the communion of saints (Eph. 4:11-16). It is also a unity that can be characterized by the presence of certain powers of soul within the "body" or "household" or "temple," and certain common practices which in combination give love, the basis of unity, a recognizable face. These powers of soul and practices all imitate the sacrificial life of Christ and can be adumbrated as follows: humility of mind *(tapeinophrosunē),* deferential gentleness *(praus),* and patience *(makrothumia).* These powers of soul manifest themselves in putting up with difficult people *(anechomai)* out of love *(agapē)* for them (Eph. 4:1-2). Such love, which is the basis of the unity God seeks, also shows itself in being kind *(chrēstos),* compassionate *(eusplanchnos),* and in the forgiveness of wrongs done *(charizomai)* (Eph. 4:32).

These practices and powers of soul give content to what it is to walk in love and to walk in a way worthy of the calling of the church. Consequently, they make visible the way in which Christ loved us and gave himself for us as an offering and sacrifice to God (Eph. 4:1; 5:1-2). They manifest the new nature of the new humankind (Eph. 4:24) and so also become the way *Adam* once more becomes the image of God (Eph. 5:1). All these powers of soul and all the practices that accompany them are now available to the church because of the power that is at work in each believer (Eph. 1:19).

Ephesians is noted for its "realized eschatology" and one certainly sees evidences of that sort of eschatology in the passages cited above. However, what commentators seem always to miss is that these eschatological powers are present in the midst of an ongoing conflict — a conflict that manifests itself not only in what we now call "the world" but also in the church. One can interpret the perorations found in the letter only as indications that the church might in fact fail in its calling.[22] The constant warnings about a former manner of life must be read in part as a testimony to its continuing presence and power even within the church. Thus, believers are urged to "put off" an old form of life that is characteristic of disunity. This is a form of life in which the mind has not been illumined by the revelation of God's secret but in fact has been given to emptiness *(mataiotēs)* The mind has been darkened *(skotoomai)* and alienated from the life of God (Eph. 4:17-18). People with such minds have not had the eyes of their hearts enlightened (Eph. 1:18). Instead, they have become hard of heart and so callous *(apalgeō)*. In this state they give themselves up to outrageous conduct *(aselgeia)* and all sorts of impure behavior *(akatharsia)* (Eph. 4:19). Their lives are also full of bitterness *(pikria)*, violent emotions of mind and spirit *(thumos)*, and anger *(orgē)* which all may be accompanied with malice *(kakia)* (Eph. 4:30).

All these manifestations of a former manner of life — one characteristic of the people of the nations — can be understood only as indications of the continuing presence in the lives even of those who now are part of Christ's body of the heavenly powers which, though defeated, are still active. Thus, the people to whom this letter was written were urged to realize that they were in a battle with powers of greater strength than merely human ones. They are warned that these powers can be fought, these clothes can be changed, these lives can be created in the likeness of God (Eph. 4:24) only through the powers and weaponry supplied by God in Christ through the Spirit (Eph. 6:10-18).

The point to be stressed is that the battle described in Ephesians is being waged not only between the church and "the world." It rages within the

22. The New Testament pictures the possibility of a disobedient church in many places, but it does not address the issue of a divided church. One can, however, use Holy Scripture to reflect upon the divided church by giving what George Lindbeck has called an Israel-like reading of the Church. In this reading, God gives up his people to the hardness of their hearts in order that they may be purified. We are in fact suggesting that we think of the Church in our time in exactly this way.

lives of believers and within the common life of the church as well. Thus, the unity and the communion it is God's purpose to establish comes to be in the midst of battle, and it is in the midst of battle that the marks by which we recognize love appear. To put it another way, the unity of the church in the present age imitates the sacrifice of Christ who gave himself. This self-offering takes the form of humility of mind, deferential gentleness, patience, willingness to simply carry impossible people, kindness, compassion, and most of all forgiveness. These powers of soul provide the space within which truth can be spoken in love (Eph. 4:15) and the unfruitful works of darkness exposed (Eph. 5:11). They provide a strategy of time wherein both truth and unity can be maintained not only within the divisive pressures of social change but also in the face of certain evil powers of soul — powers far stronger than we can cope with by intelligence, dialogue, or even (to use the phrase of TVR) mutual respect. It is this strategy of time that our more tactical, political strategies should be designed to support, and on the basis of which they should be judged.

To sum up, the problem with the account given of communion by TVR is not that its importance is overstated. The problem is rather that the nature of our divisions and our communion prior to the Lord's return is inadequately stated. As a consequence two additional inadequacies follow. In the first place, the description of the causes of our divisions is understated, perhaps even misstated; and the suggestions made for their elimination or diminishment are consequently inadequate. In the second place, the nature of the communion we are to enjoy as we wait for Christ's return is described in terms that are both far too optimistic and far too pale. We simply cannot remain true to the witness of the Holy Scriptures and lay our difficulties at the feet of historical, cultural, and technical forces. These things may exacerbate our divisions, but Christians cannot let sin simply migrate to forces that lie entirely outside the circle of our agency. We must continue to insist that the problem is in ourselves and not in our stars, and this insistence must begin with our judgments about the inner life of the churches. This being the case, we cannot leave the doctor's office with a prescription for dialogue and mutual respect and think that this sort of bromide will bring down our fevered condition. Our hope lies in a stronger medicine, and that remedy is not to declare that we are well — a holy and faithful remnant. Our hope lies in an opposite direction — in the recognition of our own part in the disease that now afflicts Christ's body. Our hope lies first in God's approval of repentance and amendment of life as the first step toward "a life created after the likeness of God in true righteousness and holiness" (Eph. 4:24).

The phrase "amendment of life" suggests that the account TVR gives of the communion we may now enjoy is indeed too optimistic and too pale. The communion of the saints open to us as we wait for the Lord's return is not a steady state of peace and harmony. Rather, it is a sort of unity that comes to be in the midst of conflict. It manifests itself in a certain way of contending with the powers of soul that disrupt our peace and in this way imitates the passion of Christ. It is certainly true enough to say that our present disputes have brought about states of "impaired communion" between various provinces of the Anglican Communion. It is also true to say, however, that prior to our Lord's return in judgment when, in the words of the spiritual, "The *Lord* [emphasis added] commands the spirit to be free," all communion is impaired. It cannot be said in terms that are overly strong. Our communion comes to be not as a steady state that we can sit back and enjoy, but in the midst of a battle. The battle is not in the first instance with historical and cultural abstractions but with forces generated by our darkened and hardened hearts. In that battle our weapons are certain powers of soul that come only from the Spirit. These are clearly presented in the Letter to the Ephesians. They are weapons of far greater strength than respect and tolerance — the great values of democratic pluralism, a form of social life built upon a presupposition of permanent, ineradicable conflict. The very character of Christian communion during the last age suggests that, though well meant, the suggestions of both Lambeth '88 and TVR that we address our problems with the democratic values of mutual respect and tolerance do not provide a way forward that will end in the sort of communion God has in mind for the church. The way God has marked traces a more challenging trail than that of civility — one that more closely resembles the passion of Christ than the marks of a well-mannered person.

## Discernment

During what Ephesians refers to as Christ's "administration *(oikonomia)* of the fullness of time" (1:10), the communion of the church is always hard-won, partial, and punctual. It is fair to say that, though TVR presents a more idealized picture of this communion than we believe Holy Scripture and the evidence of history warrant, the report nonetheless does recognize that the maintenance of communion may well require a struggle that stretches over a considerable length of time. The focus on respect and tolerance, inadequate though they may be, tells of a strategy of time — a desire to look at time as an opportunity given by God for us to become reconciled to him and to one another. Hence the report gives considerable attention to the way in which the church is to discern God's will in the midst of its divisions.

Such discernment requires first on the part of all Anglicans, be they lay or ordained, in the midst of their common worship and life, employment of the now famous "three-legged stool" of "Scripture, tradition, and reason." In the midst of this common life and worship, these become the sources of Christian knowledge.[23] The question, of course, is whether TVR gives an adequate account of the nature of these sources of Christian knowledge, and whether it takes sufficient account of the fact that at present they serve more as points of division than of unity. One must say that in both respects there are problems that need address. In respect to the Holy Scriptures, TVR, along with Lambeth '88, refers to them as a "uniquely inspired witness to divine revelation" and "the primary norm for Christian faith and life."[24] Also in line with Lambeth '88 is TVR's insistence that the Scriptures "must be translated, read, understood and their meaning grasped through a continuing process of interpretation."[25] These two statements will in all probability generate little controversy, but not so the comments on interpretation that follow. TVR comments: "Since the seventeenth century Anglicans have held that Scripture is to be understood and read in the light afforded by the contexts of 'tradition' and 'reason.'"[26]

---

23. TVR 3.12, 13.
24. TVR 3.6; cf. *The Truth Shall Make You Free*, p. 101, #77.
25. TVR 3.7; cf. *The Truth Shall Make You Free*, p. 101, #78.
26. TVR 3.7. At this point, TVR makes a claim that needs further elucidation. Though it is true that Richard Hooker viewed Scripture and reason as sources of Christian knowledge, he did not view tradition in the same light. Furthermore, he understood the nature and interrelation of the three in a very different manner than one finds in either TVR or the report of Lambeth '88 or in contemporary Anglican usage. Hooker understood reason to be a universal human capacity. It yields knowledge open to all people of good will and, for Christians, provides an instrument capable of interpreting the more difficult passages of Holy Scripture. He did not consider tradition to be a primary source of Christian knowledge. Rather, tradition is more like a form of practical wisdom that is to be followed in those cases where neither Scripture nor reason dictates a necessity for change. Thus, for Hooker, the

Tradition is defined as encompassing both the Scriptures that give expression to "the faith once delivered to the saints," and "the ongoing Spirit-guided life of the church which receives, and in receiving interprets afresh God's abiding message."[27] Tradition, the report goes on to say, includes "the ecumenical creeds" and "the classical eucharistic prayers" which serve to display the essential message of Holy Scripture."[28] However, the authors of TVR insist that tradition is not to be understood "as an accumulation of formulae and texts." Rather it is "the living mind, the nerve center of the Church."[29] The authors of TVR conclude that, for Anglicans, appeals to tradition are in fact appeals to the living mind of the church that is "carried by the worship, teaching and Spirit-filled life of the Church."[30]

There is much to recommend what TVR has to say about both Scripture and tradition. In the process of discernment, few would question Scripture as a "uniquely inspired witness to divine revelation" and as "the primary norm for Christian faith and life." Further, the authors of TVR are to be congratulated for understanding tradition as the mind of the church carried by worship, teaching and common life rather than as a collection of texts and statements. However, once more, TVR presents a triumphal and irenic view — one that suggests that the interplay of Scripture, tradition, and reason within the context of the life and worship of the church produces a unity of mind and spirit and an adequacy of grasp of "the faith once delivered to the saints" that present circumstances seem to belie. In short, the report fails to disclose the fact that, at present, the Holy Scriptures and the *traditions* (rather than tradition) through which they are interpreted seem more often than not to intensify division rather than to create unity. Thus, it is not completely accurate, when speaking of the

---

now famous three-legged stool was a seat with very uneven legs — Scripture being the longest and most important, reason being a much shorter neighbor, and tradition being an even shorter neighbor still. Further, it would never have entered Hooker's mind to pit Scripture against reason (or experience, reason's late-born cousin) as is often the case today. In short, though it is perfectly right for TVR to refer to these three sources of Christian knowledge as longstanding points of reference for Anglicans, the report makes no reference to the change that has taken place in their meaning or the way in which people understand their interrelation. As a result, the report fails to make clear the fact that the changes that have occurred render the very sources of Christian knowledge a part of its problematic.

27. TVR 3.8.
28. TVR 3.8.
29. TVR 3.8.
30. TVR 3.8.

interplay between Scripture, tradition, and reason, to attach the term "Spirit-filled" to the phrase "life of the church" in the unqualified manner found in both Lambeth '88 and TVR. The reading of Holy Scripture and its interpretation through the tradition(s) of the church may in fact display the absence as well as the presence of the Spirit, and any assessment of the sources of Christian knowledge that fails to come to terms with this possibility will most certainly fall victim to a triumphal view of the life of the church that distorts its true situation *coram Deo*.

The ambiguous character of both Scripture and tradition within the process of discernment appears rather starkly when one takes note of two aspects of their use within that collection of provinces most responsible for the current tensions with Anglicanism. I speak, of course, of ECUSA. In respect to Holy Scripture, the methods of literary and historical criticism (along with hermeneutics), as presently employed, are, generally speaking, brought into play in ways that render almost any text relative to the particular circumstances in which it is supposed originally to have appeared. In consequence, the authority of the text is, to all practical purposes, limited to those original circumstances with the result that discernment within contemporary circumstances is determined not by the witness of the Holy Scriptures but by appeals to contemporary experience and rather vaguely determined notions of "love." In short, as presently employed, literary and historical criticism, along with various forms of critical theory are, more often than not, deployed simply to take Scripture out of play.[31]

In respect to tradition, one is forced to the sad conclusion that, despite its formulaic appearance in the rhetoric of ecclesiastical debate, in fact tradition is increasingly viewed through the lens of the Enlightenment, namely, as a dead weight from the past that must be set aside if one is to gain new learning from contemporary knowledge and experience. One is confronted in reality with an ecclesiastical culture that poses as "catholic" but that in fact looks askance (save in respect to liturgical forms) at catholic tradition and views it as best a sort of jumble table from which one might with a bit of luck "retrieve" a few useful, perhaps even valuable

31. For a wonderfully clear account of the ways in which Scripture has been taken out of play in respect to current debates concerning gender see Katherine Greene-McCreight, *Feminist Reconstructions of Christian Doctrine: Narrative Analysis and Appraisal* (Oxford: Oxford University Press, 2000).

items. It is not unfair to say that in actual practice ECUSA has, for differing reasons in each case, come to the point of simply disregarding both Scripture and tradition in the conflict-ridden process of handing on the faith; and indeed one can plausibly argue that when reference is made to either, by a curious and perverse inversion, each in its own way serves more to divide than to unite.

These extraordinary circumstances require more than a historical/cultural explanation. For the Holy Scriptures of the church and the traditions that carry their message and power forward in time to become themselves primary sources of disunity cannot be explained fully (as TVR suggests)[32] by the birth of historical method, the techniques of literary criticism, and the discovery of hermeneutics. The loss of their power to bring about openness to instruction and a unity of mind and spirit must be located instead in the spiritual condition of the church itself, and God's reaction to that condition. In short, the problematic character of these two sources of Christian knowledge is best viewed as a sort of famine — a famine of hearing the Word of God that is an aspect of divine judgment upon his people.

What then is to be said of reason and the account found in TVR of its role in the process of discernment? On reading the report, one is struck immediately by the fact that reason is given two definitions. In the first instance, reason is a capacity common to human beings as such which allows them to "symbolize, and so to order, share and communicate experience" and to do so in a way that opens them to "what is true for every time and every place."[33] In the second instance, reason is a way of understanding and ordering the world that is relative to given times and places. On this account, "reason means not so much the capacity to make sense of things as it does 'that which makes sense', or 'that which is reasonable.'"[34]

Now it may be that these two views of reason are compatible, but their compatibility is in no way obvious. One is thus left with the question of whether TVR views reason as a universal power of knowledge or as a formal power whose operation is in all ways relative to particular times and circumstances. In all probability the authors wish to affirm the first and so to suggest a view that links these two definitions in a way that renders a conception of reason not far from that of Richard Hooker. That is, they

32. TVR 3.3.
33. TVR 3.9.
34. TVR 3.9.

view reason as a human capacity that opens all people to certain universals, but it is a capacity that always grasps these universals within particular historical and cultural contexts.

This reading is the most likely one. Nonetheless, TVR does not make the relation between the two definitions clear and, as a result, one can read the report as simply presenting two contradictory views of reason. One view is close to classical Christian conceptions of natural law. The other is distinctly "post-modern" in that reason is not a universal human capacity open to universal truth but a cultural construct. It is the more "post-modern" understanding that may well make possible the rather odd claim that "tradition and reason are . . . in the Anglican way two *distinct* [emphasis added] contexts in which [the] Scriptures speak and out of which they are interpreted." This claim is based upon the observation that "The gospel borne by the Scriptures must be heard and interpreted in the language that bears the 'mind' and distils the experience of the world."[35]

The manner in which the distinction between tradition and reason is here made is strange indeed in that reason as a way of understanding and experiencing the world is so sharply divided from the tradition(s) of the church. Even though both are viewed as ways of understanding and experiencing the world, they are presented in words that make them appear as two different sorts of things. Surely, however, as George Lindbeck has taught us all, even the foundationalists among us understand that tradition and so the Holy Scriptures they interpret are themselves forms of reason constituting a grammar by means of which we both understand and experience the world.[36]

Why then assign the realm of reason in an exclusive manner to "the world" and in so doing distinguish it in a way that makes it seem a different thing from both Scripture and tradition? It is indeed true to say, as does TVR, that "reason in the sense of the 'mind' of the culture" is a "necessary instrument for the interpretation of God's message in the Scriptures."[37] Of course it is. It may also be true to say that reason is a "legitimate" instrument for the interpretation of God's message. Nevertheless, in granting reason a legitimate role, it is important not to overlook the fact that the

35. TVR 3.9, 3.10.
36. See, e.g., George Lindbeck, *The Nature of Doctrine: Religion and Theology in a Postliberal Age* (Philadelphia: The Westminster Press, 1984), pp. 32-41.
37. TVR 3.10.

mind present in Scripture and the tradition(s) of the church (which are also necessary for the interpretation of the gospel message) and that present in a given culture, though both ways of understanding and experiencing the world, may in fact be in various ways at odds. The issue is how such a clash between ways of understanding and experiencing the world is to be resolved.

At this point TVR's account of the nature of the interplay between Scripture, tradition, and reason is of little help. It is, in fact, little more than a place-holder that idles and does no work. To be sure, it is certainly the case that the meeting of the "mind" present in the witness of Holy Scripture and the traditions of the churches and that present in a given culture yields insights born of the particularities of that meeting. TVR is also on firm ground when it insists that "the experience of the Church as it is lived in different places has something to contribute to the discernment of the mind of Christ for the Church."[38] It is also right to say that "No one culture, no one period of history has a monopoly of insight into the truth of the gospel."[39] However, the sharp distinction TVR makes between Scripture and tradition on the one hand and reason on the other does more to occlude than to illumine the issues involved in what TVR calls the "constant dynamic interplay of Scripture, tradition, and reason" that characterizes the process of discernment. It is precisely this overly sharp distinction (one that appears to pit reason on the one hand against Scripture and tradition on the other) that one sees at work with such disastrous results in the way in which ECUSA is addressing the internal issues that now confront it. In this debate, Scripture, tradition, reason, and laterally experience have become distinct entities that can be marshaled one against another in a process of "discernment" that simply compounds division. It would appear, in short, that, as in the case of Scripture and tradition, so also in the case of reason, in present circumstances, each contributes to the foundation of a tower once called Babel; and that our instruments for overcoming the ensuing confusion of tongues appear to do no more than multiply them. In short, TVR's account of reason could be made far more helpful if it had presented more clearly the natural-law view of reason it implies. Had it done so, it might have opened an interesting discussion about the relation between the witness of Scripture and those truths which are open

38. TVR 3.10, 3.11.
39. TVR 3.10, 3.11.

to all men as reasonable creatures but which must be grasped within the historical contexts in which people actually live.

## Reception

Despite its failure to present the extent to which Scripture, tradition, reason, and experience serve at present to compound rather than resolve differences, and despite its sometimes irenic views of the way in which the truth of the gospel is passed from generation and from place to place, TVR does recognize that at times "a desire for change or restatement of the faith in one place provokes a crisis within the whole church."[40] This crisis TVR addresses in part through the double notion of discernment and reception — strategies of time that take place within the context of the interplay of Scripture, tradition, and reason; a daily round of common prayer; and the sacramental life of the church. TVR holds that "All these resources keep Anglicans living together in fidelity to the memory and hope of Jesus under the guidance of the Holy Spirit, who leads into all truth."[41]

But do things really work in such a harmonious way? Like *koinonia,* discernment is a conflicted process that requires both grace and time for its adequate resolution. "Reception" of what TVR terms "a restatement of faith" is likewise a conflicted process that requires the grace of time, but how is this process to be managed in a way that leads both to peace and truth? One requirement is that the process not be brought to premature closure — one that perhaps reflects a pyrrhic victory for one party or another rather than a genuine reception on the part of the church. It was no doubt with this possibility in mind that the most recent Lambeth Conference, in considering the ordination of women, affirmed the principle of "open reception" set forth in the report of the Eames Commission and reaffirmed by TVR.[42] In making this affirmation, Lambeth urged the various provinces of the communion, when considering the ordination of women, to allow the process of reception to continue.[43]

Both the timeliness and the problematic character of this affirmation

---

40. TVR 3.10, 3.11.
41. TVR 3.10, 3.11, 3.13.
42. TVR 3.10, 3.11, 3.13, 4.18; cf. *The Eames Commission,* pp. 54-55.
43. See *Called to Be Faithful,* Resolution III.2.b.

are well illustrated by a decision on the part of the General Convention of ECUSA to ignore the godly admonition of the bishops assembled at Lambeth. By reaffirming with very little time for reflection or debate its previously mandated canonical requirement that the dioceses of its various provinces open the ordination process to all regardless of gender the General Convention came close to showing contempt for the views of the majority of the bishops within the communion. Here in fact one sees not a respect for the moral authority of Lambeth, but a clear attempt on the part of one member of the Anglican Communion to force an issue of particular interest to it to conclusion by political means. Sadly, the means chosen not only ignore the views of the communion's assembled bishops but also most certainly serve to produce greater division and more strife within its own ranks and within the communion as a whole.

## Interdependence

The good news is perhaps that this action on the part of ECUSA will serve to highlight the importance of the insistence on the part of the authors of TVR that a happy issue out of the afflictions of "discernment" and "reception" depends upon what it terms "interdependence" and certain "instruments of unity." Once more, the question is not whether TVR is right in its adumbration of what is needed to maintain truth and unity, but whether it has set out these conditions with sufficient clarity and strength. In fact, its account of "interdependence" calls for clarification, expansion and, at points, correction. In the first place "interdependence" is used in two senses. One speaks of the need that each province has for the others if their common life is to be maintained and their common mission is to be carried out. Another calls attention to the "interdependence of charisms" necessary for both.[44] In respect to the first of these, one must say that any ecclesiology that gives the weight TVR does to *koinonia* must give high priority to the importance of interdependence. Thus the report's insistence on the importance of interdependence is thoroughly consistent with its basic assumptions about the nature and calling of the church. However, the significance the report attaches to interdependence is undermined by

---

44. For the first sense of interdependence see, e.g., TVR 3.28-29, 5.5, 5.24. For the second sense of interdependence see, e.g., TVR 2.24, 3.14-20.

its failure to highlight a dominant aspect of Anglican tradition that, in practice, serves again and again to undermine a sense of interdependence.

The tradition is that of the autonomous national church. To be sure, TVR, in its discussion of "The Particular Church and the Church Catholic," is emphatic in its insistence that, despite the fact that "The life and mission of the Church is at its most authentic and vibrant in a particular context," it is nonetheless of the utmost importance to grasp the fact that the universal doctrine of the church is important especially when particular practices or theories are locally developed in ways that lead to disputes.[45] In some of these cases, the report goes on to say, "it may be possible and necessary for the universal Church to say with firmness that a particular local practice or theory is incompatible with Christian faith."[46]

The example given is relatively non-controversial, namely, the onetime practice in South Africa of racial segregation at the Eucharist. But does this particular agreement depend upon a sense of interdependence or upon a lower-level agreement about the iniquities of racial segregation? The clear defiance on the part of ECUSA of Lambeth's statements about "open reception," and its refusal to address the increasingly common practice of blessing of gay unions suggest a disturbing degree of hedging on the matter of interdependence, and this hedging is directly related to a sense of the autonomy of national churches or provinces that simply trumps interdependence in matters that touch a local nerve. ECUSA's behavior in respect to these matters suggests that the insufficiently qualified legacy of the autonomous national church is perhaps the gravest of all threats to the sort of ecclesiology TVR presents and seeks to defend. It is a matter that requires more direct address if the Anglican Communion is to get the balance between "The Particular Church and the Church Catholic" right.

What of the second sense of interdependence — the "interdependence of charisms"? TVR rightly notes that "The Holy Spirit bestows on the community diverse and complementary gifts" and that "The outworking of one person's gift in the Church is unthinkable apart from all the others."[47] The gifts of the Spirit, are, in short, given for the common good — "for the building up of the community and the fulfillment of its calling."[48] Having

45. TVR 4.25.
46. TVR 4.25.
47. TVR 2.24.
48. TVR 2.24; 2:26.

noted the interdependence and diversity of the gifts, one would expect, as in the case of St. Paul, some enumeration both of this diversity and the way in which each is necessary if both truth and unity are to be maintained within the church. One would expect some discussion of the way in which apostles, evangelists, pastors, teachers, administrators, workers of miracles, speakers in tongues, givers of alms, and so forth, each contribute to the truth of the church's message and the unity of its life. One might even expect some discussion of how the exercise of these gifts depends upon the presence within the life of the church of those powers of soul that are worthy of the church's calling (See again Eph 4: 1-4). What one gets, however, when next the gifts of the Spirit are mentioned, is a discussion of an ordered ministry comprised of laypersons, bishops, presbyters and deacons.

It would be a colossal mistake to dispute either the necessity or the importance of an ordered ministry, but such a discussion can hardly do justice to the diversity, interdependence, and purpose of the Spirit's gifts or to their importance in maintaining the truth of the gospel message and the unity of the church. Indeed, despite the primacy of place given to the laity in TVR's presentation of the orders of ministry, one nonetheless is left with a very clerical account of the Spirit's gifts — an account that simply submerges the identity of the Spirit's gifts in an overall sketch of church order.

To provide a case in point, let us take the example of those who have a calling to be teachers. This particular gift in no way requires ordination, but in the instance of ECUSA, it has been locked up within the narrow confines of seminary preparation for ministry and, to all practical purposes, removed from the councils of the church. On those rare occasions when the teachers of the church are allowed out of their cloisters and brought into the more public realms of the church's life their release is for the purpose of giving a blessing to one or another "position" within current debate. Within its common life, ECUSA has lost the ability to draw upon the gifts of its teachers in a way that is at the service of unity and truth. This gift, like most others, has been turned to political purposes and, as in the case of Scripture, tradition, and reason, now constitutes a barrier rather than a bridge to unity and truth.

Something similar can be said of the gifts of the Spirit. An adequate ecclesiology depends in part upon their relocation first of all within a discussion of the common life of the church and the powers of soul necessary for its peace and integrity rather within a discussion of its orders of ministry. Having said this, it is important to note the importance TVR attaches both to an ordered ministry and to what it calls "structures for taking counsel and deciding." When one addresses the question of how Christian belief and life are to be passed on, the discussion must take place on two fronts. One concerns the gifts and powers of soul necessary for communal recognition of truth and peacefulness of life. The other concerns political order and the offices that are also necessary if the truth of the gospel message and the peace of the church are to be maintained over the course of time. The discussion found in TVR of political order and office will certainly prove controversial; it nonetheless represents a step forward that is both modest and promising. The suggestions found in TVR concerning Anglican polity deserve most careful consideration.

## Subsidiarity and the Instruments of Unity

TVR's discussion of Anglican polity has its origins in the observation that "In order to keep the Anglican Communion living as a dynamic community of faith, exploring and making relevant the understanding of the faith, structures for taking counsel and deciding are an essential part of the life of the communion."[49] This initial point of departure will not meet with universal approval — even on the part of those who support the notion of the church as *koinonia*. For example, Ian Douglas, Associate Professor of World Mission and Global Christianity at the Episcopal Divinity School in Cambridge, Massachusetts, views this suggestion as the opening salvo of a group of white, male bishops — as the first step toward a western Anglican curia that will struggle to maintain the same sort of control of the church they enjoyed in the colonial period. In the eyes of Douglas, the way toward greater communion does not involve structures, but, citing Konrad Raiser, the more utopian option of "the 'mutual resonance' of a multi-cultural community dedicated to God's mission."[50] For more traditional and less ideological reasons many other Anglicans will also fear curial tendencies and so view the suggestions of TVR as simply contrary to the Anglican tradition of autonomous provinces.

49. TVR 3.11.
50. Ian T. Douglas, "Power, Privilege and Primacy in the Anglican Communion," in *Witness Magazine* 83:3 (March 2000): 14.

These concerns are not without merit, but they are overblown. In its discussion of polity issues, TVR moves in the right direction, but, nonetheless, it does require a certain amount of clarification and correction if its promise is to be realized. The first thing that needs clarification is the foundation upon which the various "structures for taking counsel and deciding" rests. In its enumeration of these structures, TVR mentions the Archbishop of Canterbury, the Lambeth Conference, the Anglican Consultative Council (ACC), and a regular Meeting of Primates. The Archbishop of Canterbury serves the process of taking counsel and deciding by providing a focus of unity for the various dioceses and provinces, by "gathering" the communion and by serving as president within the college of bishops.[51] The Lambeth Conference of Bishops serves not as a legislative but as a consultative body that exists to strengthen the spiritual and Christian principle "of loyalty to the fellowship." For this reason, TVR, though it fully recognizes Lambeth's lack of legislative authority, nonetheless calls for it to be accorded a certain moral authority because, in the words of the report, the bishops so assembled "are not free to ignore fellowship."[52] Or, as the report says elsewhere when it speaks of Lambeth, "A balance is held between denying any power of compliance or control while upholding the need for loyalty to the fellowship expressed in restraint imposed by virtue of belonging to the Communion."[53] The ACC is the creature of the Lambeth Conference and was set up to facilitate relations between the provinces of the communion during the long periods between Lambeth conferences. Finally, TVR mentions the "regular Meeting of the Primates" which was also set up by Lambeth to provide not "a higher synod" but "a clearing house for ideas and experience through free expression, the fruits of which the primates might convey to their Churches."[54] In this respect, the Meeting of Primates is to serve as a means of building personal relationships "(a) as a sign of the unity and catholicity of the Church; (b) to give high profile to important issues; (c) for mutual support and counsel."[55]

In outline, these are the political structures suggested by TVR as means of taking counsel and deciding for the communion as a whole as it faces the possible crises that may arise during the process of handing on

51. See especially TVR 3.30, 3.33, 3.35.
52. TVR 3.37.
53. TVR 3.38.
54. TVR 3.47.
55. TVR 3.48.

the faith. In the midst of this discussion, however, the report states that "The episcopate is the primary instrument of Anglican unity" and then it insists that the exercise of Episcopal oversight is properly personal, collegial, and communal.[56] It is personal because "Bishops are called by God, in and through the community of the faithful, to personify the tradition of the gospel and the mission of the Church."[57] It is collegial in that bishops both share in the priestly ministry of word and sacrament and the pastoral work of the church. They also share with other bishops "the concerns of the local church and the community to the wider Church," and they "bring back the concerns and decisions of the wider church to their local community."[58] Finally, it is communal in that bishops exercise their office within the community of local churches over whose life they have ordering responsibility. In practice, this means that the authority of a bishop is the authority he or she exercises "in synod."[59]

One may fairly summarize the import of this discussion by saying that in fact the collegiality of bishops whose authority is rooted both in their "personification of the gospel and the mission of the Church" and in the communal relations within their dioceses is the most fundamental instrument of unity open to Anglicans. TVR rightly points out that no legislative authority exists within Anglicanism beyond the diocese and the province. The point is that if the collegiality of bishops breaks down in the process of the crises involved in "restatement," the Anglican Communion has no legislative means of maintaining its unity. We regard this feature of Anglicanism to be a strength rather than a weakness, but it is a strength only as long as Anglicans continue to understand the importance of Episcopal collegiality and insist upon maintaining that collegiality, understood in the fullest of terms. It is only in this way that the unifying office of the bishop, as we have argued in the last chapter, can remain effective.

It is just this understanding and practice that a number of American bishops have lately begun to jettison in the name of a "prophetic" understanding of their office — one that launches them (in their view) out ahead of the church in ways that expose its weaknesses and disobedience. In short, as indicated in Chapter One, "The End of a Church and the Tri-

---

56. TVR 3.51.
57. TVR 5.7.
58. TVR 5.9.
59. TVR 5.10-11.

umph of Denominationalism," there is at work in certain portions of the communion a very different understanding of both the Episcopal office and the mission of the church. It is not possible here to present the complexity and seriousness of this issue, but TVR will most certainly prove ineffective if this difference in understanding and practice in respect to Episcopal office is not more clearly stated and more frankly addressed.

Indeed, it is in part due to the fact that the collegiality of bishops is at points breaking down that TVR makes its most controversial suggestions about Anglican polity. The report notes that it is now a genuine question as to whether the bonds of interdependence among Anglicans "are strong enough to hold them together embracing tension and conflict while answers are sought to seemingly intractable problems."[60] The question is in fact yet another plea for the articulation of a strategy of time. Behind TVR lies an important assumption, namely, that what might be called a final statement of Christian belief and practice lies beyond our grasp and that our history is marked by more or less successful attempts to get it right. As a part of this strategy TVR makes a suggestion, derived from Lambeth '88, that goes beyond past practice, to wit, that the primates meeting under the presidency of the Archbishop of Canterbury be authorized "to exercise an enhanced responsibility in offering guidance on doctrinal, moral and pastoral matters."[61] Further, it asks if the present arrangement whereby Anglican assemblies are consultative and not legislative is sufficient to hold the communion together "in hard times as well as in good ones."[62] The authors go on to wonder out loud "as to whether effective communion, at all levels, does not require appropriate instruments, with due safeguards, not only for legislation, but also oversight."[63] Further, at precisely this point they ask quite pointedly, "Is not universal authority a necessary corollary of universal communion?"[64]

Lambeth '88 did not move toward a universal authority but, "noting the need to strengthen mutual accountability and interdependence,"[65] it did take certain steps to affirm the responsibility of the primates "to exercise an enhanced responsibility in offering guidance on doctrinal, moral and pas-

---

60. TVR 3.54.
61. TVR 3.50.
62. TVR 5.20.
63. TVR 5.20.
64. TVR 5.20.
65. *Called to Be Faithful*, 3.6.

toral matters,"[66] to extend the jurisdictional reach of the Archbishop of Canterbury and the Primates Meeting, and to add moral authority to any decisions and/or actions the primates might take in respect to doctrinal, moral, and pastoral matters. Thus, Lambeth authorized the primates to take responsibility for "intervention in cases of exceptional emergency which are incapable of internal resolution within the provinces."[67] Lambeth further authorized the primates to give "guidelines on the limits of Anglican diversity in submission to the sovereign authority of Holy Scripture and in loyalty to our Anglican tradition and formularies."[68] The bishops assembled went on to say that these responsibilities should be exercised in consultation with the relevant provinces and the ACC or its executive but that any exercise of these responsibilities carries with it "moral authority calling for ready acceptance throughout the Communion."[69]

The obvious question is whether or not these responsibilities place judicial and/or executive authority in a body "above" that of a province or diocese and whether or not they portend a curial and more centralized form of authority than Anglicanism heretofore has known. Despite the rather disturbing question of whether or not universal authority is the necessary corollary of universal communion, it does not appear that TVR has in mind a centralized system like that of the Vatican as a means of articulating a strategy of time. The report emphasizes that the primates are to take action only after consultation with the provinces concerned. Indeed, TVR insists that a primate exercises ministry in collegial association with other bishops and that he or she is to intervene in the affairs of a diocese within the province only after consulting with other bishops; and that if action is taken it be taken if possible "through the normal structures of consultation and decision making."[70] Given this statement about the action of a primate within his or her own province, one must assume as well that if the action involves intervention by the primates in the affairs of another province, the same principle applies. One would have here a simple case of "what is sauce for the goose is also sauce for the gander."

The intention of TVR is not to set up a curia but to provide a way to deal with crises — a way that grows out of consultation and what the re-

66. *Called to Be Faithful,* 3.6a.
67. *Called to Be Faithful,* 3.6b.
68. *Called to Be Faithful,* 3.6b.
69. *Called to Be Faithful,* 3.6c.
70. *Called to Be Faithful,* 5.15.

port terms "attentiveness" to the nature of the circumstances within the province(s) in question.[71] The fact that TVR places its suggestions about an enhanced role for the primates after its discussion of "Levels of the Church's Life" and "The Principle of Subsidiarity" confirms that the intention of the report is not the re-imposition of colonial rule or the establishment of a curia or a sort of trans-provincial legislative/executive body. The principle of subsidiarity, after all, holds that "a central authority should have a subsidiary function, performing only those tasks which cannot be performed effectively at a more immediate or local level."

Clearly the intention of the report is to keep authority at a local level and do no more than provide a mechanism for the resolution of a crisis when things get out of hand, cannot be handled locally, and pose a threat to the health and unity of the communion as a whole. However, it may fairly be asked if invocation of the principle of subsidiarity is the best way to achieve this goal. The principle comes originally from the papal encyclical *Rerum Novarum* and was intended to make room for labor unions within the jurisdiction of state authority. In later encyclicals, a principle intended for the social order was transferred to the political structures of the Roman Catholic Church. Thus, the principle itself presupposes a political structure of sub- and super-ordination that is foreign to the Anglican tradition of Episcopal collegiality. Use of the term may thus begin to suggest the very sort of things its Anglican defenders wish to avoid — a curial

71. For TVR's discussion of the power of soul it calls attentiveness see especially 5.19 that says "Christian attentiveness means deciding to place the understanding of others ahead of being understood. It means listening and responding to the needs and hopes of others, especially when these differ from one's own needs, agendas and hopes. Further, Christian attentiveness means keeping these needs and agendas in mind, when making one's own decisions and developing one's own practices." Simone Weil, Iris Murdoch, and latterly Stanley Hauerwas have all pointed to the importance of "attention" as a necessary (though not exhaustive) quality of love. By stressing the importance of "attention" in the midst of the crises that may threaten *koinonia*, TVR moves closer to an adequate discussion of the powers of soul necessary if the communion of the Anglican Church is to appear in the midst of its struggles than it did in its more wooden adumbration of the virtues of pluralism, namely, courtesy, tolerance and mutual respect. In this respect it is instructive to compare 5.18-19 with 5.24. The comparison reveals, I think, that far more work needs to be done on the powers of soul that are necessary if the process of consultation and intervention TVR calls for is to strengthen rather than weaken *koinonia*. For a helpful discussion of the virtue of "attention" see Stanley Hauerwas, "The Significance of Vision: Toward an Aesthetic Ethic" in *Vision and Virtue: Essays in Christian Ethical Reflection* (Notre Dame, Ind.: Fides Publishers, 1974), pp. 30-47.

political structure with various levels of sub- and super-ordinated authority. A more helpful direction would be for TVR to emphasize the importance of the collegiality of bishops along with the gifts and powers of soul that sustain such collegiality and, in so doing, indicate that interventions by the primates are no more than emergency protocols made necessary by a lack of attentiveness, perhaps even charity, and the consequent failure of this central aspect of Anglican polity.

## Conclusion

A number of criticisms and suggestions have been made in the preceding paragraphs but their very number is a tribute to the strength of TVR. Despite the fact that it inadequately describes the extent and depth of the forces of division the communion now faces, it nonetheless, in broad outline, marks the way that must be taken if the Anglican Communion is to "maintain the unity of the Spirit in the bond of peace"; and it suggests a strategy of time which allows for the truth to be spoken in love and for evil to be exposed as the Anglican Communion seeks, in peace, to pass on the faith once delivered to the saints. Truth and unity are twins that cannot be placed in lexical order. They have been joined at conception. One does not precede the other. For this reason, space must be created in which both these twins can survive and flourish. Two things are necessary for the creation of this space. One focuses on what Victor Turner once described as *communitas,* those beliefs, practices, gifts and powers of soul that give sweetness to common life and allow its participants to live peacefully with their neighbors' idiosyncrasies and rough edges. The other focuses on what Turner called "structure" — those political mechanisms that help us order life together so that our gifts are fully realized and our aggressions peacefully contained. TVR would have been stronger if more attention had been given to the first of these, particularly those powers of soul and the gifts we can expect to find when the Spirit is present. This strategy would have given greater richness of TVR's characterization of its central concept *(koinonia)* and in so doing blunted the clericalism it often suggests. It would also have eased unnecessary fears about movements toward a more centralized and curial form of polity.

There is no neat way in which the changes and chances of time can be managed. The Anglican way, which tries to create space for the peaceful resolution of conflict within the grace of time without resort either to centralized authority or confessional overdefinition, we hold to be essentially right. The strength of TVR is that it seeks to show how that way can be adapted to the changing circumstances of our own age. We are sympathetic with, indeed, supportive of, the direction it suggests we take, but as members of the province which has done more than any other to pose the issues with which the Anglican Communion wrestles, the report leaves us with a conviction. The conviction is that, in the providence of God, the Anglican Communion is being forced through the crisis posed by ECUSA's actions in respect to the ordination of women and the blessing of gay unions to look at its common life anew and assess not only its identity but also its place within the Western Church. Thus, our present circumstances, painful as they may be, are best understood as God-given.

# CHAPTER EIGHT

# The Windsor Report:
## A Defining Moment for a
## Worldwide Communion

*Philip Turner*

I

The Virginia Report has not been the last word, obviously, in the Anglican discussion of the church's communion character. Already at Lambeth in 1988 it was clear that the stresses on the Anglican Communion noted in the Report were worsening, although few realized how quickly the Report's concerns would take flesh and tear at the communion's common life. In response to the 2002 decision of the Diocese of New Westminster to allow for the blessing of same-sex unions and the 2003 decision of the House of Bishops of ECUSA to approve the consecration of a bishop living with a same-sex partner, the primates of the Anglican Communion asked the Archbishop of Canterbury to draw together a commission charged with the preparation of a report suggesting ways in which the Communion might address the crisis these actions have brought about. That report, the Windsor Report (TWR), is now in the public domain. The primates have issued a communiqué in its support, as have the Archbishop of Canterbury and the Anglican Consultative Council. The report thus deserves careful consideration and comment. TWR, along with the Virginia Report, will for years to come constitute necessary points of reference for Anglicans throughout the world in their attempts to define both their communion and their relations with their ecumenical partners.

A distinguished colleague has said that, when placed alongside most Anglican documents, TWR is decidedly "up market." This observation is quite accurate, and the burden of this chapter is to show that, despite certain omissions and errors (some serious), TWR provides a credible way for the Anglican Communion to remain a communion rather than devolve into a federation of churches. Further, it suggests a credible way for the non-Roman churches throughout the world to respond to the potentially church-dividing tensions (both internal and external) that have arisen since the close of the colonial period. However, no matter what its strengths might be, it would be a mistake to wend one's way along the path down which the report leads its readers without pausing to take note of the fact that TWR places before ECUSA, the Anglican Church of Canada, and the Anglican Communion fundamental decisions that cannot be avoided. For ECUSA and the Anglican Church of Canada, the decision is whether they wish to be self-identified as autonomous churches within the Anglican Communion or as denominational boutiques within the fan of Protestant options that now comprise the religious scene in North America. For the Anglican Communion, the decision is whether it wishes to retain its claim to be a communion of churches; or whether it wishes to devolve into a religious federation bound together only by pragmatic arrangements and a rapidly disappearing historical memory. For the divided churches, TWR suggests a way, amid the stresses and strains of competing nationalisms, to maintain a worldwide communion without at the same time developing a centralized form of church government.

The most brilliant thing about TWR is the fact that it does not command. Rather, it offers a choice. It maps a way for Anglicans throughout the world to stay together as a communion; and basically asks it to choose something like this so as to "walk together," or choose another way and so "walk apart."[1] In placing the issue in the form of a choice, TWR both honors the autonomy of the various provinces of the Anglican Communion, and places a serious proposal for future relations before its ecumenical partners. It does not smuggle in a putative but non-existent centralized polity that can issue commands. It begins with what is — a communion of autonomous provinces that have a real choice about their future.

It has become painfully clear that there are those on both the left and the right who, in the words of TWR, have made a choice to "walk apart." The prophets on the left claim the backing of divine providence that has placed them ahead of the pack. They are content to go it alone and simply

---

1. TWR 157.

wait for others to catch up. The prophets on the right claim to be the champions of orthodoxy — charged with maintaining a faithful church in the midst of "apostasy." They are content to go it alone and await the vindication of God. TWR maps a more arduous and painful way forward — one that seeks to create a space in time within which very serious divisions within this portion of the body of Christ can be confronted and overcome. The burden of this essay is that the way TWR maps is the obedient way — one that serves as a caution to the prophets on both the left and the right, and a beacon to those for whom the maintenance of communion constitutes a fundamental obligation.

## II

The first two sections of TWR, sections that present a vision of what it means to be part of a communion of churches, are foundational to the entire report, but their significance and adequacy cannot be grasped apart from the conclusions to which they lead. In the Introduction, the chair of the commission asserts that TWR makes no "judgments" but "contributes to a process." One must indeed hope that the report does contribute to a process — one that extends far beyond the boundaries of the Anglican Communion. Nevertheless, it is important to note that, despite the disclaimer of the chair, TWR in fact contains a number of judgments. It is further important to note the specific content of these judgments because they comprise in part the way forward the authors of the report urge ECUSA, the Anglican Church of Canada, and the Anglican Communion to take.

TWR holds that it is the calling of the church to be "an anticipatory sign of God's healing and restorative future for the world."[2] The report argues that this calling has three constitutive aspects — "unity," "communion," and "holiness." To what judgments do these conclusions about the nature of the church lead? The list is extensive and severe.

1. ECUSA, the Diocese of New Westminster, the Anglican Church of Canada, along with those who have crossed jurisdictional boundaries to aid parishes and dioceses in distress because of the American and

2. TWR 2.

Canadian actions, have acted against the ideal of communion presented in the Pauline literature and the principles of communion and interdependence implied by the biblical witness as a whole.[3]

2. In acting as they have, these churches and ecclesial bodies have clearly violated communion teaching as set forth in successive resolutions of the Lambeth Conference of Bishops and subsequently affirmed by all of the instruments of unity within the Anglican Communion.[4]

3. The actions of ECUSA, the Diocese of New Westminster, and the General Synod of the Anglican Church of Canada cannot be judged to be part of a process of "reception" for the simple reason that these actions are ones that "are explicitly against the current teaching of the Anglican Communion as a whole."[5] Reception, the authors contend, is a doctrine that applies to disputed matters that have not become a part of established teaching.

4. The actions of the General Convention of ECUSA and the Diocese of New Westminster that license or promote the blessing of same-sex unions constitute "a denial of the bonds of communion."

5. The bishops of ECUSA, with full knowledge, have consecrated a person bishop whose ministry as a "bishop in the Church of God . . . very many people in the Anglican Communion" could "neither recognize nor receive." As the authors of the report go on to say, this action raises questions about the bishops' commitment to ECUSA's interdependence as a member of the Anglican Communion.[6]

6. The actions of ECUSA, the Diocese of New Westminster, and the Anglican Church of Canada have caused scandal within the Anglican Communion and placed severe stumbling blocks before the majority of its members.[7]

## III

When taken together, these judgments are sobering; and they are particularly so when one considers the fact that the members of the commission

3. TWR 122.
4. TWR 69.
5. TWR 69.
6. TWR 129.
7. TWR 87-96.

reached these judgments unanimously! The issue is, then, how adequate the foundations are upon which these judgments rest. This is the first and most basic question to be asked of TWR. On several occasions, the authors of the report remind their readers that it is not their brief to make determinations in respect to the theological and moral issues that swirl about the contested matter of same-gender sexual relations. Their brief is of an ecclesiological nature; namely, to comment on "the ways in which provinces of the Anglican Communion may relate to one another in situations where the ecclesiastical authorities of one province feel unable to maintain the fullness of communion with another part of the Anglican Communion."[8] Appropriately, the authors of TWR based their response on the "communion ecclesiology" that has shaped the recent ecumenical dialogues in which Anglicans have been involved (see, for example, the various ARCIC reports).

One can only hail this starting point if for no other reason than the authors of TWR feel bound to the ecumenical commitments of the Anglican Communion; and in so doing do not (as is now so common) act as autonomous agents utterly unencumbered by either history or social ties. Nevertheless, it must be noted that many on both the left and the right do not begin their ecclesiological discussions here. Many on the left begin with the church as a prophetic vanguard commissioned to fight within various political systems for the rights of those who are disadvantaged by those systems. Many on the right view the church primarily as the guardian of certain saving truths contained in Holy Scripture and in various creedal or confessional statements. These perspectives, different though they are, lead those who hold them to similar visions of themselves; namely, as advocates and/or guardians who must, before all else, hold to principle.

The authors of TWR, though they care mightily about truth and justice, see both as contained within and witnessed to by something more basic; namely, a form of common life that is a sign of God's will for the entire creation. Thus, they see unity, communion, and holiness of life as providing something like a circle of grace within which sinful people who have been brought into a new form of life by incorporation into Christ can struggle within the conditions of finitude and sin to bring about a faithful witness to God's purposes for the world. Thus, unity, communion, and holiness of life are constitutive of the calling of the church. Truth and justice

8. TWR 1.

(along with love) are the fruits that arise within this circle of grace and so give light to the world. For the authors of TWR, the matter of primary importance is for the church within its common life to be characterized by these three distinctive marks. Apart from them, the church loses its assigned character and so fails in its vocation.

How might such a starting point be substantiated? Only if it accords with Holy Scripture! From the beginning, accordance with Scripture (rather than with council, creed, or confession) has been for Anglicans the proper foundation for theological assertions. In accordance with this principle, the authors of TWR made a strategic decision, namely that the witness of the Bible about the calling of the church is well captured by the Epistle to the Ephesians and by Paul's Letters to the Corinthians.

What then is the witness of Holy Scripture in respect to the calling of the church? Ephesians, so TWR suggests, provides what can fairly be considered an epitome of the biblical witness. God has made known in Christ a plan "for the rescue of the whole created order from all that defaces, corrupts, and destroys it."[9] This sentence is clearly meant to render Ephesians 1:9-11. Herein lies the basis of the entire report — a starting point that would have been more effectively made with a direct quotation from the letter itself. Better to say, using the words of Ephesians, that in Christ, God "has made known to us [i.e., the church] the secret of his will in accordance with his purpose which he set forth in him [Christ] for administering the fullness of the ages so as to sum up all things in Christ, things in the heavens and things on earth." In other words, God, in Christ, has made known his eternal purpose for creation. That purpose is to unify all aspects of the created order in Christ. Further, this purpose, formerly hidden, has now been revealed to the church.

It is, therefore, God's plan, rather than human intention, that gives meaning to the existence of the church. It is God's plan that, as it were, gives the church its marching orders. Because the secret of God's will has been entrusted to the church, its common life is to be what TWR terms an "anticipatory sign of God's healing and restorative future." God's plan for the creation requires of the church that its members, in the words of the report, "live as a united family across traditional ethnic and other boundaries."[10] The characteristics of a united family, so TWR contends, requires

9. TWR 1.
10. TWR 2.

of the church a life that brings together many peoples and makes them one people — a people whose common life manifests unity, communion, and holiness of life. In this way, the church becomes an anticipatory sign of God's providential design for his creation.

The creation of a united *ethnos* constitutes the immediate purpose and issue of Christ's death and resurrection. Thus the report reads: "The communion we enjoy with God in Christ by the Spirit, and the communion we enjoy with all God's people living and departed, is the specific practical embodiment and fruit of the gospel itself." This gospel is described as "the good news of God's action in Jesus Christ to deal once and for all with evil and to inaugurate the new creation."[11] The report then goes on to make one further point of fundamental significance: the various ministries or gifts to be found among the people God has chosen to be his anticipatory sign within the world exist to "sustain" and "maintain" "the unity to which Christ's body is called." The ministries presented in Ephesians and the letters to Corinth (and specifically cited by TWR 3) are apostolic, prophetic, evangelistic, pastoral, and educational.


## IV


With one exception this précis of the biblical witness is more than adequate. Adequate or not, it serves to explain many of the negative "judgments" contained in the report. Its authors contend that, if one looks at the recent actions of ECUSA and the Anglican Church of Canada through the lens of Ephesians, the divisions these actions have brought about compromise both the very essence of the church's life and the purpose of its various ministries. They also run contrary to what TWR presents as the primary direction of the history of the Anglican Communion — a history whose major precedents support self-identity as a communion rather than a federation of churches. Thus, TWR notes that throughout their history Anglicans have been sustained as a communion by "a common pattern of liturgical life" that is "shaped by the continual reading . . . of the Holy Scriptures" (TWR #7). They have also been connected "through a web of relationships" that includes the See of Canterbury, bishops, consultative bodies, companion dioceses, and projects of common mission (TWR #7). Communion iden-

11. TWR 3.

204

tity was given "formal expression" in the third Anglican Congress that described life in communion as "mutual interdependence and responsibility [sic] in the Body of Christ" (this should more accurately read "mutual responsibility and interdependence"). This communion identity was later strengthened by the articulation of the "Ten Principles of Partnership" set forth by the second meeting of the Mission Issues Strategy Advisory Group (MISAG II). The Ten Principles are "local initiative, mutuality, responsible stewardship, interdependence, cross fertilization, integrity, transparency, solidarity, meeting together, and acting ecumenically."[12]

This historical survey is not unimportant either for Anglicans or their ecumenical partners. Anglican polity, like the British constitution, works more from precedent than written constitution. The power of these communion-making precedents is visible, TWR contends, in the way in which the matter of the ordination of women was handled within the communion. The authors trace this history to make visible a process that manifests communion identity rather than unfettered autonomy; and to show, by contrary example, the ways in which the recent actions of ECUSA and the Anglican Church of Canada move in a way contrary to both that identity and the Ten Principles that give it visibility.

The example is well chosen in that it puts to rest a major claim by those who believe that the issue of same-gender sexual relations is analogous to that of the ordination of women. Prescinding from the question of whether these two issues are of equal moral or theological weight, one can say, as does the report, that the ways in which the issues have been addressed are quite different. In one case, the principles of communion shaped the process. In the other, actions were taken in the name of prophetic truth that both ignored these principles and placed their authors beyond communal correction.[13]

## V

These actions, TWR holds, should be viewed as symptoms of an illness.[14] It is perhaps worth pausing for a moment to take in what the report is say-

12. TWR Appendix 3, 5.
13. See TWR 22.
14. TWR 22-30.

ing. *ECUSA and the Anglican Church of Canada are sick.* (This is not something institutions often say about themselves.) The symptoms of the disease are said to be both "surface" and "deep." The surface symptoms are twofold. ECUSA and the Anglican Church of Canada have taken actions in the matter of same-gender sexual relations that run contrary to what now may be considered both Anglican teaching and the majority opinion within the Anglican Communion. In reaction to these actions, jurisdictional boundaries have been crossed in various ways that run contrary to what TWR cites as ancient practice. Both sorts of action are seen as contrary to the principles of communion.

The deeper symptoms stem in the first instance from the failure of ECUSA and the Anglican Church of Canada to follow communion practice in cases where there is a dispute about the adequacy of a development in doctrine. Thus, neither the Diocese of New Westminster nor ECUSA "made a serious attempt to offer an explanation to, or consult meaningfully with, the Communion as a whole about the significant development of theology which alone could justify the recent moves by a diocese or a province."[15] Further, neither ECUSA nor the Diocese of New Westminster "went through the procedures which might have made it possible for the church to hold together across differences of belief and practice."[16]

Behind these symptoms lay others that, one might say, contributed to their severity. Many consider the issues in question to be *adiaphora:* matters not essential to the gospel witness and so subject to local determination. Thus, these persons believe that they were free, on the basis of the principle of subsidiarity, to take decisions locally that "the rest of the communion believe can and should be decided only at the Communion-wide level."[17] In combination, these factors have produced a fifth symptom; namely a lack of trust that has issued in a dispute that has become "adversarial, not to say abusive."[18] Finally, these symptoms have revealed one of profound significance; namely, that there is a lack of clarity within the communion as a whole about the nature and function of authority in circumstances where communion-threatening disputes arise.

TWR's analysis of symptoms leads directly to its second chapter —

15. TWR 33.
16. TWR 35.
17. TWR 39.
18. TWR 40.

one in which principles are set out that might allow for treatment of the sickness it has identified. These principles demand careful consideration, but first several brief comments on TWR's account of "The Purposes and Benefits of Communion" are in order. The first is that the depiction of the calling and ministry of the church found in the report is only partially in accord with the biblical witness. Ephesians and the Letters to the Corinthians make it clear that the same forces that crucified the Lord, even though defeated, continue to roam abroad and do their divisive and destructive work. Consequently, the life of unity, communion, and holiness to which the church is called is not lived out in a perfect manner. Rather, these characteristics manifest themselves only in a fearful struggle in which sin must be met and overcome both within the common life of the church and at the intersection where the life of the church meets that of the surrounding world. As was the case in the Virginia Report, the account given in TWR of unity, communion, and holiness of life does not address the character of this battle; and it fails to give an account of the weapons to be employed as it is waged against a divisive enemy that lies both within and without. The result is an account of the life of the church that omits its cruciform nature. There is no call for the church to take the "whole armor of God" and to "stand" in a battle that can be won only by Christ. Further, the call for repentance, though present, is stated in such a modest way that it can easily be missed.[19]

This sanguine account of the life of the church leads to an inadequate diagnosis of sickness the report rightly identifies. It leads also to a serious omission in its account of unity, communion, and holiness of life. If one reads the account of the symptoms of the disease that has infected Anglican churches in North America, it appears at first that the illness has been produced by a simple failure to follow proper procedure. However, one must ask what has led ECUSA and New Westminster, despite the universal disapproval of the instruments of unity within the Anglican Communion, knowingly to take unilateral actions that not only failed to follow procedure, but also served to divide and scandalize the communion. And what lies behind what the report terms "adversarial not to say abusive behavior"? According to Ephesians, the appearance of arrogant, adversarial, and abusive behavior within the life of the church must be read not as a procedural problem but as a sign of the presence within the life of the church it-

19. See TWR 134.

self of the very powers of darkness that crucified the Lord. The presence within the common life of the church of what Ephesians calls "a former manner of life" and "a darkened understanding" is made visible by the appearance of bitterness, wrath, anger, clamor, slander, and malice. One can only sadly admit that these little germs are far more common in the present life of ECUSA and the Anglican Church of Canada than are the signs of the counter-reality it is the calling of the church to manifest.

It is also the sanguine character of TWR's account of unity, communion, and holiness that leads to a serious omission; namely, a discussion of the place of discipline within the common life of the church. The very people who are responsible for tearing the fabric of the Anglican Communion are rather naïvely called upon *voluntarily* to absent themselves from communion functions until they bring their practice into accord with that of the rest of the communion. It is true that TWR mentions that Paul in his letter to the Corinthians does not hesitate to administer "severe discipline in the case of scandalous behavior."[20] TWR also suggests that the Archbishop of Canterbury has the authority both to invite and refrain from inviting to functions of the communion. Nevertheless, apart from these brief and undeveloped references, no further mention is made of a factor that throughout the New Testament is considered crucial for the maintenance of the unity, communion, and holiness of the church. It is difficult indeed to imagine the clear intent of TWR being realized apart from a rather careful, even extended, discussion of this issue.[21] Apart from a serious attempt to grapple with the form discipline might take within the sort of polity that characterizes the Anglican Communion (or any other global ecclesial body) it will most certainly not long remain a communion.

## VI

The last remark provides a convenient way to begin discussion of the second section of TWR. Here are presented the principles the authors of the report view as a cure for the sickness whose symptoms they have de-

20. TWR 4.

21. For a proposal about the form discipline might take in the Anglican Communion see Anglican Communion Institute, *Communion and Discipline: A Submission to the Lambeth Commission by the Anglican Communion Institute* (Colorado Springs: The Anglican Communion Institute, 2004).

scribed. Not surprisingly, the first of the principles mentioned is what one might call the preexistence of communion — one rooted both in "our shared status as children of God" and "in our shared and inherited identity."[22] This inherited existence "subsists," says TWR, "in visible unity, common confession of the apostolic faith, common belief in Scripture and creeds, common baptism and shared Eucharist, and a mutually recognized common ministry."[23] From the given reality of communion, TWR draws an important conclusion; namely, "in communion, each church acknowledges and respects the interdependence and autonomy of the other, putting the needs of the global fellowship before its own."[24] When this principle is not observed, states of "impaired communion" result. In such circumstances, TWR goes on to say, the constitutional status of several member churches of the Anglican Communion is called into question because "many . . . mark out their identity in terms precisely of being in full communion either with Canterbury or with all other churches in communion with Canterbury."[25] The authors of the report thus, in the strongest possible terms, issue the following caution: "the divine foundation of communion should oblige each church to avoid unilateral action on contentious issues which may result in broken communion."[26]

These principles serve to make clear how seriously the authors of TWR view the present conflict within the Anglican Communion. The very identity of Anglicanism hangs in the balance. Thus, their presentation of "the bonds of communion" is central to their suggestions as to how the various provinces of the Anglican Communion might continue to walk together rather than apart. Communion is a reality given by God, but God maintains the communion he gives in various ways. Chief among them is the reading and singing of Holy Scripture within the context of common worship. It is through this medium that God continues to exercise authority over the church. The authority of Scripture, according to the authors of TWR, actually refers to the authority of God exercised through the reading of Scripture within the common life of the church.

It is at this point that a careful reader of the report ought to have a problem. Surely, the authority of Scripture must also be viewed, as it were,

22. TWR 45.
23. TWR 49.
24. TWR 49.
25. TWR 50.
26. TWR 51.

from below as well as from above. That is, Scripture must be viewed not only from the way in which God speaks through it but also from the way in which it is used within the church to discern God's will. Thus, the authority of Scripture, among Anglicans, has traditionally meant that a given theological or moral claim must be judged "in accord with Holy Scripture." When disputed matters arise, Anglicans have always claimed that Scripture has authority in that it must be *the* locus for testing any theological or moral claim. The authority of Holy Scripture does not share equal authority with reason, experience, and tradition. It must be the final and decisive testing ground for any theological claim.

The obvious issue is this. Given its central importance within Anglicanism, how is Scripture to be interpreted so as to maintain unity, communion, and holiness of life within the body of the church? In response to this issue, TWR has a number of useful things to say, each of which has a fundamental bearing on the present conflict. If the witness of Scripture is to be rightly discerned, it is of central importance that there be *teachers of Scripture,* chief among whom are bishops who aid the church in its efforts at discernment.[27] In the end, however, it is the church, through agreement among the faithful, that judges what is and what is not in accord with Scripture; and it is here that a fearful problem is revealed. In the current conflict, the very writings through which God unites the church have themselves become a source of division. The dispute over sexual ethics has revealed that they are read and inwardly digested in different ways in different parts of the world. In response, TWR does not hurl insults like, "Fundamentalist!" or, "You deny the authority of Scripture!" Rather it calls for the Anglican Communion to "re-evaluate the ways in which we have read, heard, studied and digested Scripture."[28] In particular, TWR calls for "a shared reading of Scripture across boundaries of culture, region, and tradition."[29]

This call makes visible a central aspect of what it is to be a communion. One cannot claim communion and at the same time, in one's reading of Scripture, refuse correction from outside the boundaries of one's own province. It is precisely such refusal of correction that now so threatens the Anglican Communion (and, one must add, other global Christian

27. TWR 57, 58.
28. TWR 61.
29. TWR 62.

bodies). Consequently, TWR rightly goes on to ask how a shared reading of the Bible is possible. Central to its answer is an interpretation of the role of the episcopate. Bishops are not only the primary teachers of the church; they also occupy an office through which the unity of the church is expressed and maintained. They are more than local pastors of pastors. They represent the local church to the church universal and the church universal to the local church. Thus, TWR concludes, "that the churches of the Anglican Communion, if that Communion is to mean anything at all, are obliged to move together, to walk together in *synodality*."[30] Clearly, such synodical walking together is expressed most visibly among Anglicans through the office of bishop. The question that places this response in a wider ecumenical context concerns the manner and effectiveness of other means of procuring the same end; but no matter what the answer may prove to be all other churches face the same issue.

Differing answers to this question pose one of the thorniest of ecumenical issues. The answer given by the authors of TWR make it plain that from their perspective the actions of ECUSA and the Anglican Church of Canada do not accord with the kind of practice that manifests a commitment to communion. Anglicans are, however, called to "the specific unifying task of a common *discernment in communion*."[31] How then might discernment in communion take place? Discernment takes place, say the authors of TWR, through a process of *reception* that brings about agreement among the faithful *(consensus fidelium)* in respect to a disputed issue. This process clearly presupposes that forbearance and mutual subjection in love are prized practices among the faithful as well as among the bishops who represent them. The process requires both space and time for a godly resolution of conflict to take place.

This process, if allowed to take place, will issue, the authors of TWR believe, in a common decision about what matters may rightly be considered appropriate for local decision *(adiaphora)* and which are matters that affect the communion as a whole. The process yields those issues that may be decided by autonomous provinces of the communion and those that must await general agreement. There is, however, a significant limitation TWR places upon the notion of *reception.* "It cannot be applied in the case of actions which are explicitly against the current teaching of the Anglican

30. TWR 66.
31. TWR 67.

Communion as a whole, and/or individual provinces."[32] In these cases, the issue is not "reception" but how the members of a communion are to respond to actions destructive of their inner peace.

Consequently, the authors of TWR insist that autonomy within communion is a limited notion. Autonomy does not imply unfettered freedom. Within a communion and within the process of discernment, provinces are "autonomous *only in relation to others.*"[33] Autonomy is rightly understood within communion only in relation to the principle of *subsidiarity* that demands that only those decisions be taken locally that properly may be so taken. Thus, again, the actions of ECUSA and the Anglican Church of Canada are displayed as contrary to and subversive of the God-given gift of communion.

## VII

With what then is one presented at the end of this rather lengthy discussion of "Fundamental Principles"? One is left with an admittedly slow process of discernment the purpose of which is to insure that the church has read, marked, learned, and digested the Holy Scriptures rightly; and in the process maintained the communion that is God's gift and God's destiny for the entire creation. One is left also with a sharp criticism of ECUSA and the Diocese of New Westminster as having acted in ways that threaten, indeed violate, communion within this part of God's sadly divided church.

In response, the authors of TWR suggest certain steps, some short-term and some long, that they deem necessary for the preservation of communion. The suggested steps are varied, but all share a common feature deemed necessary for the preservation of communion. This common feature is the practice of *mutual subjection in Christ.* This practice is bracketed by what the report terms "the imperatives of communion," namely, "repentance, forgiveness and reconciliation." From the outset, no party to this dispute is exempted from these demands. In respect to short-term measures, the report first makes clear what is demanded as a sign of repentance by the principle of mutual subjection of those who supported the consecration of Gene Robinson.

32. TWR 69.
33. TWR 76.

- ECUSA (as a whole) is invited "to express its regret that the proper constraints of the bonds of affection were breached" and "for the consequences which followed." Such an expression of regret would, TWR holds, "represent the desire of the Episcopal Church (USA) to remain within the Communion."
- Those who took part in the consecration of Gene Robinson are invited (in order to create the space necessary for healing) to consider "whether they should withdraw themselves from representative functions within the Communion."
- ECUSA is invited "to effect a moratorium on the election and consent to the consecration" of anyone "living in a same gender union."[34]

In respect to those who have approved the blessing of same-gender unions, TWR notes, in surprisingly firm language, that liturgical provisions of this sort constitute "actions in breach of the legitimate application of the Christian faith as the churches of the Anglican Communion have received it, and of the bonds of affection in the life of the communion. . . ."[35] Consequently, the authors of the report call for the following measures.

- TWR calls upon all the bishops of the Anglican Communion not to authorize the blessing of same-gender unions.
- The authors of the report also call for a moratorium in ECUSA and the Anglican Church of Canada upon all such public rites.
- The authors of the report also call upon all bishops in ECUSA and the Anglican Church of Canada who have authorized such rites "to express regret that the proper constraints of the bonds of affection were breached by such authorization."[36]

The points mentioned above are all directed to those who have violated the witness of Holy Scripture, the clear teaching of the Anglican Communion, and the principles of communion that bind its member churches together. What, however, are the steps to be taken by those who have been scandalized by these actions? What do repentance and mutual subjection demand of them? The authors approach this question by asking

34. TWR 134.
35. TWR 143.
36. TWR 143, 144.

what care is to be given to dissenting groups within ECUSA and the Anglican Church of Canada who find the above actions unacceptable and whose relation with their bishops has been damaged. Their response amounts to a double-edged sword. On the one hand, they recognize that the actions of bishops in both the U.S. and Canada have caused a breach of trust so serious that in some cases a parish or diocese "has found itself unwilling to accept the ministry of a bishop associated with such a contrary action."[37] In response, bishops from elsewhere have been asked to provide pastoral and sacramental oversight. TWR makes it "quite clear" that, though its authors believe the matter should have been handled differently, they nonetheless "fully understand the principled concerns that have led to those actions."[38] Thus, they express support for the proposals for delegated Episcopal oversight approved by ECUSA's house of bishops in 2004, and they suggest that the Anglican Church of Canada adopt "a broadly similar scheme."[39] They even go so far as to say that the oversight they have in mind might, in principle, be provided by bishops from other provinces within the Communion.

## VIII

It is clear that the feasibility of these short-term measures is dependent upon the very principles from which they have been derived.[40] In particular, their success depends upon a communion-wide commitment to the fundamental practice of communion — mutual subjection. If an ethos of this sort is not in place, there seems little reason to believe that the various provinces of the Anglican Communion will in fact accede to suggestions such as these. For this reason TWR contains long-term as well as short-term suggestions. A number of these suggestions concern the position and

37. TWR 149.
38. TWR 149.
39. TWR 152, 153.
40. The recent struggles over provision of delegated or alternative oversight within ECUSA already indicate a lack of such commitment. At the same time, this lack of commitment has raised the question of how clergy whose bishops clearly do not accept the principles of communion are to relate to the Communion as a whole. What form of oversight is appropriate for clergy whose relation to the Archbishop of Canterbury and the Primates of the communion is either broken or in doubt?

role of the "instruments of unity" the Anglican Communion has developed to cope with divisive issues; namely, the Archbishop of Canterbury, the Lambeth Conference of Bishops, the Meeting of the Primates, and the Anglican Consultative Council. The report recommends a number of measures (some wise and some not so wise) that might be taken to make these "instruments" more effective.

Two of these measures are of central importance. The first, and most basic, is a suggested "Covenant" to be adopted by the member provinces of the Communion — a covenant that seeks to make clear the nature of communion and the importance of mutual subjection. The second, with the same purpose in view, urges on the part of each province the incorporation into their constitutions and canons of a set of "communion" measures that support and help define communion membership. Anglicans will hotly debate the contents of the covenant for years (not months) to come. However, the suggested covenant, even in its present imperfect form, deserves careful examination. It succeeds splendidly in making clear both the nature of communion and the meaning of mutual subjection.

The suggested covenant, the purpose of which is "to foster greater unity and to consolidate our understandings of communion,"[41] is divided into five sections: (1) common identity; (2) relationships of communion; (3) commitments of communion; (4) exercise of autonomy in communion; (5) management of communion issues. Part I *(Common Identity)* locates Anglican identity within the broad stream of catholic Christianity. Thus, Anglicans are said to belong to a communion that is part of the One, Holy, Catholic, and Apostolic Church; and as such participate "in the apostolic mission of the whole people of God." Immersed as they are within this tradition, member churches undertake "to preach God's Word authentically." The standard of authentic preaching is Holy Scripture that contains "all things necessary for salvation" and provides "the rule and ultimate standard of faith." The essentials of such faith are summed up in the Creeds. The order of the Communion, as it seeks to be faithful in its service, is maintained by a three-fold ministry of bishops, priests, and deacons that (along with the order of the laity) is given by God as an instrument of grace.

Communion among Anglicans, so the covenant contends, is rooted in a common faith, grounded in Holy Scripture, and ordered by a catholic

41. TWR Appendix 2, Preamble.

form of holy orders. The covenant specifies, however, that common faith does not "require acceptance by every church of all theological opinion, sacramental devotion, or liturgical practice" that may be found in other provinces of the communion. It does require, however, that the members of the communion, particularly when there are divisions, seek to interpret the Scripture conscientiously in the light of tradition and reason and "to be in dialogue with those who dissent from that interpretation with a view to "heal divisions."

The content the covenant assigns to "common identity" is sufficiently thick to distinguish the communion its architects have in mind from any form of federalism or alliance that links churches more by common heritage and interest than by unity of belief, practice, order, and mutual accountability. Communion is even more clearly distinguished from federation and alliance by the next two sections of the proposed covenant; namely, *Relationships of Communion* and *Commitments of Communion* (TWR Appendix Two, Articles 6-17). Communion is founded not in human contrivance but in "a gift of God." Thus, no member church "may declare *unilaterally* [emphasis added] *irreversible* [emphasis added] broken communion with any fellow church." God's gift of communion means further that the provinces of the Communion are "interdependent." Their interdependence subsists, among other things, in a relationship with the See of Canterbury, relationships of mutuality and "personal" communion between the members of other provinces, a shared purpose of common witness, and a dedication to "fostering and protecting a common mind in essential matters; and . . . achieving greater unity," and "mutual acknowledgement of a common identity."

A range of more specific commitments is suggested in support of communion relationships. Each church within the communion is to "act in a manner compatible both with its belonging to the One, Holy, Catholic and Apostolic Church and with its membership in the Anglican Communion." Accordingly, no church is to act in essential matters without consideration of the common good. In particular, bishops are to ensure that Holy Scripture is rightly interpreted. Indeed, ministers along with their bishops are to "be a visible sign of unity" and are to "maintain communion within each church and between it, the See of Canterbury and all other Communion churches." Both ministers and bishops are never to act "without due regard to or jeopardize the unity of the Communion." Thus, in "essential matters of common concern" each church is to "place the interests and needs of the community of member churches before its own"; and in respect to such matters every effort is to be made to resolve disputes through respect for the counsels of the instruments of unity and by "reconciliation, mediation or other amicable and equitable means."

The above summary of the contents of the proposed covenant in no way exhausts its provisions. It is sufficiently complete, however, to indicate the central significance of communion for Anglican ecclesiology, and the fundamental importance of mutual subjection for the maintenance of communion. Nevertheless, the proposed covenant does not seek to defend the centrality of communion at the expense of the traditional Anglican emphasis on the "autonomy" of each province. Thus Part IV stipulates, "Each autonomous church has the right to order and regulate its own affairs through its own system of government and law." To borrow a phrase from an earlier period of mission thinking, each church is to be self-governing, self-supporting, and self-propagating. The "three self formula" defines the meaning given to autonomy in TWR. However, autonomy is understood as a relational rather than independent term. It is to be both understood and exercised within the constraints of communion; and is not to be exercised apart from a "fiduciary duty to honor and not to breach the trust" accorded to each member church by the communion as a whole. The provinces of the Communion are, therefore, to exercise their autonomy being governed by the principle of mutual subjection and with regard for the common good.

# IX

One way of describing the present conflict within the Anglican Communion is to say that it is a conflict between two views of the relation between communion and autonomy. In one view, autonomy in many ways trumps communion. On this view, communion is adequately defined simply by the practice of mutual hospitality and aid.[42] The boundaries of autonomy are both broad and porous; and the obligations of communion are defined by tolerance of difference, mutual respect, and mutual aid. TWR contains a different account of both communion and autonomy. According to TWR,

42. See, for example, Michael Peers, "Power in the Church: Prelates, Confessions, Anglicans," The Arnold Lecture (Halifax, 2000).

communion is the more fundamental of the two notions. It has as thick description that, while allowing for different theologies, forms of worship, and pious practice, it nonetheless limits the exercise of autonomy by locating each member of the communion within the broad stream of catholic belief and practice, and by requiring, in cases of serious conflict over essential matters, deference to the views of a body of churches far larger and wider than the boundaries of a single diocese or province encompass.

The surface manifestation of the present conflict within Anglicanism is an argument over the way in which the relation between communion and autonomy is to be understood and assessed. However, the conflict presents both Anglicans and their ecumenical partners with a more fundamental issue. The issue is generated by a question all churches must address. How does the church both remain faithful to the apostolic witness and yet address the issues of its own time with clarity and cogency? The response of TWR is neither that of Roman Catholicism, which relies upon a central teaching and governing authority; nor that of Eastern Orthodox Christians who rely upon the decisions of ecumenical councils; nor of classical Protestantism that has, until recently, relied upon confessions of faith and catechisms; nor of evangelical Protestantism that has relied upon the ability of each believer to understand and interpret the biblical message for themselves. The answer that is contained by implication within TWR centers on the creation of a space in time that is sustained by a form of communion that, while allowing for the free expression of diverse opinion, is rooted in relations of love and mutual subjection and preserved by a protracted commitment to maintaining unity in respect to the defining features of Christian belief and practice. The Anglican answer to the question of fidelity and cogency on the part of the church is not addressed by magisterial, fixed conciliar, or confessional authority, but by the shape and form of the common life of the church itself. That shape is given form by a thick notion of communion and by the graceful practice of mutual subjection. It is a strategy of time that depends upon dedication to both communion and mutual subjection and upon a willingness to abide over extended periods within the internal conflicts of the church. Absent a dedication to communion and a willingness to be subject one to another in love the Anglican strategy for addressing time's vicissitudes will surely fail. Many will say that communion and mutual subjection are very undependable foundations to serve as the rock upon which to build the church of Christ and maintain its fidelity over time. These foundations may be too fragile, but if indeed they prove to be so it may also be the case that the edifice built without them turns out to be a house unworthy of the Lord of the Church.

TWR presents Anglicans with the question of fidelity and relevance; and, if Anglicans in fact accept its view of how they are "to walk together" in the midst of time and change, the Anglican question will be the one with which they in the years to come present their ecumenical partners. If Anglicans do not accept its view of how to make use of the grace provided by time, they will in fact have little to offer a divided church.

# CHAPTER NINE

# Conciliarity and the American Evasion of Communion

*Ephraim Radner*

There *is* something that Anglicanism can offer the larger church. That has been a motivating conviction behind this book. But the offering is, in fact, under enormous threat. Perhaps its thwarting can itself be a gift. But surely faithfulness demands some greater hope.

In the chapter that follows, we take up again the question of communion and mutual subjection, issues we examined earlier in the context of the topics of authority and episcopacy especially. Now, however, our reflection will be informed by some of our discussions of the Virginia Report and our last chapter describing the Windsor Report. In particular, we want to address the matter of communion and mutual subjection within the context of those practical pressures towards autonomy and interdependence as that context is given within the structures of common council. It is true that Anglicanism, as the Windsor Report has suggested, understands "communion" in terms of a "thick" character of habits, virtues, practices, and commitments that cannot easily be contained by the fixed parameters of a few accepted ecumenical councils, as in the Eastern Orthodox churches. Yet councils there are within Anglicanism — the so-called "Instruments of Unity" of which the Windsor Report makes so much are, even in the individual, though highly networked, role of the Archbishop of Canterbury, all bound to the practices of "taking counsel." And despite their acknowledged fallibility and hence repeated and corrected subjection to Scripture, these structures of common gathering, discussion, and decision have an essential place within the communion character of Anglicanism that cannot be dismissed. "Conciliarism," as it developed in the Western Church in the late Middle Ages, is precisely a response to this thick reading of communion, and we have argued that it is one that Anglicanism, perhaps more than any other Christian tradition, has sought to embody in its emergent communion.

Here we will consider why it is that a single national church, ECUSA in this case, does not have the right or the means to "do whatever it wants" in its local and provincial councils, most especially in its largest synod, the General Convention. From a theological perspective, there are a number of avenues by which appropriately to address this question. But here we will dwell on the character of ECUSA as a Christian *church,* and therefore on the character of the structures that order this church. Many American Episcopalians have, after all, reacted to the appeals, claims, and demands of other world Anglicans — offered in the form of, for example, Lambeth Conference resolutions, primates' letters and meetings, the Archbishop of Canterbury's appeals, Anglican Consultative Council resolutions, commissions, and of course the Windsor Report itself — as if ECUSA's juridical autonomy reduced these counsels from around the world to interesting "suggestions," to be taken or left behind as "seems best to us" according to the votes of our convention. What follows will be a response to several versions of this argument for American juridical autonomy, with what is perhaps an obvious but nonetheless clearly difficult reality that must fundamentally relativize this sense of autonomy: that is, that ECUSA is a member of the "One, Holy, Catholic, and Apostolic Church." This reality informs our understanding of "communion," as the Windsor Report discusses. But it must also inform, in a very concrete way, our understanding of what it means to "take counsel" and be "in council." In this case, the reality will point us to the sometimes overlooked and often misconstrued tradition of "conciliarism" that sits at the foundation of Anglicanism itself, and that surely represents a central aspect of our calling as a church today. And at the heart of this calling is the spiritual act of embracing "what others want," and letting this become our own. It is precisely the way in which we take counsel with one another in these often quite formal ways that constitutes the substance of mutual subjection.

## Can a Local or National Church "Do Whatever It Wants"?

The Windsor Report has elicited a vigorous debate over the proper character of the Episcopal Church's decision-making process. From one perspective, the debate is healthy, because it has created a widening interest among clergy and laity in a fundamental aspect of ecclesiology that, in the past, has been the province of only a few theologians and church bureaucrats (for better and for worse). From another perspective, however, the debate has proven debilitating — contributing to the paralysis of faithful decision-making itself by which the church might move forward with her proclamation and mission. "Time" is a gift God gives the church for her repentance (2 Peter 3:9); if not used, it becomes a stumbling block to her renewal. It is this danger that the Windsor Report itself warns against as imminent, with a weary and pleading tone.

A church in this situation must try hard to face and answer rightly this fundamental question, and act accordingly: can it do whatever it wants, and if not, why not? Perhaps the question seems impertinent, in the sense that a negative answer is obvious. But this is surely not the case, based on the claims of many at the moment; and even the negative answer is fraught with implications many church leaders seem unable to accept.

Let us ask the question in an extreme form: could a church, like ECUSA, if it chose, affiliate itself with the structures and teachings of Mormonism? It would appear that, should the proper process be followed, ECUSA's General Convention could change its Constitution to reflect such a decision. Would it be "legal," in a civil sense? Perhaps. Although even here it is likely that questions would be brought before the civil courts regarding property and fiduciary expectations.

More importantly, there would clearly be enormous theological and moral discomfit aroused among clergy and members by such a change and by such decisions — in the same way as if the Pope declared Muhammad an inspired prophet whose words should be received as Holy Scripture by the church. So outrageous would this appear that a range of internal mechanisms would be put into motion by which to constrain and reverse such decisions. In a real sense, the political structures within which such decisions might be pursued would cease, in a very straightforward way, to be the primary vocabulary of discernment, and other — and we would suppose "deeper" or "thicker" — criteria would come into play. When the putative seventeenth-century Messiah Sabbati Zvi, after whom it seemed that much of the Jewish world of the time ran, embraced Islam under pain of death, an entire set of pneumatic protocols by which discernment was thought to be achievable in the matter went out the window. Instead, some bedrock understanding of the faith emerged as a non-transgressable constraint, and this even in the face of a few continued Sabbatean followers who, consistent with their previous judgments, assumed the Messiah's Muslim conversion was divinely revelatory and authoritative.

It is reasonable to assume that, even in the context of current Episcopalian doctrinal chaos, this kind of "bedrock" constraint would emerge in the case of an ecclesial-political conversion to Mormonism. And just this likelihood raises important questions as to the character of a given church's autonomy.

For certainly within ECUSA's current constitution, for instance, it is clear that the church cannot "do whatever it wants." The constitution's preamble — adopted as an "integral part" of the constitution in 1967 — refers to a number of identity markers that obviously form some limit or constraint upon the church's actions: "constituent membership" in a worldwide "fellowship" of "Anglican" churches, "communion" with a particular See (Canterbury), and the propagation of the "historic faith and order" "according to the *Book of Common Prayer*" (the *Book of Common Prayer*, as authorized by the church, being referred to as the standard of practice for all dioceses, within the constitution's articles).

The *Book of Common Prayer* itself, in its original Preface, speaks of certain constraints on change in terms of not "depart[ing] from the Church of England in any essential point of doctrine, discipline, or worship." In the course of the *Book of Common Prayer*'s prayers and liturgies as well as its Catechism, other constraints are also mentioned — e.g. the primary standard of the Word of God, the test of scriptural consonance, and so on. The notorious Righter trial of the 1990s used the concept of "core doctrine" as a constraining criterion (suggesting its form in something like the Apostles' Creed), presumably in analogy with this language of "essentials."

These general observations about constraints inherent in the foundational documents of a denomination are commonplace. The arguments arise and have arisen with vengeance over what actually defines these limits. But the fact that there *are* acknowledged limits upon the church's decision-making in and of itself is highly significant in pointing to some undergirding reality about, in this case, ECUSA itself, a reality which ought to inform the shape of the arguments themselves. Why are there limits? Simply because this is a "Christian" church? Does a commitment to the Creeds define exhaustively or even primarily who the church is and the nature of its "communion"? It would seem not, precisely because none of these standards sufficiently determines the distinctions we make about ourselves that in fact order our lives *apart* from various other Christian and creed-accepting churches. But what else is there?

## Why Are There Limits?

Perhaps we can first ask ourselves why we have constraining limits at all upon our decision-making, however we end up defining them. Returning to our example, why would the embrace of Mormonism contradict "who we are" in such a way that it would forbid the embrace from the start? Why are we not "free" simply to "choose to be different"? From a Christian perspective, there is an obvious answer to this: on the most fundamental level: we are "not our own, but have been bought with a price" by God in Christ's life and death (1 Cor. 6:19f.). This sets out, from the beginning as it were, a basic dynamic of accountability to God in Christ by which legitimate choices on our part are made only within the ambit of God's will and purposes.

On an ecclesial level, this divine ambit is given form in the relationships by which we are ordered in common life as a church or churches. The Windsor Report speaks of this form in its decision-making aspect primarily in terms of the relationship between "autonomy" and "communion," two elements that are "thoroughly compatible, interdependent and directed to the same goal, namely the mission of the Church" (par. 84). These concepts touch upon the heart of the matter, although they have yet to be addressed by critics of the Report in any thorough fashion. It is worth reviewing some of these criticisms on the basis of these primary categories, precisely to see the different ways Americans, in particular, have addressed the question of the nature of ECUSA's inherent constraints.

### Pure Autonomy

A common approach among some Episcopalian critics of the Windsor Report has been to deny the fundamental relationship between autonomy and communion altogether for ECUSA, and to lift up instead the autonomous rights of the American church as primary. Louie Crew, a member of ECUSA's Executive Council and an advocate for the inclusion of gay and lesbian persons within the leadership and the conjugal liturgies of the church, has described the Windsor Report's purpose in terms of an "intervention" into the autonomous affairs of the "democratic assembly" that governs ECUSA. Crew uses the term "monstrous" to characterize this "interference" (and, by implication, the Report itself), because it has "taken sides" against a set of tightly held (if contested) local values on gay inclusion that he believes the General Convention has established and represents. These are values that are evidently not shared around the world among the representatives of most Anglicans, but Crew believes that their external challenge, a challenge leveled against the local church constituted by ECUSA, debases the Report to the level of the grotesque.[1]

Crew has worked hard and skillfully to be in a position where these kinds of charges can be made on just this basis: if ECUSA is solely governed by General Convention, as Crew would insist; and if General Convention has spoken in favor of specific orders of gay inclusion (this has been Crew's partial achievement), then we must rebuke those who would "interfere" in ECUSA's sovereign affairs and thereby taint their moral ignorance with the sin of political oppression, thus transforming the transgression into a blasphemy.

This is mostly political rhetoric which, once peeled away, looks like a claim to naked autonomy for ECUSA. But it is a claim, not an argument. And its foundations are obscured when, as many who share his views do, Crew in fact posits some inherent constraints upon ECUSA's mission in terms of Jesus' Great Commandment — loving God and neighbor. The reasons, however, for such a general standard (over and against any number of other potential general Christian standards) and the means of its application, are hard to give. They clearly do not rule out, for example, the Mormon option. Nor do they offer much illumination on the particularities of ECUSA's separatist ecclesial existence. Regardless of whether pure autonomy is really something some Episcopalians believe defines their church, it is likely that most who default to this claim do not really accept it themselves. And if not, some other avenue of thinking must be pursued.

The Windsor Report, in any case, affirms some basic elements of au-

---

1. Crew's remarks can be found, among other places, on his Web page: http://andromeda.rutgers.edu/~lcrew/rel.html.

tonomy as fundamental to the church and to Anglican churches in particular. But it places these elements within limits — limits that are, at least in some form, explicitly assumed in ECUSA's founding documents. If there *are* limits to autonomy, something more must be said than that ECUSA has the right to do what it wants.

### Autonomy of Pneumatic Council

Ellen Wondra, a professor of theology at Seabury-Western Theological Seminary in Evanston, Illinois, has argued, in a way that puts some clothes on naked autonomy, that ECUSA's legitimately unconstrained decision-making process must rightly be understood within the context of a complex process of pneumatic inspiration. That is, there is a process of discernment that rightly *belongs* to a local/national church like ECUSA without external constraint upon its resources, progress, or outcome; it "rightly" belongs to ECUSA, as to any other church, precisely because such unconstrained decision-making is a divine gift and vehicle for the "new working of the Holy Spirit" as it leads the church "into all truth."[2] This is one of the most common arguments against the notion of communion as we have been developing it, and therefore it is worth examining in detail.

Wondra underlines a number of particularly "American" characteristics that set ECUSA apart from other Anglican churches, specifically in the realm of electoral representation, General Convention, and forms of debate and decision-making (e.g. "serious talking" vs. "consensus" as the American mode of "consultation"). Although she does not say so explicitly, there is a hint that ECUSA hereby functions positively in a way that reflects aspects of the United States' political process: Congress acts, often in conflictual and messy ways; then its actions may or may not find a place in the international community's acceptance; but this place-finding represents yet another stage in the larger messy process by which truths — in the church's case, the truths of the Holy Spirit — are discerned and received. The point here is that, for this pneumatic/political process to work, ECUSA — like a nation state — must have its sovereign decision-making apparatus left unchecked, in an *a priori* way, from the outside.

---

2. See Wondra's October 18, 2004, Inaugural Lecture at Seabury-Western, entitled "The Highest Degree of Communion Possible," available on the Internet at http://www.seabury .edu/mt/archives/2004/11/ellen_wondra_in.html.

One immediate problem with this picture — one suggested by Wondra positively, but without definitive approbation — is that the "sovereignty" of a church in its decision-making is not congruent with the notion of inherent constraints upon her choices. If there *are* inherent constraints, where do they "come from"? Obviously, the United States' current place within the judgment of the "community of nations" is precisely what ECUSA (according to her own leaders) does not want itself, as a church, to assume — the "rogue" or "cowboy" nation. And a nation is *not,* in any case, an analogy to a church or to a member of the church; a community is not the same thing as a communion. The question of "apprehending the truth," dealt with earlier, is particularly pertinent to this discussion: communion apprehension is instrinsically "conservative," not innovative.

Yet local sovereignty for Wondra is a means of preserving the possibility of dissent, innovation, and thereby the work and leading of the Holy Spirit. Why this presumption? It is a peculiarly American one, of course ("serious talking" not "consensus"), but has no logical (nor, increasingly, any demonstrated historical) basis: why cannot discernment and the Holy Spirit operate corporately on a first-order basis? When the Apostles concluded their counsel in the (alas) now infamous gathering at Jerusalem, recounted in Acts 15, the statement was that "it has seemed good to the Holy Spirit and to us" that a certain course of action be followed (15:28). Why is it pneumatically "freer" to move, the smaller the unit of decision-making? This is *not* what "subsidiarity" is about. The Anglican principle of history that "councils can err" (Article 21 of the Articles of Religion) does not nullify the necessary usefulness of councils nor the necessary existence of "corporate constraint"; it means simply constant testing (according to the Word of God) through recognized means. "Prophecy," thus and as displayed in the Old Testament, is rightly construed in relationship to a whole; the whole is not construed in relationship to a singular prophetic action. Hence, the Prophets of Israel spoke in relation to a known corporate Covenant with God; the Covenant was not construed in relation to the articulations of an individual prophet.

In light of Anglicanism's Reformation identity, this American presumption for the pneumatic priority of the individual (or individual unit) stumbles not least on the failure to place the Holy Spirit's guidance and Scripture into an ultimately intimate relation within the church in its corporate reality. It is worth noting that Hooker himself argued not only for the domestic usefulness of giving priority to the "definitive" judgments of a corporate council over "private judgment," but asserted that God's providence — the "eye of His understanding" — would make beneficial use even of such a corporate council's "erroneous sentence," and even in the case of the interpretation of Scripture. In the long run this would be for the upbuilding of the church, in such a way that individual conscience could, with confidence, submit to such corporate judgments (*Laws*, Preface 3). Hooker's point, with which Wondra would agree, is that there is a historical "process" through which the Spirit's guidance emerges; but he would interpret this not in terms of the conflictual and messy forms of democratic debate (although they are not excluded as one element) so much as in the embrace of the corporate discernment of Scripture's meaning which itself is moved through time, even in such discernment's errors, by the Spirit of God.

Just here, Wondra's attempt to link women's ordination and gay unions and ordination on an "inseparable" footing (in a way similar to certain self-proclaimed "orthodox" commentators), as well as in terms of a political/ecclesial analogy, fails adequately to address this pneumatic character of the church's corporate interpretation of Scripture. She is right about the Windsor Report's simplification of the history of women's ordination (a history still ongoing); but she is wrong in questioning the actual contrast between this history and the current debate over gay inclusion painted by the Report. For there *is* a contrast between the two, and in it the issue of Scripture's corporate construal is central. Indeed, Lambeth (affirmed by all three other "Instruments of Unity") lifted this issue up and made a quite clear distinction between the two questions just on this basis: on the matter of women's ordination, scriptural teaching was viewed as inconclusive (though hardly irrelevant, a distinction which explains much of the conflict), while on the matter of gay inclusion, Scripture's teaching was viewed as clearly prohibitive. The very communion-rending character of the present crisis proves this contrast with the past, and explains in part the Windsor Report's concern to place Scripture at the forefront of its analysis of the practical implications of "communion."

The fundamental notion of an ongoing and "new work of the Holy Spirit" is itself — whether locally or more widely discerned — open to serious question as an adequate way of describing the ordering of the church's life through time. Part of Wondra's argument for leaving ECUSA and other local churches unconstrained — raised in terms of a question rather than a certainty — is that this may be the only way pneumatic "innovation" can take place, as if this is what in fact the Holy Spirit does in "guiding" the church. But "newness" is not, once again, something we can assume *a priori* characterizes the work of the Holy Spirit. Some of the analogies she raises — permitted divorce and remarriage, for instance — are ones she presumes are obvious goods of the Spirit's leading, when in fact many are reconsidering their justifications, and the corporate process of "reception" that gave rise to their acceptance in the first place. (Communion life is, almost by definition, self-correcting.) At many periods of the church's life, pneumatic inspiration was understood as leading precisely into a discovery of "things past." And if "progress" and "retrogression" together characterize the Holy Spirit's leading, there is perhaps a more helpful and inclusive set of categories for describing pneumatic action and its ecclesial discernment altogether.

In any case, ECUSA's "inherent constraints" are at least partially (and significantly) defined externally: the "essential doctrine, discipline and worship" of the Church of England, "communion" with Canterbury, and so forth. Part of decision making, under such circumstances, demands a discernment and integration of, for instance, the judgments of relevant churches as to the meaning of "accord" and "communion" in such cases. For if an assertion is made by, say, the Church of England that ECUSA is not in accord with an "essential discipline" of her life, what is the meaning of counter-claiming that one is in fact *in* accord? The definition of a church-dividing issue is one that divides churches. To assert otherwise is like starving to death, while insisting that, nonetheless, this wasting away does not constitute "real" hunger. Autonomy of council, whether naked or clothed, and given inherent constraints that are partially defined externally, is an impossibly fulfilled task, since council in this case always requires council *with others.* And the projection of American democratic debate and decision-making onto any church is clearly incoherent just here: it cannot subsume the elements of external council that *always and inherently* must inform local discernment, however peculiar its forms and methods, just because of the reality of the church as communion.

### Defined Boundaries for Autonomous Action

Perhaps it is possible simply to define in advance what might be the appropriate spheres of "autonomous" and "mutual" counsel in decision-making. If one were able to do this, then one would have safely outlined the area of local sovereignty within which churches could simply be "left alone." Robert Hughes, a theology professor at Sewanee, takes this approach with respect to his critique of the Windsor Report.[3] Is it not the case, he argues, that we can know which matters belong to ECUSA's particular council, and which matters ECUSA must not touch, apart from deciding with others? This would appear a commonsensical hope, and even assumption. After all, the Prayer Book Preface itself distinguishes between those things ECUSA can "change" and those she cannot. Don't we know the difference? And therefore, can we not parcel out the "corporate" from the "local" in advance, as it were, and so avoid a constant (and hence bothersome) dynamic of mutual subjection?

Hughes enters into this argument by noting the way that the Scriptures are properly seen as being embedded in something larger than the mind of an individual bishop. He thinks the Windsor Report moves too directly from scriptural authority to the teaching authority of the dispersed episcopacy. In this, he perhaps misses the Report's overriding location of the bishop's work within a "collegial" enterprise; but he is surely right in insisting that there *is* a context for scriptural interpretation and application that goes far beyond what this or that bishop may personally think. In pursuing this point, however, Hughes also wants to parse Scripture's pertinence to the church's decision-making in advance, to distinguish, for instance, those elements of Scripture that are "universally valid" in the faith and discipline of the church — and hence that are subject to at least external judgments as to their adequacy — from those that are subject wholly to the autonomous judgments of the local church.

Here we come to a matter that touches upon the "thick" character of communion from the start: all things, in all their Scriptural context and reference, are embraced by the demands of mutual subjection, even at all times. Hughes' desire to cordon off for the local church a large area free of "outside" interest demands a kind of propositional definition of what is "essential" and what is "non-essential" to the faith. These categories are then divvied up according to spheres of power: what is "inessential" can be determined and changed locally; what is "essential" cannot. Hughes — along with many others — uses the Chicago-Lambeth Quadrilateral as a guide here: the fact that the Quadrilateral describes the Creeds as a "suffi-

---

3. See Hughes' public lecture, "Thoughts on the Windsor Report," given in Nashville on November 13, 2004.

cient statement of faith" makes them the only element that is "essential," and therefore subject, in their referents, to external judgment in cases where a church somehow undermines their authority. Everything else (including teaching on and standards of "morals") belongs wholly to the sphere of autonomous local definition and discernment. (This is the kind of standard used in the Righter trial decision, which distinguished between "core doctrine" and "morals.")

It is important to see what the practical payoff for this kind of boundary-setting is. Apart from Creeds, Hughes has constructed an arena wherein there is no need among churches to reach "consensus" about any matter at all, since all non-creedal disputes are over matters that are, in fact, non-essential. Local autonomy is granted a far-ranging sphere of action, and the Anglican Communion is redefined in a way in which all current conflict is rendered otiose.

This goes counter to a great deal of Anglican tradition, not least Hooker, for whom the demands of understanding Scripture's pertinence and guidance are given — often simply discovered — in the course of the church's "conciliar" life. Far from raising a protective wall against "conservative" inflations of moral standards, Hughes' approach buys into a boundary-constructing project that, for all its differences in conclusion, mimics many forms of "orthodox" propositionalism. It certainly limits Scripture's role in the fullness of the church's life, which is precisely something the Windsor Report, with whatever lack of clarity, attempted to counteract.

Curiously, standards of "essence" are never defined in ECUSA's founding documents — only that there is such a thing. What is the difference between "essential discipline" and "non-essential discipline"? Or "essential worship" and "non-essential worship"? Are "morals" tied in any "essential" way to "discipline"? If nothing is to be established in the church that is "contrary to the Word of God," does this include the distinction between "essential" and "non-essential" discipline and worship? It is possible that Hughes believes that the Quadrilateral itself provides the definitions we need for this; certainly there are many who wish this were so. But such a use of the Quadrilateral is internally incoherent (not to say historically misapplied as to its stated purpose for the sake of ecumenical discussion). If the Creeds were "sufficient" in terms of defining the "boundaries of essence" exhaustively, there would be no Quadrilateral at all: Creeds do not mention Scripture, Eucharist, or Historical Episcopate, all of which the

Quadrilateral makes essential in its "sacred deposit." But if we accept these other elements as defining "essence," where do they come from, and what does their origin say about the character of "doctrinal, disciplinary, and liturgical essence" itself?

The reality of "inherent constraint" points not to a set of articulated boundaries and categorizable propositions — the Trinity, the Incarnation, and a few other things, but no more — but rather to the nature of the church herself. The church is inherently constrained because of *who* she is. Who is she? And what is any local church, like the Episcopal Church, in relationship to this? On this score, we can be reasonably clear: both the Nicene Creed and the Preamble to ECUSA's Constitution answer the question this way: the Episcopal Church lives "within" the "One, Holy, Catholic, and Apostolic Church." She is a "member" of a "fellowship" "within" this Church. She is a *part of something larger than herself.* And surely this is what we would wish to say about any local, national, or denominational church.

While this is straightforward, the implications of such an identity claim have always demanded struggle to embrace. As early as 1814, for instance, the Episcopal House of Bishops felt it necessary to respond to confusions afoot as to the real nature of the Episcopal Church, and General Convention that year adopted a resolution that affirmed the continuity of the Episcopal Church with the Church of England, the difference lying only in a "civil distinction." In every other respect, the two "churches" were in fact the "same body," sharing the same "religious principle, in doctrine, or in worship, or in discipline," despite their different ecclesial "names." In other words, one apprehended implication of being part of the "One, Holy, Catholic, and Apostolic Church," was that there is a common "body" defined by common "doctrines, discipline, and worship" within which the autonomous actions, now defined "civilly" in terms of particular and geographically distinct and distinctly ordered gatherings, in fact function.

The lack of definition of "essence" within the Prayer Book and elsewhere, therefore, is explained by the fact that the essence is given in a membership within something living and larger, deeper and thicker — "inclusive" here without meaning "exhaustive." It is within this that Scripture functions as "ultimate standard and rule," in the Lambeth Quadrilateral's formula — that is, as the grammar, vocabulary, and epistemological referencing of the larger Body's speech and praise of God; it is within this that the Eucharist has a necessary meaning beyond an optional ritual, but as the one "body discerned" (1 Cor. 11:29); it is in this that the historical episcopate emerges, orders, and is ordered in accordance with the fullness of the whole, as an articulating witness to the means of common life in Christ.

Autonomy functions not as a separate sphere from this reality, as some like Hughes might define it, as an over-and-against realm of power, as some space that is taken, in a zero-sum game, from the other: autonomy is a local perspective upon the single and integrated action and life of a member within the whole. Autonomy is thus defined, not as an alternative to, but in actual terms of, "interdependence" and "communion" itself, just as the Windsor Report has said.

## What Is the Meaning of These Limits?

If a local church like ECUSA is a part of a whole, how should it function in its partiality?

The Windsor Report spends a good deal of time on matters of "subsidiarity" — "the principle that matters should be decided as close to the local level as possible" (par. 38). It does this as a practical focus for discussing the matter of autonomy and communion among "parts" of the church. But the purpose of its discussion is not to define a set of boundaries and spheres of power within which this or that decision is properly made (e.g., "flowers on the altar" are local; the clauses of the Creed are "communion-wide"). The Report's discussion of who decides and where decisions are made and what they are about is rather designed to sketch a way that "communion" itself works. And while "communion," as we know, forms the theological basis for the Report's entire discussion, the history of "subsidiarity" and its referents derives more particularly from another source, what is called "conciliar" thought — more recently Roman Catholic, more broadly the pre-Reformation milieu that deeply influenced elements of the English Reformation itself. (This use of the term should be distinguished, although only partially, from the Eastern Orthodox use of the term as a reference in particular to subjection to the acknowledged "Ecumenical Councils.") Conciliar theology in the West derived from the reflections of church people on how decisions are made "in council," with the goal of explicating more largely how *parts* of the one Body of Christ might live in a whole faithfully and harmoniously.

The mixture of concepts deriving from "communion" with those deriving from "conciliarism" is fraught with some potential misunderstandings. Bishop Mark Dyer, the only Episcopalian on the Commission that produced the Windsor Report, for instance, spoke positively of Anglican "conciliarism" as a defining feature of ECUSA's tradition. But he defines this in terms of "conversation" (just as, for instance, Wondra describes the American version of "consultation" as "serious talk"). This kind of definition is quite foreign to the tradition of conciliarism, and it points to some of the confusions bound up with talking about "communion" in a way that is meant to inform seamlessly the character of the church's decision-making. There is a real danger, as we have seen in earlier chapters, inherent in "communion ecclesiology's" vaunted reliance on trinitarian relations, that God's own "inner" character of unobscured and unobstructed mutuality among Father, Son, and Spirit may be misapplied to the human relations of the church. The ironic outcome to this is, that by attributing divine characteristics to the church (God as Father, Son, and Holy Spirit can happily "converse" with each other, so why can't we?), one actually devalues the embodied form they might take on earth. We cannot, in fact, "converse" among ourselves with the oneness that characterizes the trinitarian persons; we need something better ordered and structured to achieve communication, decision, and action.

In any case, "give and take" has nothing to do with the Trinity as far as its life is presented in the gospel: the Father "sends" the Son to die in the world; and the Spirit is sent likewise to lead the Son and his members to the Cross in a witness of glorious self-giving. Athanasius' favorite text was Philippians 2:6-11 — the divine Son taking the "form of the slave" and becoming "obedient" even to "death." If communion is to be based on this reality of God's "inner relations," it has little to do with "conversation" and "consultation" in any first-order sense. "Consent" is the more appropriate word — the one Paul uses himself in Philippians 2:5 ("being of one mind"), and the character of "consent," while its establishment may be difficult, is one of common and mutual subjection that represents God's life, not so much in its coming-to-be (conflict) as in its accepted form. Conciliarity, as an expression of how the church of Christ is to function in its parts, was founded on this notion of "consent," the means by which the church, at her various "levels" of council, is pulled together into a multi-layered figure of consensual and mutual servanthood within the world. In this sense alone is "conciliarity" an equivalent term to the structural dynamism of "communion's" common life in time.

234

"Subsidiarity" in this context is not so much a "right" to determine locally as many things as possible, but rather represents the "principle" that "consent" must work its way down to the deepest, widest, and thickest levels and ranges of the church's life, so that all the "parts" can indeed be drawn through a "common mind" into the life of the whole. A local church like ECUSA cannot do whatever she wants, not simply because of her Constitution, nor because the Holy Spirit tends to reveal new things to the locally sensitive, nor because there is a template which parses the "essential" from the "inessential" and so provides a legally protected realm of sovereignty. She cannot do whatever she wants because she is a part of the One, Holy, Catholic, and Apostolic Church, defined by a "being-in-fellowship" with a range of other members of this Church, that takes the form of a subjected "consensual" life that is cantilevered, as it were, through extended forms of decision-making that adjoin into the "one mind" of the church. In this sense, the relativizing claim that the British, unlike the Americans, see "consultation" as "consensus" is not so much the description of a cultural difference as it is an unwitting statement of the conciliar challenge as it faces a self-asserting American church in particular. It is, of course, a challenge that faces all self-assertion in any church.

Many of the English Reformers were knowledgeable and supportive of the conciliarist understanding of the church, especially as it sought to elevate the fullness of ecclesial council to the same level as, or to a higher level than, the Pope's authority. Theologians like Thomas Starkey, in Henry VIII's court, were in fact full-blooded in their conciliarist commitments. But the conciliarist tradition disappeared as a vital Anglican influence in the wake of the mutual isolations of Protestant bodies and Roman Catholicism. Christianity took on its developing nationalist, local, and denominational forms, within which the conciliarist vision had little logical force. Hooker himself — who raised, with Cranmer earlier, the possibility and even need of a General Council in the text alluded to earlier (quoting Beza's wearied hope that "in some common lawful assembly of churches all these strifes may at once be decided") — seemed resigned to such a gathering's impracticability, and accepted therefore "national" church councils as second-best alternatives. Conciliarism received a new interest (apart from its vestigial Gallican incarnations, obliterated in the French Revolution by the original forces of "secularism") only with the coming of Vatican II (cf. the magnificent early work by Hans Küng), which was forced to confront the expanded realities of Christian life in the world's multiplying Christian environments. And it was this process that stood — and continues to stand — in some parallel relationship to Anglicanism's need to deal with the growth and multiplication of non-Western churches, something for which the concept of "communion" took on an accelerating reach.

The question arises, then, as to whether the Windsor Report's notion of "communion" is better explicated in terms of the church's common "conciliar consent," at least with respect to its practical ecclesial implications, than in terms of outlining more broadly "how God acts" and "who God is" (questions of the Holy Spirit, of the Trinity, of mutual relation). That does not mean that the concept of "conciliarity" has no profound theological dimension. But that dimension is not simply extrapolated from some image of God prior to its historical ordering of the church's life in time.

To be sure, the greatest conciliar theologians — and the conciliarist tradition is not well known any longer, despite recent work by historians — were certain that the way the church sought to live in its decision-making was bound up with the very nature of God. But it was bound up in the sense of having its structures accountable to a way of life congruent with God's own will and purpose. Even a neo-platonist like the idiosyncratic Nicholas of Cusa in the 15th century — perhaps the most creative of the conciliarists — understood that the "concordance" of the Trinity's Three-in-Oneness called the church, not to some iconically re-presentative Trinitarian life so much as it demanded the careful commitment to a vocation of consensual mission that did honor to God's character. This it would do through mutual "council," ranging from the local to the "universal" level, through which the great purposes of God would be discerned on the basis of Scripture read and interpreted in common.[4]

For Cusa, there was no strict set of lines defining autonomy and the responsibilities of a larger community: rather the church as a whole represents an ordering by which common life is fulfilled through the best self-giving of individual members, working together in various geographical arrangements. "Concordant Consent" forms the highest kind of authority, as it is based on the represented levels of local "consent" gathered into "one." This is something, Nicholas says, that heresies can never achieve, for

4. See his *The Catholic Concordance,* Books I and II, in a rich English version by Paul Sigmund, and published by Cambridge University Press in 1991. There are good bibliographical references in this edition to other recent works on the Conciliar Movement.

they are almost by definition an embrace of the local as a definitive discernment. (This astute judgment should stand as a warning to all local churches, including ECUSA and her General Convention.) As the church fulfills her mission in time, her vision necessarily moves from the local — the least authoritative council, if in some instances adequate to the moment — and expands itself to the fullest range of conciliar consent, the General Council. Nicholas's *concordantia,* embodied through the working out of interrelated and upwardly cascading consents, is precisely that gift yearned after more generally in the opening to the common intercessions of the *Book of Common Prayer:* "Receive these our prayers which we offer unto thy divine Majesty, beseeching thee to inspire continually the Universal Church with the spirit of truth, unity, and concord; and grant that all those who do confess thy holy Name may agree in the truth of thy holy Word, and live in unity and godly love."

The Windsor Report's reiterated "ancient canonical principle that what touches all should be decided by all" (par. 51) represents a deep conciliarist commitment to the notion of "oneness in Christ" as it calls forth mutual self-ordering towards the fullness of the whole. (Nicholas himself provides a wealth of examples, dating back to e.g. Canon 62 of the Council of Carthage.) Levels of locality find their own fulfillment as "members" of the Body in their deliberated movements towards an ever-widening circle of consent, within which autonomous action discovers its means of serving the whole. This is not about the "self plus others," but the "self *given over to* others." Conciliarity applies Paul's Christian "freedom" to become "through love, slaves of one another" (Gal. 5:13) to local churches themselves.

Conciliar consent, in this light, is not simply one action among many that a local church might engage if it so chose or felt it to be useful and possible; it is the ultimate goal of any local church's efforts to live faithfully in its role as a "part" of the One, Holy, Catholic, and Apostolic Church. And its attainment represents the measure of our faithfulness. Thus it makes no sense to consider the present debate and conflict within Anglicanism as a matter of parties — local provincial churches — with equal standing figuring out a way to press their views, as in a political struggle; and if neither is willing to "compromise," to find a way to give ground or "admit they're wrong," thereby to "bring down the government," and necessitate a break-up. (This judgment has been made by an increasing number of observers.) Given our identity as a "church," the present debates and their enormous Christian import call instead for recognizing the inherent constraints of our life as Christians as they are embodied in the proper levels of consent, and submitting to them (much as Hooker intimated). A failure to embrace this calling is simply an admission that there is no church at the center of the debate itself. Many historians believe that the disintegration of the Conciliarist "movement" in the fifteenth century, a decline of interest that created the vacuum into which at least a significant impetus for the Reformation divisions of the sixteenth century rushed, derived directly from the inability of its proponents to enact its hopes — a failure, that is, to reach "consensus" and to live its meaning appropriately. In a similar way, the alternatives of ecclesial separation or considered absolutism retain their unfortunate viability for the present, not only in America, but around the world.

The complaint by American autonomists that the Lambeth Conference (from which came the 1998 teaching on gay inclusion's "incompatibility" with Scripture) is not really a "council" because it did not set out, in 1867, to be such a gathering is beside the point: Lambeth's "representative" character (given Anglicanism's catholic episcopal polity) and its recognition as speaking consensually on behalf of a range of more local provincial voices, grant it a conciliar status *de facto*. This has always been the measure of councils, apart from some kind of papal approbation; and their consensual acceptance by member churches, "in accordance with Scripture," has marked their decisions as pneumatically authoritative. That the American General Convention should act as if this is not the case only underlines a local church's alienation from the larger church and the way it has turned pneumatic discernment on its head.

There is, furthermore, a sadly missed opportunity and calling in a local church like ECUSA's continued insistence on "going it alone." The conciliarists had a deep and historically significant commitment to proper "representation," in council through election (cf. Nicholas, Bk. II.13, 19). The purpose of this was not to protect or maintain "rights," but rather to integrate individuals into the fullness of the Body. As someone like Wondra properly appreciates, the eighteenth-century American Episcopal Church taught the English about this fundamental element of conciliarity (at a time when their own Convocation was prorogued); it was a great and reviving gift for the whole Church. But now ECUSA must learn her own gift's meaning as shared with the world. The levels of integration that form the "concord" and "consent" of the Body's life are now multiplied beyond the dreams of eighteenth-century Anglicans. Rather than parsimoniously denying ECUSA's integral ecclesial relationship to other churches in the world — as some American Episcopalians now insist, in their efforts to protect their own perceived rights from the claims of the larger church — we should recognize that the conciliar vocation of representative consent, begun in eighteenth-century America, is the same today, now properly explicated within the life of a global church. If the fate of communion moves in this direction, it is a blessed destiny.

Our very incompleteness and imperfection as a "part" of a dismembered Body, of which the Anglican Communion itself is only (with others in different ways) a pale shadow, underscores the plaintive tenor of this calling, seemingly undesired by many. Many Roman Catholics today actually look to Anglicans as a sign of their own transfigured conciliarism — one with and through the Pope, to be sure, as Anglican–Roman Catholic dialogues have sought to point us towards; but only within the synodal dynamics that Vatican II began more fully to unfold, and which seem to many to be unclearly directed at the moment. The failure to honor this call, echoed thus even by ecumenical friends, would prove a desperate rejection of God's evident will. We would be throwing away a calling to live for the sake of the whole church, in favor of local and (even locally) highly contested discernments whose consequences are, even now, proving a ruination to the hopes of our creedal prayers: "I believe in One, Holy, Catholic, and Apostolic Church." This is surely the only constraint — and privilege — from which our decisions might rightly take their form.

Thomas Cranmer's career was framed by a particular hope it is worth recalling. First, Cranmer took up early on Luther's 1518 call for a "free general council" to bring reform to the larger church. Years later, from the darkness of his last imprisonment he appealed once again, looking backwards at the turmoil that had led him there and forward into the violence awaiting him, for a council "lawfully gathered together in the Holy Ghost, and representing the holy catholic church."[5] The Windsor Report is not an "answer" to Cranmer's appeal so much as it is a recognition of its abiding purposefulness. Even now however, in this portion of the church, and, alas,

---

5. Some details on this can be found in Diarmaid MacCulloch's *Thomas Cranmer: A Life* (New Haven: Yale University Press, 1996) and in the anthology *A History of the Ecumenical Movement, 1547-1948,* ed. R. Rouse and Stephen Neill (Philadelphia: Westminster Press, 1967).

in a growing number of others, the *meaning* of this call, with all that it reveals about who we are and what we can and cannot do, is still a cause for stumbling and evasion. In the two chapters that follow, we ask: is this stumbling such as "to fall" irreparably (cf. Rom. 11:11)?

PART IV

# THE FUTURE OF COMMUNION

# CHAPTER TEN

# ECUSA's God and the Idols
# of Liberal Protestantism

*Philip Turner*

## I

This chapter seeks to describe and assess what might be called the "working theology" of the Episcopal Church U.S.A. I have undertaken this exercise because recent actions on the part of the House of Bishops and the General Convention of this church have, as has now been discussed at length, provoked a crisis within the Anglican Communion that might well issue in its dissolution, its "final" stumbling. The presenting issue of the crisis concerns a matter of sexual ethics of course, but ECUSA's most profound problem is not moral. Rather, it is theological. As I hope to show, ECUSA in fact suffers from a theological poverty that is truly monumental. In the end, it is this theological poverty that has issued in the moral missteps recently taken by its governing bodies. It is also the case that the theological poverty I hope to describe has for a number of years been apparent to many of ECUSA's ecumenical partners and to her critics within the Anglican Communion itself — particularly to those from the Global South. To this degree, ECUSA stands as a kind of "portent" to all who have eyes to see. But the outcome to her fall is not one that affects only herself. As a church, her stumbling is a scandal to the very life of communion that God would give us in Christ.

How then does one both identify and assess the "working theology" of a church? There are theological articles and books of theology. There are liturgies, and confessional statements. Nonetheless, the contents of these documents do not necessarily control the working theology of a church. The theology contained therein may in fact not appear in the texts of Sunday's sermons. Neither do the theological views that are to be found in these documents always comprise the content of what clergy say to parishioners in perplexity and distress.

In this day and age, to find the working theology of a church one cannot go to a canon of theological works. One can, however, review the resolutions passed at official gatherings, and listen to what clergy say Sunday by Sunday from the pulpit. One can listen to the conversations that occur at clergy gatherings; and one can listen for the advice they give to troubled parishioners. The working theology of a church is, in short, best determined by becoming what social anthropologists are wont to call a "participant observer." One can "be" in the midst of a church, observe its language and practices, and present a descriptive and critical account of what one sees and hears.

Such is the nature of this account of the working theology of the Episcopal Church. It grows out of 35 years of traveling about, listening, and observing. It focuses on the clergy because, despite constant assertions to the contrary, ECUSA's clergy in fact control its ethos. The picture that emerges in the course of this account lacks the sort of coherence and consistency one would expect from a systematic theologian, but one should expect no such thing. The working theological universe of most people and most groups contains gaps, even contradictions. These lacunae and confusions are not in all ways a bad thing. They provide grist for the mill of social life that gives it a certain dynamic. So it will not be my purpose to pick out gaps and contradictions, and then carp. My purpose is rather to describe, and then stand back and ask how "Christianly apt" is the day-to-day theology and practice of the Episcopal Church.

## II

Having spent ten years as a missionary of ECUSA in Uganda, I returned to this country and began graduate work in Christian ethics at Princeton University. Three years later I took up my first academic post at the Episcopal Theological Seminary of the Southwest. Full of excitement, I listened to my first student sermon, but was simply taken aback by its vacuity. The student began by asking a wonderful question: "What is the Christian gospel?" His answer through the course of an entire sermon was this: "God is love. God loves us. We, therefore, ought to love one another." I waited in vain for some word about the saving power of Christ's cross or the declaration of God's victory in Christ's resurrection. I waited in vain for a promise of the presence of the Holy Spirit. I waited in vain also for an admonition to wait patiently and faithfully for the Lord's return. I waited in vain for a call to repentance and amendment of life in accord with the pattern of Christ.

The contents of the preaching I had heard Sunday by Sunday from the pulpits of the Church of Uganda (and from other Christians throughout the continent of Africa) was simply not to be found. One could, of course, dismiss this instance of vacuous preaching as simply another example of the painful inadequacy of the preaching of most seminarians; but, over the years, I have heard the same sermon preached from pulpit after pulpit by experienced priests. Only the examples change. The standard Episcopal sermon, at its most fulsome, begins with a statement to the effect that the Incarnation is to be understood (in an almost exhaustive sense) as a manifestation of divine love. From this starting point, several conclusions are drawn. The first is that God is love pure and simple. Thus, one is to see in Christ's death no judgment upon the human condition. Rather, one is to see an affirmation of creation and the persons we are. The great news of the Christian gospel is this. The life and death of Jesus reveal the fact that God accepts and affirms us. From this revelation, we can draw a further conclusion. God wants us to love one another, and such love requires of us both acceptance and affirmation of the other. From this point we can derive yet another. Accepting love requires a form of justice that is inclusive of all people, particularly those who in some way have been marginalized by oppressive social practice. The mission of the church is, therefore, to see that those who have been rejected are included, and that justice as inclusion defines public policy. The result is a practical equivalence between the gospel of the Kingdom of God and this form of social justice. The statements "It's a matter of the gospel" and "It's a justice issue" stand on all fours one with another.

This latter statement is of particular importance if one is to understand the fervor of many who support the recent actions of ECUSA's House of Bishops and its General Convention. For many who view these events from the "outside," the actions in question represent a denial of something fundamental to the Christian way of life. For many "inside" they constitute a primary expression of gospel truth. The simple fact is that neither party to this dispute considers the present conflict a matter indifferent (adiaphorous). Both in fact believe that their stand is a matter of gospel truth. "Tradeoffs" are inappropriate in the eyes of both. A deadlock of this sort suggests that the Anglican Communion is faced with what in fact may be more a theological divide than an ethical one.

## III

The theology of divine acceptance (rather than redemption) that underlies the working theology of ECUSA is at present expressed in more serious ways than the ethical change in respect to sexual relations its adherents support. A more fundamental expression of the theology of acceptance is to be found in the increasingly common practice of inviting non-baptized persons to share in the Holy Eucharist. The invitation is given in the name of "radical hospitality." It's like having a guest at the family meal, so its advocates claim. It's a way to invite people in and evangelize, say its proponents.

Within ECUSA, a sure test of whether an idea is gaining favor and a practice acceptance is the appearance of a question on the General Ordination exam that seems to point in the direction of acceptance of a practice or belief that previously has been considered unacceptable. Questions on divorce and remarriage, the ordination of women, sexual behavior, and abortion all have preceded changes in ECUSA's teaching and practice. Now there is a question about "open communion." I do not mean to suggest that all these changes have proven ill founded, for they have not. I suggest only that "open communion for the non-baptized" is far more than a cloud on the horizon within ECUSA. It is a change in doctrine and practice that is fast becoming well established, and perhaps should be of even greater concern to the Anglican Communion than the recent changes in moral teaching and practice.

Indeed, it is important to note when examining the working theology of ECUSA that changes in belief and practice within ECUSA are not made after prolonged investigation and theological debate. Rather, they are made by "prophetic actions" that give expression to the doctrine of radical inclusion. Within ECUSA, prophetic action has become the favored way of effecting change. Such action has become common in large measure because it carries with it no cost. Since the struggle over the ordination of women, ECUSA's House of Bishops has given up any attempt to act as a unified body or to discipline its membership. Within a given diocese, almost any change in belief and practice can occur without penalty. Three justifications are given for such laissez-faire practice. One I have mentioned; namely, the claim of the prophet's mantle by the innovators. Claim of the prophet's mantle is followed by a claim that the Holy Spirit is doing a new thing — one that need have no perceivable link to the past practice of the church. Following these two claims comes another that portrays the nature of the church according to a congregationalist model. Backed by claims of prophetic and Spirit-filled insight, each diocese can justify its action as a "local option." Local option within ECUSA is a term that refers to the right of a diocese or parish to go its own way (in contradistinction to common practice and belief) if there seem strong enough internal reasons to do so.

To return to the matter of open communion (now claimed by many as a local option) one can see hovering about a congeries of theological and moral innovations all of which stem finally from the doctrine of radical inclusion. One can see also an accompanying reduction in the significance of Christ's death and resurrection; and one can see also the eclipse of participation in Christ's death through growth in holiness of life as a fundamental marker of Christian identity. With the notion of radical inclusion and acceptance comes also the view that one need not come to the Father through the Son. Christ is a way, but not the way. The latter view is exclusionary and thus unacceptable, not being in accord with the open acceptance that has been revealed in the Incarnation. The Holy Eucharist is a sign of radical acceptance on the part of God and God's people, and so should be open to all and sundry should they wish to partake. Further, this invitation need not be accompanied by a call to repentance and amendment of life.

## IV

I make this latter point to underline the fact that the doctrine of radical inclusion that now serves as an epitome of the working theology of ECUSA works itself out in two directions. In respect to God, it produces a quasi-deist theology that posits a benevolent God who favors love and justice as inclusion, but acts neither to save us from our sins nor to raise us to new life after the pattern of Christ. In respect to "the neighbor" it produces an ethic of tolerant affirmation that carries with it no call to conversion and radical holiness.

ECUSA's working theology is also congruent with a form of pastoral care designed to help people affirm themselves, face their difficulties, and adjust successfully to their particular circumstances. The primary (though not the sole) vehicle of pastoral formation offered ECUSA's prospective clergy has for a number of years been Clinical Pastoral Education (CPE). CPE takes the form of an internship generally located in a hospital or some other caregiving institution. The focus of this form of education tends to be the expressed needs of a "client," the attitudes and contributions of a "counselor," and the transference and countertransference that define their relationship. In its early days, CPE supervisors were heavily influenced by the client-centered therapy of Carl Rogers, but the theoretical framework employed by supervisors today varies widely. A dominant assumption in all forms, however, is that the "client" has within the answer to his or her perplexities and conflicts. Access to personal resources and successful adjustment is what the pastor is to seek when offering pastoral care.

I would be the last to say that this particular form of pastoral formation is without merit. Nevertheless, it does not lend itself easily to the sort of meeting with Christ that in traditional Christian terms leads through faith, forgiveness, judgment, repentance, and amendment of life. The sort of confrontation often necessary to spark such a process is decidedly frowned upon. The theological stance associated with the form of pastoral care most frequently practiced by those who have been through CPE is not one of challenge. Rather, it is one in which God is depicted as an accepting presence not unlike that of the therapist or pastor.

It may seem that I am laboring the obvious when I say that many, if not most, of the classical themes associated with pastoral care can find no place within a theology dominated by the notion of radical inclusion. The atoning power of Christ's death, faith, justification, repentance, and holiness of life, to mention but a few, appear at best as an antique vocabulary to be either outgrown or reinterpreted. So also does the notion that the church is a community elected and called out by God from the peoples of the earth for a particular purpose. That purpose is to bear witness to the saving event of Christ's life, death, and resurrection and to call people to believe, repent, and live in an entirely different manner. It is this witness that defines what many call "the great tradition," but a theology of radical inclusion must at best trim such robust belief. To be true to itself it can find room for only one sort of witness, namely, inclusion of the previously excluded. Indeed, the connection of the existence of the church to a saving purpose makes little sense because salvation is not an issue for a theology of radical inclusion. God has already included everybody, and now we ought to do the same.

I have said enough by this point to contend without undue fear of misunderstanding that perhaps the most serious problem with the working theology of ECUSA is that, within ECUSA, Christianity is no longer presented as a religion of salvation. Salvation, which normally refers to the restoration of a right relation between God and his creation, cannot rightly be the theme of Christian witness because God has accepted us all already (save perhaps those guilty of exclusionary practice). No! Salvation cannot be the issue. The theology of radical inclusion as preached and practiced within ECUSA must define the central issue as moral rather than religious, because exclusion is in the end a moral issue even for God.

## V

I feel compelled to apologize for this truncated and admittedly impressionistic sketch of the working theology of ECUSA. I am fully aware that many will say things really can't be that simple (or that bad). There must be a more complex working theology than this. I know also that many will claim, rightly, that a theology of radical inclusion has its location in what I have called the Great Tradition. It certainly does; but, within this tradition, God's loving embrace is never divorced from his sacrificial act of atonement, his judgment upon all unrighteousness, and his call to holiness of life. Defenders of ECUSA's working theology have in fact divorced their articulation of a theology of inclusion from its full historical expression. Indeed, the credibility of ECUSA's working theology depends upon the obliteration of the complex nature of God's love in the name of a new revelation in which the true nature of God's relation to his people and his world has been fearfully distorted.

In fairness, one can raise questions about this presentation of ECUSA's working theology. I have tried to anticipate some of them. Nevertheless, when all is said and done, it seems to me that ECUSA's message, even when it comes from the mouths of its more sophisticated spokespersons, does amount to a long exposition of what can fairly be called "inclusion without qualification." If I am right in this assessment, then the second of my initial questions becomes relevant, namely, how adequate is this everyday fare as sustenance for the lives of Christians? In looking back over the sketch I have provided, I was distressed to realize that the epitome I have presented is little different from the basic message communicated during the course of my own theological education. And I thought it could easily be myself that I have just described. But for one eventuality, that description might have proved accurate. Fortunately, God provided in my case an intervening event. I lived for some ten years among the Baganda, a people who dwell on the north shore of Lake Victoria. They have a proverb which, roughly translated, says, "A person who never travels always praises his own mother's cooking." Travel allowed me to taste something different. It was not until I spent a considerable time outside the confines of my own denomination that I came to realize that its working theology stood miles away from the basic content of "Nicene Christianity," with its thick description of God as Father, Son, and Holy Spirit; its richly developed Christology, and its compelling account of Christ's call to holiness of life.

Not everyone has such an opportunity, but there are many ways to travel. One is interior rather than exterior. It requires nothing more than to listen to someone who is different, and take to heart what that person may be saying, no matter how strange it may seem. The voice now addressing ECUSA in theological tones that seem not just strange but unacceptable comes from the Global South, and particularly from people who in the biblical sense are poor. What they are trying to point out is that the working theology of ECUSA does not accord with the great Christian tradition they received from the very people who now seem to be preaching a different gospel. Rather than dismissing this alien voice (as, say, the voice of fundamentalism or as the voice of people who have never experienced the Enlightenment) it might be more Christianly apt to adopt a more humble attitude and ask if what this strange voice is saying has any merit. In particular, it might be not only prudent but also charitable to ask if its criticism of ECUSA's working theology has the ring of truth.

It is likely that the future of Anglicanism as a communion of churches depends upon ECUSA finding the resources to dare pose such a question. For it will not do in the end, as official spokespersons for ECUSA tend to do, to reply by reference to ECUSA's *Book of Common Prayer* with the comment, "You see we are orthodox just like you are. We affirm the two testaments as the word of God, we recite the classical creeds in our worship, we celebrate the dominical sacraments, and we hold to Episcopal order." The challenge now being put to ECUSA is not about its official documents. It is about its "working theology" in which most of the Anglican Communion does not recognize the great tradition that gave it birth. And from this "theology" issue stumbling blocks upon which the Communion as a whole may founder.

# CHAPTER ELEVEN

# The Humiliation of Anglicanism
# and Christian Life

*Ephraim Radner*

The Christian nadir represented by ECUSA's "working theology" raises a tragic question: What will happen if the gospel is, in fact, no longer recognized at the center of our church? One of the great criticisms of the kind of emergent communion life that characterizes Anglicanism is its inability to deal decisively with such failures. The Windsor Report stops eerily short of addressing this looming incapacity. There is no *magisterium* capable of bringing matters into line; there is no clear manner of disciplinary separation. The struggle of the Anglican Communion over the past few years is a study, some would say, in just this kind of failure and confusion. At the center of Anglicanism and at the heart of various provincial churches within Anglicanism, lies the reality of corruption, whether in morals or in "working theology"; and in its face a sense of powerlessness.

Yet over and against this reality, time and again, the vocation of communion is given and, in a real sense, proven. Herein lies the valued aspect of Anglicanism's "agony," and that aspect of her life that constitutes a witness for the larger church and world. For part of what constitutes the Christian life in communion is, as we have repeatedly noted at various points in these chapters, a willingness to face the corruptibility of the church itself with a special form of exposed and endured witness. Communion involves, that is, "suffering" in the deepest of Christian senses: the suffering for the church herself and for the members of her body, which is Christ's (Col. 1:24); suffering that is joined to the very sufferings of Christ himself in suffering on our behalf. The "communion [*koinonia*] of his suffering" (Phil. 3:10), is exactly how Paul describes this (cf. Rom. 8:17). And that suffering involves, even at its roots, the elements that make up the assault upon the church's communion itself: lies, slander, heresy, abuse, division in its small and embracing features together. This suffering of the church's fractured communion for the sake of and as the expression of communion itself represents one of the deepest paradoxes of the "church as communion" that has so exercised the theological imagination of the past decades. It is, however, no more difficult to grasp than the fact that God would suffer the assault upon his own life — the Cross — and thereby prove before all creation more than anywhere else that *here* he *is* God most manifestly (cf. Phil. 2:1-11).

Historically, then, this paradox of communion is embodied in the seeming material demise of churches themselves, churches constructed through the failures of communion life, and now suffering, as it were, the character of their provisionality in the face of the world's attack upon the weakness of communion's seeming failure. Suffered in love, this demise becomes transfigured into the form of divine communion itself. It is a paradox that transcends, frankly, the ecclesiological "strategies" often associated with communion theology as it has attempted to chart the reconciliation of this or that estrangement, or to resolve this or that challenge in common life. This holds true even for the kinds of simple "recommendations," however laudable, of something like the Windsor Report: in the end, the church's communion will assume a certain shape, given to it by God in Christ, and our life in faithfulness to this gift will be one that is formed around this shape simply and without reserve.

It is critical to understand this historical aspect to communion's "fate." For it necessarily provides an answer — a non-strategic answer — to some of the deepest questions that arise — and ever arise — in the midst of the church's temporal life: "when the foundations are being destroyed, what can the righteous do?" (Psalm 11:3). What are we to do when leaders of the church, upon whose episcopal office and betrayed "authority" communion thrives, teach error and drive the flock astray? What are we to do when the communion of the church — the teaching of the Scriptures and the witness of the Saints, and other inestimable gifts of God — are themselves alienated from our midst by neglect and open contempt? What are we to do when congregations of the "little ones" are thrown into turmoil by such error and by such driving and alienation, and when hopes are starved and faith grows cold? The "working theology" of any number of churches — local and global — elicits such questions around the world.

But instead of moving in the direction of communion "exposure," attempted resolutions to these desperate pleas have historically often stoked the church's continued resignation to the actual *impossibility* of communion life, most usually through the encouragement of a sense of communal self-protectedness, escape, and division. Indeed, the most common way of responding to an individual church's woes is familial, parental, and exceptional: it is *our* church, I am defined by it, I am beholden to its bloodline and its patrimony, I am the mother, she the cub, and thus we circle and defend. And the responses members give, from this posture of such exceptional regard and concern, will vary on the basis of how we define the exceptional itself. The answer to "what are we to do?" in such cases, the cases of the divided church, will depend on our careful, detailed, and exceptional definitions of "what is our church?" What is Anglicanism? What is Lutheranism? What is evangelicalism or Catholicism? Such questions reveal an almost Mormon fascination with genealogy as the vessel of ecclesial redemption, rather than with a communion-orientation that makes or re-creates genealogy in its very experience.

## The Humiliation of the Church

A communion-oriented approach to the temporal assault upon the church in her churches, will move from the question, What are we to do? — the strategic ecclesiological question — to the question, What is God doing? The first question has no meaning outside the second, and may well simply need to be put aside in its shadow. Here we move into the realm of reflection upon God's providential ordering of the church's life, a form of theological and devotional discipline woefully under-practiced within modern Christian life.[1] The agony of communion itself is apprehended only through such reflection as this.

For those who gaze at the church, whose memories and hopes are ones that are still filled with a sense of wonder at the gifts, exceptional or not, that were given us, who, as it were, say to our Lord, "Look, Teacher, what

---

1. See Ephraim Radner, *Hope Among the Fragments: The Broken Church and Its Engagement of Scripture* (Grand Rapids: Brazos Press, 2004), esp. the Introduction and Chapter 3.

wonderful stones and what wonderful buildings!" To these the Lord repeatedly replies, "Do you see these great buildings? There will not be left here one stone upon another, that will not be thrown down" (Mark 13:1-2). Since the church is One, the demise of the particular represents something touching the whole church; and the reality of the church's communion will therefore be given only in apprehending this movement by which "assault" becomes the work of God, to be embraced with the "whole Christ," in his own "demise" as divine mission.

If we look at the church's communion in this way, we will see something different than merely the failure of an institution, surely; but also something other than the disposable results of faithlessness in this or that place, whose redemption is simply tied up with reparative strategies. We will see, rather, the strange work of God, who creates good and evil (Isa. 45:7), and whose call to servanthood includes, nay ushers in, the "plucking up and breaking down" even as it does the "planting and building" (cf. Jer. 1:10). The potter thus speaks aloud and proclaims to his beloved, "O house of Israel, can I not do with you such breaking down and plucking up that all might turn from and amend their ways and their doings? That I might again build up and plant?" (Jer. 18:6-11) — that is, might tear down for the sake of exaltation. For what God does is seen before the world: a lifting up through the humiliation that lies at the heart of his mission in the world, the humbling for the sake of sin's destruction (Col. 2:14), for the sake of rising up before the doubled knee and praising tongue of every creature "in heaven, on earth, and under the earth" (Phil. 2:5-11). "The Lord alone will be exalted in that day, and the pride of men brought low" (Isaiah 2:17).

The communion life of the Christian is one that both apprehends this history and follows the Lord into its enfigured midst, wherein the Christ makes alive the forms of his own subjection to time within the shape of the church's life.[2] Is this not he in whom we are baptized?, the Christian asks. He "in whose humiliation justice was denied," and into whose "death" we are led by Ethiopians and their mutilated questions and desires (cf. Isaiah 53:7-8 and Acts 8:30-38)? He calls: "whoever exalts himself will be humbled; whoever humbles himself will be exalted" (Matt. 23:12), and the church has long enshrined this vocation as the prophecy of her own life

---

2. See the classic book on this theme: Nadejda Gorodetsky, *The Humiliated Christ in Modern Russian Thought* (London: SPCK, 1938).

(cf. James 4:10; 1 Pet. 5:6). So that when she "sees" that "he has humbled her," she might find life in his word (cf. Deut. 8:3).

The "church as communion" represents, theologically, the way in which the church finds, in her common life doggedly pursued amid all its imperfections and mutual failures, the forms of her Lord's life. As God lives *this* life, the Christian finds answers to the questions of communion's weakness by discovering the words of Jesus' given form in her own responses. To return to the earlier question of Jesus, "Do you see these great buildings? There will not be left here one stone upon another, that will not be thrown down," he provides a series of temporal reactions: "And when you see the desolating sacrilege set up where it ought not to be, then . . ." (Mark 13:2, 14), then flee, or then perhaps stay put, or then look around (vv. 15ff.). "When you see these things taking place, then know that he is near, at the very gates" (v. 29). When "they have roared into the midst of the Holy Place . . . hacking with axes, breaking down with hatchets and hammers, setting sanctuary on fire and desecrating the dwelling place of his name," when we cry out that "we do *not* see signs, that there is no longer any prophet left" (Psalm 74:4ff.), when "no stone is left upon another," when we in fact see such things that veil our eyes, *then*. . . . The scriptural form of Christ's own life provides the temporal outcome to this sequence. It is a sequence prophetically described, and thus divinely given from all eternity, and visible within the forms of scriptural promise. Even now the "desolating sacrilege" is set up, even now we are gazing at the "now" of the church's humiliation, the perpetuity of the church's end, *because* . . . : "He has torn that he may heal us; he has stricken, and he will bind us up; and after two days he will revive us, and on the third day he will raise us up, that we may live before him" (Hosea 6:1); *because* "He answered them, 'destroy this temple, and in three days I will raise it up'" (John 2:19); *because* the "temple is his body" (v. 21).

As the very divine gift of the Body of Christ given over to humankind, the "communion answer" to the question of what God is doing in communion's own disintegrating assault is this: the humiliation of the exalted, for the resurrection of the debased. It is an answer whose embodiment has been explicated before, by those like Tertullian whose lives beheld the building up of the church through her tearing down, or by those like de Maistre, who recognized the terror of the world's assault upon the church as the field of her planting. But because this church is given *as communion,* then we cannot seek to escape her humiliation, even as we know that her preservation lies beyond our powers. Humiliation, if of God, demands that Ishmael's murder of Gedaliah give way to Another's schemes (cf. Jer. 41–42). Humiliation, bound to the "church as communion," is the wrecking of each exceptionalist ecclesial strategy in the face of the only exception divine exalting might embody.

This is so wherever we might find ourselves, in whichever "church" the descent begins. The point is first to frame our vision from the act of God, and not upon the basis of some putative character instrinsic to a given church, unless that character itself is understood as that of need and turning and of trust. The only "theology" here that matters is that which articulates such awareness; the only ecclesial attitudes those that mark such conversion; the only people indicated those who see and know. Traditional exceptionalism — Anglicanism, Lutheranism, evangelicalism, Catholicism — can only be seen here as each together marking the figure of God's doing. Humiliation without exception — the pride of all will be brought low — is therefore strategically powerless, by definition. And the "fate of communion" can be embraced only in a kind of "straight-ahead" manner, where there are openness and candor, where plainness and consistency, where neither looking to the right nor the left distracts direction, where being somewhere becomes the place of witness wherever that may be — fleeing or staying, captivity or sword, each becomes the frame of perseverance, however it is given (Mark 13:15ff.; Rev. 13:10). "And the multitudes asked [John], 'What then shall we do?' And he answered them, 'He who has two coats, let him share with him who has none; and he who has food, let him do likewise'" (Luke 3:10f.). Communion leaves the church "without agenda," in the words of Rowan Williams.[3]

## The Miracle of Humiliation: Two Figures

Paul's own practical response to the church's humiliation — "they all turned away from me! . . . therefore be strong in the grace entrusted and share in suffering" (2 Tim 1:15–2:3) — does not follow a coherent structural strategy. Nor then can we expect the church's history within this figure to embody such coherence either. The search for "precedent" for the present

3. Rowan Williams, Presidential Address to the Anglican Consultative Council, June 20, 2005.

humiliation of so many Christian bodies precisely in their fractured communion cannot therefore be one that has as its goal the composition of a blueprint for action; it can only aim at discerning what forms our confession might take within the giving over of our witness to God's shaping judgment and mercy. The fate of communion emerges in just these forms.

In this light, two very different examples of humiliation can be instructively offered as lived forms of communion's agony, both in its depleting and fertile aspects: the "Nonjuring Church" of late-seventeenth-century and early-eighteenth-century England, and the church under the French Revolution. In each case, the "exalting" gifts of God follow diverse patterns, and through them, the pattern of communion itself, exposed to time, is embraced in various ways. Communion's fate is certain, but also variegated.

Furthermore, in each the context for the church's humiliation is one which still holds ties of genesis as well as effect within today's environment of ecclesial disorder and dejection. We would be willfully ignorant if we refused to articulate the hopes that have fed our demise; if, that is, we refused to acknowledge that the liberative strategies that have pulled us down — in terms, for example, of the politics of race and gender and sexuality — come from a well of human yearning that is deep, because deeply demanded, in a history for which the church of Christ bears shameful responsibilities. The desire to escape religious violence and oppression; the search for freedom to orchestrate political and economic growth and alliance outside the constraints of exclusive religious demands; the inescapable practical demand that human welfare not be the slave to the political hypocrisy of ecclesial greed, compromise, and tyranny — these remain yearnings of today, however deformed and calcified, and they exist in continuity with a past the church has already struggled through. So the two examples outlined below belong already to our lives, in ways that are perhaps more intimate than the many other examples one might have lifted up.

Yet in each of the two cases below, although one in a peaceful and insidious cultural violence, the other in an overt series of physical assault and destruction, the paradox of freedom's demands upsetting the religious order by which human lust is restrained and transformed, was made clear. The church's complicity in evil was exposed and deflated by the very forces her own gospel was called to overcome; and in such open ridicule and humiliation, the gospel was given new life. God has done these things for our instruction even today. For perhaps these are not examples, after all; but broken crests upon a massive tide, encircling the world, in whose one current we too are caught.

### Nonjurors[4]

The Nonjuring division of the late seventeenth and early eighteenth centuries in England represents one of the few precedents of ecclesial humiliation *within* Anglicanism itself, and in this light alone deserves our attention. Its outcome is instructive both as promise and warning for the current crisis in ECUSA and Anglicanism in general, churches bound to a communion ecclesiology who have found its demand a burden difficult to bear. This is so, particularly in light of the kind of non-strategic communion life that is both the confessional core of that burden and its most fruitful response to the burden's contextual weight.

The Nonjuring episode was brought on by the conflict between a Christian leadership within the Church of England committed to a straightforward expression of responsible "word-keeping" before God on the one hand and the ecclesial press to adapt to changing political and cultural permissions and goals on the other. When James II issued the 1688 Declaration of Indulgence (which probably sought the restoration of Roman Catholicism within the realm), seven bishops, led by Archbishop of Canterbury William Sancroft, refused to publish it in their dioceses. After withstanding a brief imprisonment and trial, their popular support effectively brought about James's flight from England and the invitation to William of Orange to replace him as monarch. However, the same bishops, along with over 400 clergy, remained clear that their moral adherence to the Reformed religion of the State was also tied to their allegiance to the

---

4. The following resources, among others, cover the period and events well: William Lisle Bowles, *The Life of Thomas Ken, D.D.: Deprived Bishop of Bath and Wells* (London: J. Murray, 1830-1831); Robert D. Cornwall, *Visible and Apostolic: The Constitution of the Church in High Church Anglican and Non-Juror Thought* (Newark, Del.: University of Delaware Press, 1993); William Gibson, *The Church of England, 1688-1832: Unity and Accord* (New York: Routledge, 2000) (a salutary perspective on the relative tranquility of the Church of England during the limited anguish of the nonjuring crisis); Thomas Lathbury, *A History of the Nonjurors* (London: W. Pickering, 1845); J. H. Overton, *The Nonjurors: Their Lives, Principles, and Writings* (London: Smith, 1902); J. W. C. Wand, *The High Church Schism: Four Lectures on the Nonjurors* (London: Faith Press, 1951)

divinely ordained monarch — in this case, as they believed, still James, despite his failures and disobediences.

For this reason, even though they had steadfastly opposed James's romanizing policies, Sancroft and his colleagues also refused to accept William as the rightful monarch of England in James's place. They believed that their Oath of Allegiance to James was morally and religiously still valid, and they therefore withheld the oath now demanded for William (hence the name "Nonjuring" or "non-swearing"). Within two years the seven bishops (joined by two others and still including Sancroft) along with the hundreds of Nonjuring clergy had been deprived of their ecclesial livings within the parochial and diocesan structures of the Church of England. The fact that this wholesale purging of bishops and pastors took place "uncanonically," without the legal permission of the church's own councils, represented a complete capitulation of ecclesial existence, with the open connivance of her leaders, to the demands of state.

The Nonjurors based their actions on the integrity of their oath — their word before God — and the oath itself upon a deeply religious understanding of the Divine Right of the Monarch, a theological position that, although now bemusedly discredited, had in different guises been at the center of Anglican ecclesiology and scriptural interpretation since the sixteenth century (enshrined, for example, in the Elizabethan Homilies). The Nonjuring response in the face of government (and church establishment) leadership demands for conformance to a religious commitment they now judged immoral and heretical, because it voided a previously sacred oath, was simply to refuse to go along, to accept the ecclesiastical consequences, and to continue in their personal and corporate Christian witness as best they could, without however (at least initially) attempting to overturn the establishment itself.

Many of the Nonjuring clergy and bishops, having been "fired," were forced into immediate penury; they survived only barely and through the charity of friends and colleagues (much as the older ones had survived during the Commonwealth). New congregations of Nonjuring laity were formed here and there, but without gathering a dynamic following. In 1694, several new Nonjuring bishops were secretly consecrated, something that perpetuated the movement but that also (along with other actions) propelled it into a formal schism until 1804. By this point, many had either returned to the Church of England's communion, or simply died out. Indeed, already by the 1720s, with the new Hanoverian dynasty well in place, the debates within Convocation silenced by the government's suspension of its business gatherings, and a division within the Nonjuring movement itself over Prayer Book usage sapping its leadership energies, the "confessing" character of the Nonjuring Christians in England was a spent force.

Spent or not, the power of the Nonjuring confession was considerable as a response to the Church of England's unraveling witness in the face of political chaos. First of all, the Nonjurors upheld the authority, not of conscience, but of the demands of God over those who commit themselves in his name to the divine ordering of the church (at least as they perceived it). This has proved to be a still-disturbing testimony to the moral grandeur of faithfulness to one's sworn responsibilities, accountable to God, over personal and political expedience, however prudent the latter may seem. "I am not ashamed" to do what I have sworn to do.

Secondly, the response of the Nonjurors was one wholly consistent with the forms of these responsibilities themselves and of the order they had sworn to embody. Thus, there was an astonishing coherence between principle and action, that gave rise to the stark demands of non-resistance and passive obedience — virtues lived before the divinely ordained monarch — even in the face of the unjust treatment meted out to the dissenters. The integrity that informed the *shape* of "nonjuring" — the acceptance of deprivation, the avoidance (initially) of setting up structures of opposition, the tenor of quiet disengagement from what was immoral and dishonest — was one of its most distinctive features.

Thirdly, Nonjuring bishops and clergy committed themselves to the care of their flock, but in ways that demanded purity of order only as far as possible. That is, they presented themselves as examples of confessing rigor, yet exercised prudence where it came to the pastoral constraints of those placed in their care, trusting that God would order what they did not have in their moral power to invent. It was mainly later in the movement's history that scrupulosity was preached as a popular gospel, and it only fed into the sectarian tributaries of Nonjuring dissipation.

Fourthly, the confessing focus of personal testimony fueled a brightly burning flame of holy witness on the part especially of the movement's leadership, one that shone in sharp and convicting contrast to the theological permissiveness that was part of the Latitudinarian program of the day. Many (although by no means most) of the leaders of "juring" clergy — people like Burnet and later Tillotson, who dared to take Sancroft's place at Canterbury — were individuals of extreme moral probity and effort. Yet their often flaccid religious purposes only encouraged the spread of wide-ranging deistic and atheistical attitudes, and it came as no surprise that the wider the reach of religious "toleration" stretched through the Whig policies, the less frequented were the churches of *all* denominations. Treating the populace to a freedom for all faiths, they discovered that competition killed. The holy living of the Nonjurors, on the other hand, informed by a substantive theology of Christian truth, produced spurs to Christian conversion that were influential for some time (cf. William Law's influence on Wesley, or the repeatedly used Christian apologies of Charles Leslie).

Indeed, fifthly, the Nonjurors renewed in the eyes of the English church, through their lives, the divine integrity of the "confessing vocation" itself, and sowed one of the few fields that provided a consistent harvest of sanctified example for mission and Christian service for over a hundred years following. To be an Anglican "saint" was no longer, in the public eye, an oxymoron.

Sixthly, the Nonjuring witness was suffused with and motivated by an abiding hope, coupled with a deep repentance, that unveiled for many the priority of God's ordering providence within the life of the church, over and against the plotting and manipulation of ecclesial existence that had long infected the English church (and that today has been translated into the religiously vacant management strategies of contemporary leaders). By giving themselves over, in a concrete way, to the unforced outcomes of events, they embodied within themselves their own accepted humiliation, and the primary promises of divine resurrection in a way that was "of another kind" than the "bodies" through which their church was being beaten down.

Finally, the willingness to consider, to reflect, to discern, and to articulate this in writing — all elements made possible only by their submission to the extension of time through hope — offered to the church the most useful legacy of their witness. Ken, Dodwell, Brett, Leslie, Law, and others, although rarely read today, informed the consciences, theological skills, and moral ballast of many of the great churchmen England was still able to produce, from Berkeley to Wesley to the Oxford renewal.

On the other side of the balance, it is worth noting the difficulties caused by the very virtues of the Nonjurors' steady disinclination towards active resistance. Their careful disengagement from efforts to manipulate a change in the establishment's policies of orthodox discipline created a vacuum of direction and authority within their own internal relations. This lack of interest in positive self-ordering in turn transformed itself, if only in terms of group dynamics, into growing pressures for organizing new structures, whose only fuel now derived from an identity of resented opposition. The acquiescence to the consecration of new bishops, done in careful concert with the exiled court of James, demonstrates how an open hope, because unaccompanied by efforts at organized formation and oversight, could be remade into a political strategy, which itself demanded the structures of a separate church.

Thus, a formal "schism" came into being, almost despite itself and certainly in contradiction to the original principles of the Nonjuring leaders: communion, in its embodied forms, is not invulnerable to the perversities set deep within the heart even of faithful Christians. The later writers of the movement, following theologians like Hickes, often tended towards a stridency of condemnation that eventually, as the political hopes of the Jacobites dissolved, took on the rhetorical and polemical characteristics of sectarianism. It is not surprising that many Nonjurors, in this climate, quietly slipped back into the fold of the Church of England.

It was a church, however, that had already been denuded of some of its finest leaders, that is, precisely of those Nonjurors who had previously left it. And as a result, it was a church now theologically diluted and spiritually decimated in the face of the creeping and in places rampant secularism of the age. As J. W. C. Wand has written, the original Nonjurors were "the very cream of the ministry at that time." Yet, "it is possible that their humility disguised from them the fact that in satisfying their own conscience they might still be doing harm to the church . . . isolating the men of strongest church principles and allowing them to withdraw from the church of the country [thereby] laying the whole field open for William's scheme of latitudinarian comprehension."[5]

Despite the fact that Nonjuring writers like Charles Leslie were effective apologists for orthodoxy, they carried on their battle from outside the established church, and therefore never had the social credibility with which, not to mention the rhetorical arena within which, to influence those whose hold on cultural sensibilities might most critically have been touched by their arguments. Further, the scandal of actively fomenting schism itself simply undercut the claims to ecclesial integrity Nonjurors had originally defended. "It was difficult to maintain the traditional doctrine of the minis-

5. Wand, *The High Church Schism*, p. 12.

try in the face of attacks from Deists and Latitudinarians while those who stood most strongly for that doctrine were consecrating bishops without a see and without a single assistant at the imposition of hands."[6]

In sum, the *humiliation* of the church proved for the Nonjurors to be a tide they were unable — as much as anyone in their day or ever — to resist, and whose debasing effects they could not escape anymore than could the time-servers of the establishment. The very strategies of such attempted resistance, when once articulated and carefully pursued — even in the form of suffering and orchestrated loss of power — themselves proved impotent and degrading of faith, leading to schism and to bitterness. This illustrates a tremendously important truth regarding God's self-humbling work and its transposition into saving judgment, even through (and perhaps especially through) the effort to maintain the form of communion: humiliation is not a selective force; it envelops the faithful and the unfaithful together, even as its healing takes on different forms for each. The fate of communion is to engage this enveloping force: negatively, it is to press aside the resistances to communion's disciplinary demands; positively, it is to find life within subjection to such a vast demand that clears away even one's claim to exceptional assertion.

Thus, only out of this subsuming act of divine degradation, which left the Nonjurors in some sense as tainted as their foes, did the clarity of their "straight-ahead" responses bear sanctified fruit. Saintly Thomas Ken, "accepting a retirement into insignificance" as one writer put it, strangely remains one of the most quoted poets in the church's acts of adoration: "Praise God from whom all blessings flow; Praise him, all creatures here below; Praise him above, ye heavenly host; Praise Father, Son, and Holy Ghost," a doxology that came from his heart and pen, and a paradox of history that only God could have construed for his glory.

### The Refractory Church of the French Revolution[7]

A hundred years after the Nonjuring witness first emerged, another, more pointed and drastically more tragic confrontation between the

---

6. Wand, *The High Church Schism*, p. 82.

7. For material on this topic, see: Nigel Aston, *Religion and Revolution in France, 1780-1804* (Washington, D.C.: Catholic University of America Press, 2000); Paul Christophe, *1789, Les Prêtres dans la Révolution* (Paris: Les Éditions Ouvrières, 1986); Emmet Kennedy, *A Cul-*

parties of faith and her enemies bound in mutual humiliation took place in France. We all know enough about the French Revolution to realize its ultimate hostility towards Christianity. But the actual life of the Christian church within the course of this assault is less familiar, despite the fact that its forms set the course and defined the players for much of Continental Europe's ecclesial existence since. And while the Revolutionary ideology is preeminently visible as an anti-Christian attitude, in fact its textured genesis and ongoing character are deeply informed by a host of modern hopes whose powers still exert themselves, even through the Christian institutions it sought first to co-opt and then to destroy. They are hopes not without ties to the Latitudinarian dreams of the earlier revolution of late- seventeenth-century England. Indeed, the connection between the two clearly indicates how difficult it is simply to extricate the Christian gospel from the legitimate yearnings for religious freedom, however difficult it may be to turn such longings aside from gnawing away the core of the gospel itself. Over and over again, divine humiliation resolves the religious contradictions of human political failure.

The central facts regarding the church during the French Revolution are simple in their legal referents, but very messy in their lived details. On July 12, 1790, the Constituent Assembly of the Revolution voted in the so-called Civil Constitution of the Clergy. This act, among other elements, sought to reorganize the French Catholic Church along new diocesan lines which conformed to the new "departments" of the reorganized state, simplified the structure of the hierarchy, made clergy paid civil servants of the state, and made episcopal appointment subject to civic election. Although the Pope was still offered recognition as doctrinal "head" of the church, all practical, disciplinary, and pastoral authority was transferred to the French government. Four months later, a formal oath of allegiance to the new Constitution was imposed on all clergy. During this first year, the new Constitutional church jockeyed for position, both in parishes and in dioceses, with priests and bishops who refused to accept the Constitution or

---

*tural History of the French Revolution* (New Haven: Yale University Press, 1989); C. S. Phillips, *The Church in France, 1789-1848: A Study in Revival* (New York: Russell & Russell, 1966 [orig. 1929]); Ivan Strenski, *Contesting Sacrifice: Religion, Nationalism, and Social Thought in France* (Chicago: University of Chicago Press, 2002); Timothy Tackett, *Religion, Revolution, and Regional Culture in Eighteenth-Century France: The Ecclesiastical Oath of 1791* (Princeton: Princeton University Press, 1986).

take the Oath. The dissenters were known as "Refractories," and the church still loyal to the Roman allegiance known as the "Refractory Church."

In 1791, when Pope Pius VI finally condemned both the constitution and the oath in an official brief, the struggle between Constitutionals and Refractories became heated and rose to a level of extreme and often brutal violence, with the Constitutionals backed by State arms, and the Refractories upheld, if at all, by local popular resistance. By 1793, however, the Revolution had moved into its Jacobin phase: Christianity itself was increasingly seen as an enemy of freedom, and new forms of deistic religion were being promoted by the State, to the detriment of both Constitutional and Refractory Churches together. At this time many of the Constitutional clergy themselves left the church and joined in promoting the new "faith." In the Terror that followed, priests and bishops from both groups perished.

With the fall of Robespierre and his party in mid-1794, a period of relatively secure religious toleration was imposed. The Constitutional church withered without government support, so that when, in 1801 Napoleon and Pius VII established a new Concordat between the French state and the Roman Church, making the latter the official religion of France once again, the shell of the Revolutionary church was easily discarded. Although the Concordat was subsequently modified in a way that placed new state controls over the church's life, Roman Catholicism remained the only recognized "catholic" religion in France.

These simple dates and facts, however, mask the intricate complexity of lived experience within the church(es) of this period. In effect, two "catholic" churches existed side by side for ten years in France, each considering the other "schismatic" and, more than that, seeing the other as dangerous to the physical and spiritual safety not only of its members but of the citizenry at large. In addition, there was a wide area of blurred commitment between the two groups, not only among clergy but among laity. This was true especially in the early years of the Revolution. Both these realities are useful in discerning several important dynamics at work in the process of ecclesial humiliation such as was imposed upon Christian France at this time.

First of all, the Constituent Assembly's legislative imposition of a new form for the church — a kind of singular ecclesial reconstruction — obscures the fact that there had already been a long and gradual movement, among many clergy and even some bishops, in search of just some of the elements the new Civil Constitution embodied: lay engagement, accountability, commitment to the principles of justice as a part of the church's economic and political existence, openness to new learning, and so on. Although the Constitution was greeted with hostility by most of the bishops from the start, this was hardly true for the parish clergy, nor for the people. For years the French church had been a place where "Gallican" ideals (based on the principles of "national" sovereignty within the church, analogous to certain "Anglican" principles) were rampant within highly orthodox and prominent Catholic circles (e.g., Bishop Bossuet) as well as more suspect groups (the Jansenists). A certain kind of reforming "primitivist" outlook prevailed in these quarters, carried through to the end of the eighteenth century and governed by the yearning to "restore the church" to her early simplicity and organization. By the time of the Revolution, these attitudes were part and parcel of broad swaths of the French church, and the Civil Constitution, in many ways, seemed simply to bring them to a kind of political fruition, to the delight of many.

The faultlines that began to appear with the Constitution's promulgation and then with the imposition of the oath, then, had less to do initially with "ideas" or "theology," than with a dawning sense that the church herself had been literally taken over by secular forces, both politically and ideologically: the Assembly, after all, had made the decision, and had oddly enough thrown the church's governance over to citizens at large, many of whom were obviously neither Catholic nor even Christian. The appearance of "two churches" was therefore a gradual reality. Clergy and people were uncertain of the meaning and implications of the Constitution for some time, and wavered between their moral and political commitments, on the one hand, and the sense that the church they had known was actually under structural assault. There were regional differences, of course: in some areas up to half or more of the local clergy were willing to take the oath. In those regions where the majority of the clergy refused it, some were forced out of their cures by authorities and replaced with "constitutional clergy"; others were simply left in place, supported by their people, and deemed relatively unproblematic in the face of larger challenges to the government. Parallels with contemporary splits within single Anglican Churches are apparent here.

Among the "jurors" — the new Constitutional clergy — there were many who were upholding their long-held views. But there were also many who saw this as the opening to new career advancements, middle-aged men whose sense of being trapped in rural parishes was suddenly overturned by the prospect of election — with local government support — to positions they had never dreamed accessible. Finally, there were those who simply understood that taking the oath was their only means of maintaining their positions — *"il faut vivre"* (one must live), as one aristocratic clergyman confessed to his astonished friends on taking the oath. For some time, even into the Terror, the "real" motives for many Constitutional clergy were uncertain, a matter that caused confusion in their confrontation with refractory clergy, and finally made them suspect to the radical secularizers when they let loose their fury on clergy of all brands.

Things changed dramatically, in any case, when the Pope declared the Constitution heretical in 1791. The waverers, as well as many of the self-servers, quickly declared their allegiance to Rome; many constitutional clergy retracted their oaths, and the battle of the "two churches" was officially launched. The question of the "true nature" of the church was now at the center of debate (where such debate was possible). While the issue was "discipline" less than "doctrine" or "liturgy," to be sure, discipline was seen by the Refractories as but an element — visible and critical — of a larger cultural relaxation of commitment to the "church Universal" and the communion of saints. If Gallicanism had a reason, it was now seen to be one that must be constrained by the larger church's demands of common order and mutual commitment, and as being possibly dangerous from the start in its potential for abuse.

As time wore on, and the spectacle of Constitutional clergy marrying and divorcing and marrying again, or of abandoning parish work in favor of political agitation, gained a shocking profile, it became obvious to many that the cult of the "primitive" vaunted by the jurors was turning out to be a means of shedding Christianity bit by bit and altogether itself in favor of a number of abstract ideals closer to political ideology than to historical theology. From the point of view of the Refractories, this was a clear case where "forms of life" had been shown to be absolutely necessary to the maintenance of faith itself. This became obvious after 1793 when the government's assault on Christianity itself turned against the Constitutional church, even while some of its fiercest and bloodiest proponents were lapsed Constitutional clergy.

Yet although the lines of confrontation and difference became clearer and clearer, it was also immediately apparent that the larger church — Rome and the faithful Roman Catholic leaders who were friends of the

French church — was powerless in the process of resistance. In the three years leading up to the Terror, despite a wide regional diversity, thousands of priests were thrown out of parishes, hounded into penury, imprisoned, or simply forced to flee. By 1793, with the coming of harsher measures, it is estimated that about 40% of the French clergy — 30,000 to 40,000 — had been forced to leave France. Murders, killings, and executions began to spread, with estimates varying wildly as to the numbers of clergy and religious put to death, but probably reaching into the several thousands (not to mention the over 200,000 killed in the various counter-revolutionary uprisings in, e.g., the Vendée, which largely supported the Refractory Church). Some of these executions, done for instance by mass drowning, represented extremes of grotesque cruelty. By 1794 Christian worship itself was outlawed, and the Refractory Church became largely an "underground" reality. Early on, the Refractory clergy understood that "they were on their own." As even now many Christian leaders sense their location.

And in this place of abandoned confession, a wide variety of postures were taken, not coordinated, few driven by a common set of practical ideals: from mass emigration, to opposition and deprivation, to imprisonment and death, to miraculous survival, clergy and their supporters struggled to work openly or in hiding, in any way they were able to tolerate according to health, money, local encouragement, temperament, and principle. Some distributed "Refractory catechisms" (in polemical response to "Constitutional catechisms"), pamphlets, and collections of devotions and sermons in order to sustain the flock. Others preached openly or celebrated the Mass in parishes where they were simply left alone by the authorities (very few by 1794). Others still moved about in stealth by night and day (among these was a priest known as *"March-à-terre"* for his constant hiking from one place to the other), consistently informed by the fact that no long-term strategy existed, and there was little communication with the outside church. Instead, there was only the hope of humiliated waiting and overcoming through divine resurrection. As one village priest named Marchais from the Vendée put it:

> Such is our lot in the present circumstances: we must resolve to be martyrs, either in fact or by inclination. I mean by that either in dying in anguish or living in tribulation. Thus are all things ordered now, and after what it has pleased God to sanction against us, it is impossible that we

can escape one or the other fate, and we must either shed our own blood or live on in destitution.[8]

The horror of the church's survival, and its slim margins of perdurance is something worth pondering. The Constitutional church, despite leaders of acknowledged integrity like Bishop Henri Grégoire, simply disappeared; whereas the Refractory Church of Roman Catholicism remained, but barely. As Aston (whose work is the best summary of recent research) remarks, given the persecution, abandonment of faith by many, outlawing of Catholicism, and the State imposition of an alternative "Religion of Reason," "the public practice of Catholicism ceased, to such an extent that by the spring of 1794, it has been estimated, only about 150 of the 40,000 pre-1798 parishes in the whole country were openly celebrating Mass" (p. 215). By and large, the final resisters were young, educated, missionary-minded priests, urban as well as rural, whose faith and resilience (physically and intellectually) allowed for their perseverance in the face of enormous odds. Yet there were not many of these still standing when the cloud finally lifted.

And when the smoke had cleared from the wreckage, the larger church's reaction was both cautious and flexible. When Napoleon finally concluded his Concordat with Rome in 1801, the Pope (Pius VII) sought to recognize the challenges not only of the Revolution's ending, but of its beginning. He demanded that all pre-Revolutionary bishops — many of whom had survived in exile — resign their sees in order to bring in a fresh leadership untainted by the original outrage of the reformers. Beyond these, the Refractories — those still in France and the many more thousand émigrés — were ready simply to repossess the empty churches (with much of their property still in the hands of the State, however). They had survived, if not flourished, but the survival itself left them as living tools for the church's replanting in France. The old clergy were reinstalled. But the Pope also allowed for the reintroduction of many of the surviving Constitutional clergy as well (although they too were not numerous), looking to the side of their juring infidelities and permitting them to stand with their "confessing" brethren. The church herself was in such dire and humiliated straits, needing and receiving a full re-creation, that the kinds of puritanical party lines were no longer useful in sustaining her, and the beaten were seen, to some extent, as having become one, through having

8. Aston, *Religion and Revolution in France,* p. 242.

come through the furnace "together." It proved an odd and probably wise conjunction of forgiveness and (enforced) political prudence. Napoleon quickly imposed an interpretation on the Concordat that in fact carried with it many of the impediments the Civil Constitution clergy had demanded at the beginning; and the Pope, this time acquiescing, and in fact submitting for awhile even to the emperor's imprisonment, simply waited for the tyrant's death. It was patience soon rewarded.

No religious person gazing at this sight could deny the clarity of God's work in it, precisely because of the scattered remains of human failure lying about it. Chateaubriand, in his *Mémoires,* spoke of the church's halting resurrection in terms of a quaking emergence from the catacombs, at once astonishingly beautiful and ghastly. De Maistre saw the entire episode as the revelatory philosophical basis for a historical theory about sacrifice. According to this theory, time and the politics of nations and peoples are understood as God's crucible for human purgation, a plan embodied in Christ and now shared in the grand sacrifice of his church. The spilling of blood, for de Maistre, is both a crime and the means by which that crime's judgment is enacted, as the bleeding of the innocent ends by covering over the initial sin itself.[9] It was a theory few political scientists could affirm, yet one about which the sober Christian historian remains unsettlingly perplexed, and to which the Christian disciple rests intractably bound.

The experience of the French church in the Revolution, finally, brings into profile a number of consistent elements within ecclesial humiliation that still inform our conflicted Christian life today, as it struggles within and against communion life together. First the nature of conflict is interior to the church and to the inquiries of faith itself — the motives for reform and the ideals of the Revolution were those, initially, of Constitutional and Refractory together in many cases. We should beware of assuming a clarity of difference as an essential element of Christian life (and this wariness should beget both self-examination and charity). But once emergent, this difference becomes inescapable and engorges the whole of life, of mission, and of prayer. The blurred lines of origin and motive bring a common judgment to us all; but they also demand a particular confession once acknowledged, from which we dare not step down.

Secondly, the impotence of the church to enforce a resolution is a mark of divine humiliation from the start. The whole process in France

---

9. This is discussed at length in de Maistre's 1821 *Soirées de S.-Pétersbourg.*

was left within the weak hands of the individual confessors — laity as much as clergy — whose skills were constricted, whose faith was varied, whose hopes were often unfocused. St. Paul's admission that "we have this treasure in earthen vessels" is both a prelude to his catalogue of "death's work" in his "body," and the historical ground upon which the testimony can be made that "transcendent power belongs to God and not to us" (2 Cor. 4:7ff.). No one should imagine that help might come from Egypt, from Zealots in our midst, from leaders of acute political judgment and power ready to bring their gifts to bear on behalf of the oppressed and beleaguered. The vessels are ours alone; and they will break, though without the loss of hope.

Thirdly, the divine character of this reality, as a gift that is, is demonstrated through the impossibility of strategic organization proving useful or doable. Among the confessing Refractories, faithful prudence coexisted with and often struggled against daring sacrifice — emigration and martyrdom, secrecy and extravagant display, quiet prayer and theological polemic, perseverant presence and catechetical formation, all represented together the uncoordinated character that marked the unheralded and unplanned matrix of divine grace.

Fourthly, the fruit of a few, strong, well-formed, and young was given as a final stay against the church's annihilation. This cannot be overlooked or granted as a coincidence. And in the face of the present judgment God brings upon us, we cannot help but cry out for mercy given our acquiescence over years to the graying of the clergy and the evacuating of their divine knowledge. Whether coordinated or not, the humiliated church can and must form the young within its midst, and grant them the wisdom of the church's still unsquandered truths and gifts.

Fifthly, we should note the strange compromises of God's renewals; that is, how when the Terror lifted, and respite was gained, and finally Napoleon grudgingly permitted the Roman Church again to live, the Pope went forward quietly, even openly permitting aspects of the rejected Revolution's secular claims over the church, at least for a moment. These compromises, to be sure, proved to be tactics for the times, for time itself, a kind of willingness to let the Providence that had "torn" now take up the very rods of its discomfiting to do its "healing" and to achieve the final overturning of those instruments of his wrath.

Finally, we should consider the divine irony and turning inside-out of the church that God performed upon a recalcitrant people in France, by acknowledging the strange character of post-Revolutionary French Catholicism: for here emerged a church in which, in theology and devotion, we see the triumph of "grace" in an institution that had raged against its Augustinian (and evangelical!) foundations and promises for two centuries. We see, that is, a church that had officially squeezed out the Dominicans and Jansenists from its hierarchy of influence only now, after its near-destruction, in the nineteenth and early twentieth centuries, being transformed into an ecclesial culture in which "grace" becomes the dominating theme of revival itself. (The sociocultural analysis of the modern French church is rightly illuminated by the icon of someone like George Bernanos and the literature and spirituality of humiliated Jansenism that it represents.) A humbled church to this day, filled with saints, in a desiccated culture, French Catholicism still "bears the marks of Jesus on its body" (Gal. 6:17). True hope is seemingly fulfilled.

## The Historical Failures of Anglican Exceptionalism

Nonjurors and Refractories unveil the truth about divine humiliation as communion is exposed to her assaults, even as such humiliation moves into our midst. This is the sort of thing, in other words, that we should expect to experience if "life in communion" is to be the church's vocation and destiny in this world: purity was no guarantee of and granted no rewards; good motives did not preserve moral outcomes; organization led to schism, while confused confession maintained the marks of humbled flesh, "useful" to resurrection; faithful and simple labor, straight-ahead, done in the face of persecution and rejection, is seed; holiness and patience is a flame; teaching and catechizing is a gift; where no one triumphs, God reigns.

But through all this, the humiliation of the church moves to its end without exceptions. It gathers up humankind, and works through this or that body of the church as it chooses, drawing all together "through the Cross" (cf. Col. 1:20). And when its grip becomes the stuff of time, it manifests itself, not as a selective or a partial work, but as a death and resurrection. The communion of the church manifests itself through this history. The humiliation of Anglicanism, in this church or another; the humiliation of Catholicism, in America or Africa, or all of it together as it suffers in each and every portion of its communion, can hardly be parsed, then, in terms of discrete levels of debasing — brought down as low as this, but no lower; touching this branch but leaving all the others fully leafed; destroying the post-1976 or 1979 church, but sparing all that came before or looks before; pruning theological excesses and encouraging ecclesial virtues here and there, and only thereby making us all better Anglicans or Lutherans or Catholics; heartening the intelligent and menacing the stupid. For the Temple tumbles without "one stone left upon the other"; and it rises as a whole — no bones broken. Anglicanism's humiliation, along with every other church's, is, in its root derivation, the human race's; it cannot represent some divine strategy to protect an exceptional church from exceptionally bad people. In this, the communion that is the church is given profile.

It is important to see, then, that the fate of communion is actually resisted by those who seek to maintain the exceptional nature of their particular churches, even in the sense of "mutuality in diversity." Communion in and as the church is, in a sense, "sweeping" in its destruction of exceptionalism, precisely because the Christian life in communion is willing to expose its exceptional characteristics to their own demise.

"'Brethren, what shall we do?' And Peter said to them, 'Repent, and be baptized in the name of the Lord Jesus'" (Acts 2:37-38), "buried with him in death, so that as Christ was raised from the dead by the glory of the Father, we too might walk in newness of life" (Rom. 6:4). In this way, we are called to recognize the failures of these exceptionalist visions of the self, called to see one's own similarities, complicities, and genealogies with all who have been humbled for their boasting, called, that is, to be readied for life. As one church among many, Anglicanism for instance is at best an imperfect analogy to the details of another's humiliation — of North Africa's and Asia Minor's, of China's and Japan's, of Russia's and France's, each inclusive of a breadth of ecclesial diversity within itself, each governed by its own polity and marked by its own trail of inadequate perception and preparation.

But that is just the point. Anglicanism or any other church, of yesterday or of today, is no "model" of anything. It is simply a "figure," a "living-out" of the given, that is, of the vocation, purely, to be who one is created to become in the following of Jesus *here*. And "from here," from this overwhelmed locale, "testimony" is given by those willing to open their mouth in wonder and confession, to be "bound and carried where they do not wish to go" (John 21:18). It is the testimony that gives "account for the hope that is in us" (1 Peter 3:15), the "reminder" of the "gospel for which we" and all those before us "suffer, bound in fetters" by the world, by its people, and by its times (2 Tim. 2:8-9) Others will do what they must do to be faithful where they are. The paradox of communion's fate is that, in the face of its assault over time, remaining in place — even within the unholy precincts of a painful division — becomes the expression in the end of communion's divine promise, made in the face of all the dividing strategies of Christian exceptionalists.

> The saying is sure: "If we have died with him, we shall also live with him. If we endure, we shall also reign with him; if we deny him, he also will deny us; if we are faithless, he remains faithful — for he cannot deny himself." (2 Tim. 2:11-13)

# The World Is Waiting for Holiness

*Ephraim Radner*

## Sanctified Council

Communion is an ecclesial vocation, a call by God to the church to live *as* the church of Christ. It is also, as bound to Christ himself, a stumbling block in its own right to those who reject it (cf. Lk. 20:17f.), a divine reality that triumphs even among and in the face of the seeming power of its enemies. How then shall we describe today the actual shape of this dangerous and sublime vocation?

There has been an evangelistic explosion in the late twentieth century. It has seen the Christian faith spread, often with unheard-of rapidity and breadth, in Africa and Asia, and is probably the most decisive and striking global religious phenomenon of the present era. This is all the more so in the face of rather opposite predictions — the demise of Christianity worldwide — that were made not that long ago.[1] But the concomitant search for communion is probably the most important ecclesial and theological reality that is now informing this expansion.

There is a kind of historical mystery to this phenomenon, however.

---

1. See the pointed arguments, with historical background, of Lamin Sanneh, *Whose Religion Is Christianity? The Gospel Beyond the West* (Grand Rapids: Wm. B. Eerdmans, 2003). For a theological exposition of the meaning of this historical phenomenon, in creedal terms, see George Sumner, "The Ascension of Christ and the Mission to the Gentiles" *The Rule of Faith: Scripture, Canon, and Creed in a Critical Age,* ed. Ephraim Radner and George Sumner (Harrisburg, Pa.: Morehouse Publishing, 1998), pp. 136-48.

For, as communion is apprehended as a global fate, the very press for its embodiment is being met with internal obstacles that have transformed the image of communion into a crucible of division. This is so not only as non-Western and Western churches face off in arguments regarding standards of morals and doctrinal expression, but as independent churches within the growing areas of the Christian world split off from established orders and create multiplied centers of affiliation.[2] Anglicanism has been typical in this regard, not only now finding itself embroiled in a seemingly intractable struggle for definition as a worldwide and globally related body, but also spawning (even before the most immediate debates) a host of smaller independent churches both in the West and in the areas of the newer provinces.[3] Thus, the mutual subjection in Christ Jesus that informs the center of communion life is taking the form of a divine humiliation that is gripping many churches even in the midst of an otherwise brilliant moment of growth.

If God is at work in the world, even in the agony of Anglicanism's struggle with the vocation of communion, it is a work whose contours touch the world's larger church directly at the center of its own unfolding historical experience of growth visible within assault, understood in the broadest terms possible. Thus, the last fifty years of political struggle, violence, suffering, and economic struggle that have in fact engulfed many ar-

2. The phenomenon and history of "independency" among churches and Christian movements in Africa and Asia is complex; but its influence on the actual policies and attitudes, as well as its lens upon their meaning, of established churches is enormous, and little appreciated in current debates. Well-known recent works like Philip Jenkins' *The Next Christendom: The Coming of Global Christianity* (New York: Oxford University Press, 2002) tend to overlook these aspects. For important links to current research, see the South African Missiological Society's webpage on AICs (African Independent/Initiated/Indigenous Churches) at www.geocities.com/Athens/Parthenon/8409/aic.htm, including a link to its unique database. See also the works of Allan H. Anderson, with references: *African Reformation: African Initiated Christianity in the Twentieth Century* (Trenton, N.J. & Asmara, Eritrea: Africa World Press, 2001); *Asian and Pentecostal: The Charismatic Face of Christianity in Asia* (Oxford: Regnum, 2005). For particular cases in Asia, see Robert C. Salazar, ed., *New Religious Movements in Asia & the Pacific Islands: Implications for Church and Society* (Manila: De La Salle University, 1994).

3. I.e. the so-called "Continuing" Anglican churches (some of which have spread into Africa and Asia), more recently the Anglican Mission in America (AMiA), loosely affiliated cross-jurisdictions (to which the Windsor Report gives some pointed attention), breakaway independent churches in Africa led by former Anglicans (this probably extensive phenomenon is not well documented at present).

eas of Christian growth cannot be seen apart from this movement of God, and from the church's place within it. The global fate of communion can be apprehended only from within the earthen vessel that is the church's own difficult transformation into a subjected body (cf. 1 Cor. 15; Col. 1).

Many of the quite concrete elements of ecclesial life and form discussed in this book — forms of counsel, postures of mutual response, episcopal leadership, provincial interdependence, and the rest — must therefore be seen as aspects of a divine work within the world's churches as God forms the one church in history. The struggle of American Christianity in this regard, and the struggle of Anglican polity and mutual engagement and service in witness to the one Gospel of Christ, from within American and Western postures of relation with their Anglican sister provinces, are exemplary of this movement. They cannot be judged simply as local phenomena. The form of their own outworking belongs to God, and therefore to the future of the church as a whole. One of the most notable dynamics now informing this whole is precisely the growing acknowledgement of the communion imperative within the non-Western churches, however confused may be the efforts at embracing it, and the experience of its contradictions in the failures of these churches. It is a kind of confrontation that exposes the divine work of human transformation in Christ at the deepest level. The search for conciliarity has become a search for sanctity, exposed to view not simply in the relations of ecclesial politics, but in the most difficult situations even of political turmoil and violence.

The conflagration in central East Africa of Rwanda and Burundi (and in different ways now in the Western Congo) — not only in 1994 and after, but also in the preceding decades — is paradigmatic of this search and its motives. And since aspects of this history have received wide public exposure, it is worth examining its outline as a kind of exemplary manifestation of the church's present destiny in the terms of communion's imperative.

Thus, although there was enormous Christian growth in these areas after colonial independence, not only through the predominant Roman Catholic Church, but through a host of smaller Protestant and independent churches (including Anglicanism), the churches themselves, precisely in their almost frantic expansion, proved unequal to the task of maintaining a unified and hence effectual witness in the midst of social disintegration. Formal decisions, by church leaders, actually sought to minimize such witness, while continuing in the fragmenting assertions of ecclesial dispersion.

In Burundi, for instance, following the genocide of 1972, the country was ruled by a military regime whose political principle was based on an explicit refusal to engage the past violence and tragedy of its populace. Public acknowledgement of that violence was effectively outlawed, even while acts of reconciliation between groups and persons were repressed. Not everyone conformed, and there was a simmering political unrest, marked by arrests, exiles, imprisonment, even occasional execution. By the 1980s, this environment of escalating unrest and nervous repression began to encroach even upon the church's life. Bishops and church leaders at the time struggled with this. On several occasions, they met to grapple with a real issue of Christian duty, centering on discussions of Scripture — like Romans 13 — about the relation of Christians to the established state. There was, in other words, a press toward common decision-making, although no formal "council" was ever held. The leaders' — Anglican, Catholic, and Protestant — decision about this was nonetheless made clear through indirect and private counsel: political passivism, silence, and focus on the work of evangelization were to be the churches' vocation, without talk about the past and about repentance or forgiveness.

One must rightly wonder about the "authority" held by these informal decisions, made around the edges of conciliarity. For the outcome to this way of "being church" followed a trajectory of almost predictable disintegration. By the mid- to late 1980s, the political situation deteriorated — churches were closed and pastors were intimidated and sometimes arrested; individual church members went off in different directions of response (resistance, flight, schism, and mostly sullen conformance); there was a near collapse of many churches' institutional structures when mass arrests and deportation of foreign church workers took place, along with closure of church schools. And finally, one saw the complete unraveling of the nation's human fabric in the drawn-out civil war that began in 1994, with its murders, violence, refugees, and hunger.

While the churches survived, and have, in many cases, resumed their growth especially as the civil war has slowly moved towards an unsteady political resolution, the character of Christian ecclesial witness during the past decades remains unexamined. One can nonetheless make some initial observations: the decision of the church leaders around passages such as Romans 13 had integrity; it may have been "true" (after all, why *not* passive martyrdom?). But it had little spiritual substance in people's minds and hearts. It was "truthful" in an abstracted doctrinal way, perhaps; but made

279

without a certain honesty (that is, without discussion and testing among church members). The decisions for politically-tinged quietism were also made in ostensive unity — bishops and other leaders of the churches were all in major agreement; there were little debate and acrimonious division in the churches on this general matter. But this turned out to be a nominal unity, because it was made among leaders who dealt with each other out of many personal, regional, and even ethnic mistrusts and sometimes hostilities. There was unity, of a sort; but no charity. Finally, the bishops and others *did* offer leadership. But in too many cases, it turned out to be leadership without witness (there were, of course, some brilliant exceptions, among even bishops). By and large, the suffering of the *episcopē*, even among Protestant churches, was highly limited in comparison with, as the years rolled on, the tribulations of local people and pastors caught on the ground in places of conflict without escape.

The situation in Rwanda was, of course, far more explosive, though no more tragic. The documentation, furthermore, of the Rwandese genocide is, if only for legal reasons, far more detailed. Thus, slowly the horror of the outcome is being faced and pondered by Christians.[4] Still, the question of common counsel for the sake of the witness to Christ, even in the midst of these two relentlessly expanding Christian ecclesial spheres, has been left ignored, a fact emphasized not least by the continued forces of fragmentation taking place among Christian bodies, even as the total numbers of Christian adherents rises.[5] In a context wherein the decision making of the church's leaders was not upheld by the embodied virtues of the Spirit's sanctifying life, the witness of individual Christians was severely constrained: integrity — of which there was and is much in the Burundese and Rwandese churches — proved *powerless where the councils of the church were unsanctified.* While there were many who struggled mightily to do the right thing, to be faithful, to be true in a time and place of darkness and fear, that struggle was most often suffocated by the churches' deeper and more hollow character.

The desperate need for a different kind of church and witness is one, therefore, that is obvious in the world, and that founds the imperative of

4. See Carol Rittner, John K. Roth, and Wendy Withworth, eds., *Genocide in Rwanda: Complicity of the Churches?* (St. Paul: Paragon House, 2004).

5. Cf. the work of Gerard Van't Spijker on the enormous growth of AICs in Rwanda after the 1994 genocide, referenced on the South African Missiological Society's webpage noted above.

communion facing global Christianity. At the same time, that imperative is heard — as it always has been — in the midst of the vying powers of corruptibility and sanctity seeking common embodiment.

At stake is the witness of hope we offer within a world that denies God, in act and not only in word. And God's hope is therefore also what is at stake in the character of the church's council, of whatever kind. It is not for nothing, but for everything, that Jesus prayed that we might "become *perfectly one,* so that the world may know" that, in Christ, the Father has acted in love for us (John 17:23). For without this visible testimony, hope itself becomes an imaginary virtue. Hubert Jedin, the great scholar of the sixteenth-century Catholic Church, once remarked, on the failed attempt to reconcile Protestants and Roman Catholics at the Conference of Ratisbon: "It is easy to say that at Ratisbon the impossible had been attempted. But was not the unity of the church as Christ willed it, so great a good that even the impossible must needs be tried?"[6]

## The Character of Conciliar Authority and Its Modern Loss

If we take a moment to reflect on the shape of the kind of "council" that upholds communion in its largest reach, we must see how, in fact, the power of communion can therefore rest only upon the sanctified character of common decision-making. It is possible, of course, to speak of "councils" in a simple functionalist fashion: any gathering of the church where, through some kind of legitimate representative action, matters are adjudicated somehow. By a "council," in this sense, we would mean any group of church leaders that gathers to make a decision about the church's common life — from a local congregation's vestry or board to Nicea, from the convention of an Episcopal diocese to the Lambeth Conference. There are many councils in the church, then, and they come in all kinds. But for a council to be, in a Christian sense, "authoritative," something more limiting must be envisioned: that is, a council whose decisions adequately reflect *God's* will to use the church for his good purposes. Thus, a council is "authoritative," when God makes it *effective* for positive divine purposes. This is the sense of Jesus' "authority" *(exousia),* as described in the gospels.

---

6. Hubert Jedin, *Ecumenical Councils of the Catholic Church: An Historical Outline* (New York: Herder and Herder, 1960), p. 152.

But we must note that the presence of the "truth" — to the degree that the truth is apprehended, understood, articulated, and taught — is not sufficient to make a person or a council authoritative in this sense of divine efficacy. There are countless individuals and councils that have known and taught the truth; but which were utterly without authority, and have been lost in the turmoils and eddies of history. In only one person — Jesus himself — are truth and authority necessarily coincident. So, an authoritative council will be truthful; but not all truthful councils will have authority. The working of the Holy Spirit in and through a council is thus the mark of its authority, and this mark is thereby and by definition bound up with the pneumatic holiness of a council's character. Communion, in this light, goes far beyond adhering to structures of mutual counsel; it is founded on the character of that counsel even more.

The notion that authority in council derives from the sanctity of its participants is venerable, although, in the history of the church, this notion became increasingly obscured. The early councils — Nicea, Chalcedon — were fueled and steered by the ascetic movement that nurtured the early leaders of trinitarian and christological articulation — Athanasius, Basil, Leo. Despite the disputes, even the acrimony, surrounding these councils' establishment, their work was quickly identified as authoritative in large measure *because* their teaching was moored in the holiness of its teachers. The Synodical Letter of the Council of Constantinople (382), for instance, establishes, in part, the authority of the participants in term of their *suffering* for their faith, much as St. Paul does in 2 Corinthians 11, when he claims he is a "better" apostle because he has suffered more than others: "Who could tell the tale of fines, of disenfranchisements, of individual confiscations, of intrigues, of outrages, of prisons? . . . perhaps because we were paying the penalty of sins, perhaps because the merciful God was trying us by means of the multitude of our sufferings; thanks be to God for all these things!"[7]

Councils were quickly given the epithet "holy" — sometimes they were even described as a "synod of saints" (so Hilary of Poitiers, speaking about the Council of Antioch in 341) — because of the gifts of the Holy Spirit evidenced in the lives and work of the participants together. As historians have observed, these councils of the early church rarely framed their decisions in

---

7. Synodical Letter of the Council of Constantinople (382). Available online at http://www.fordham.edu/halsall/basis.const1.txt, and elsewhere.

terms of faithfulness to Scripture itself, but rather in terms of faithfulness to the teaching of earlier saints, including the apostles. So Session Two of Chalcedon (451) proclaims: "This is the faith of the fathers, this is the faith of the apostles. . . . Peter has spoken thus through Leo; Leo and Cyril taught the same thing!"[8] Obviously, the issue of truth was fundamental, but holiness, it was thought, *displayed* somehow the truth unveiled.

This perspective on conciliar authority continues in the Eastern Orthodox tradition. It underlies the Orthodox commitment to the process of reception, by which the whole church takes time to assimilate both the decisions of a council, and also the *character* of its participants in the course of their own lives as a whole, the witness of martyrdom, of course, being a compelling seal upon any teaching. One of the most astonishing examples of the power of holiness to determine a decision about doctrine came at the Council of Florence, in 1439, when an attempt to reunite Western and Eastern churches took place, with some initial success (soon after squandered). After a stalemate on the central vexed question of whether the Holy Spirit proceeds from the Father alone or from the Father and the Son (the so-called *filioque* clause), an attempt was made to examine the teachings, not of the theologians alone, but of Greek and Latin *saints* on the matter. "For it was an axiom with the Greeks that the Saints, whether they were Greek or Latin, could not disagree about the faith, for they were all guided by the same Holy Spirit."[9] In the course of their examination, they thereby identified different formulas provided by the saints themselves regarding the Holy Spirit's procession — "from the Father," "from the Father through the Son," "from the Father and the Son." Since they were all uttered by acknowledged saints, they reasoned that these formulas must mean the *same thing* because all were uttered by holy men. Thus agreement was reached.

This notion of sanctity as the foundation of a council's authority was not totally lost in the West. Among Latin "conciliarists" during the time of the great papal schisms, we see the principle expressed repeatedly, e.g., by someone like Jean Gerson. Still during the sixteenth century, we can find someone like Cardinal Reginald Pole opening the second session of the Council of Trent (1546) with a fervent statement of this vision: addressing

8. Session Two of Chalcedon (451). Available online at http://www.fordham.edu/halsall/basis/chalcedon.html, and elsewhere.

9. Joseph Gill, *Personalities of the Council of Florence* (New York: Barnes and Noble, 1965), pp. 120-21.

all the bishops and others present, and echoing earlier councils, he called participants, not to right choices and orthodoxy, but to penitence and to renewal: "We ourselves are largely responsible for the misfortune [in the church] that has occurred — for the rise of heresy, the collapse of Christian morality — because we have failed to cultivate the field entrusted to us. We are like salt that has lost its savor. Unless we do penance God *will not speak to us* . . . only if Christ is our peace will the Spirit of God be poured out upon us, only then will he himself say to us, See here I am!"[10]

Still, Pole's attitude was unusual, and by the sixteenth century in the West, this view was largely disappearing among Western Christians. In its place were three rival views of ecclesial authority, elements of which continue to inform our sense of what an ecclesial council is all about:

First, the "conciliar view," in a technical sense, saw a legitimately assembled council as, in itself, holding authority "directly from Christ, to which every person, of whatever rank, including the pope, must be obedient" (*Haec Sancta,* Council of Constance, 1415). Or, as Seripando said at the opening of Trent, "the door is now open, the mouth is open that only utters unadulterated truth."

Second, there was the "papalist" view, for over two centuries in struggle with conciliarism, that reversed the order and made a council authoritative only when convened by and ordered by the Pope, whose own directives in council with curia were considered the ultimate criterion of truth. The struggle between conciliarist and papalist views continues to the present, informing not only Protestant-Catholic divisions and debates, but also ones internal to the Roman church itself.

Finally, there was the "dispersed" view of authority, that defined the church essentially in terms of its individual members, and therefore located the authority of the church, not in council at all, but ultimately in the integrity of an individual's faith. William of Ockham's claim, made during his own struggle with the papacy during the thirteenth century, is paradigmatic of this attitude: the indefectibility of the church — the promise of God that the church could never fail — could rely on a single individual's faithfulness, all others being faithless. If only *one* person is faithful, the church exists in truth.

This last view becomes the basis of the whole Protestant principle vis-

10. Hubert Jedin, *A History of the Council of Trent* (London: Nelson, 1957-1961), vol. 2, p. 26.

à-vis church councils: basically, councils have *no* authority, according to this principle; only speakers of the truth have authority. It was this conviction that allowed reformers like Luther and Calvin (followed by English reformers, even up to Richard Field) to identify the "true church" continuing in the midst of "apostate" Roman Catholicism of the Middle Ages. The "truth," for the Reformers, is defined in terms of accordance with Scripture, interpreted by the Holy Spirit. The principle, furthermore, is enshrined in Anglican theology and polity, from the start via the 39 Articles of Religion. Article 21 (omitted from the American Prayerbook in 1801, but also explicitly accepted in substance) states: "When [General councils] be gathered together, they may err, and sometime have erred, even in things pertaining unto God. Wherefore, things ordained by them as necessary to salvation, have neither strength nor authority, unless it may be declared that they be taken out of Holy Scripture."

Since one of the arguments of this book has been that Anglicanism *in fact* embodies a certain kind of conciliar impetus and character, one that has emerged in time with the embodied force of a communion imperative, it is worth noting in what ways this foundational *anti*-conciliarism has manifested itself within the Anglican Church. For it is just this internal tension in Anglicanism that has made its historical fate in the current of divine communion life so difficult; and that has ended up by unveiling the divinely humiliating nature of historical communion as itself an ecclesial vocation, so marking out a path for the church's wider history.

## Anglican Anti-Conciliarism and the Yearning for Communion

A fundamental fact about Anglicanism in relation to the question of councils and authority is this: Anglicanism has *no* structures to promote and sustain the virtues of the Spirit that alone grant authority to the church's witness. And there is *nothing* intrinsic to Anglicanism's structures (from bishops, to vestries, to councils, to the Eucharist) that might so promote and sustain communion's pneumatic virtues for a simple reason: in line with Protestantism in general, Anglicanism is committed to a *rejection* of such structures altogether as intrinsically (as opposed to coincidentally) authoritative. And since councils were never intrinsically authoritative within Anglicanism (even the councils of the early church), sanctity could not ever be their certain guarantee.

A simple grasp of the English Reformation's general shape makes this clear.[11] The evangelical sincerity and fervor of the English reformers, including Cranmer, ought no longer to be at issue. They were sincere, fervent, and imbued with a lively faith. But, rejecting the intrinsic authority of church councils, what were the means appropriate to the pursuance of the Reformation for people like Cranmer? The answer (perhaps more common to most church leaders than we care to admit) was: any means at all that would work.[12] The individually apprehended and accepted "truth" of the gospel was alone what mattered to them, not the character (i.e. sanctity) of the context in which it was promoted.

In England's case, the prime instrument of reformation was the secular Privy Council to the monarch, a body of lay and clerical counselors chosen for a host of political and policy reasons. Archbishops like Cranmer sat on this Council, which, under the young Edward VI, was driven (for much of the time) by a committed Protestant, Edward Seymour, the Duke of Somerset. There were other important councils — Parliament, the two Convocations of York and Canterbury, and so forth — but the Privy Council pulled the strings, by manipulating Parliamentary elections and debate, orchestrating voting through, for example, the imprisonment of conservative bishops at important moments, and sending out, under their control, official "visitors" to dioceses, charged with implementing reform and punishing resistant priests and bishops. The use of select "mobs" to destroy statues, disrupt processions and Masses, for instance, proved an effective means of ecclesial change. Thus, while the great doctrinal and liturgical bequests of the English Reformation — *Book of Common Prayer,* Ordinal, and so on — were indeed "great," and deservedly cherished, they were not the product of the church "in council" as we generally understand the word today, nor as we have defined it earlier in this chapter.

Politically, then, we could say that the various reforming instruments of council in the Reformation period in England proved "authoritative,"

11. For details to this kind of overview, see Diarmaid MacCulloch, *Thomas Cranmer: A Life* (New Haven: Yale University Press, 1996); John Guy, *Tudor England* (New York: Oxford University Press, 1990).

12. Cranmer, however, on more than one occasion (as we have had occasion to note in Chapter 9 above) looked to a General Council for the resolution of the divisions of the Church. But this was initially spurred as much by his pragmatic vision as by any deep theological principle.

insofar as the Roman church was eventually displaced and the Church of England was established. But were they ever truly "authoritative" in a spiritual sense? Did they embody the spiritual gifts — of honesty in truth, of charity in unity, of courage in leadership, and so on? Whatever the case, no one in fact ever *claimed* that the Reformation decision-making bodies needed to embody such virtues, this, not only according to the Protestant principle regarding councils, but also according to the standard pragmatic impulses of most church leaders of this time and of most others. But history, in a sense, also demonstrates that even in providential terms they did not: the history of the English church from the Reformation on, even including the vaunted "Elizabethan Settlement," is a movement that began in an ecclesiastical *coup d'état,* and ended in a religious civil war in the 1640s and beyond, the evangelical embarrassment from which Christian life in England never recovered (the rise of deism and atheism and the Methodist schism being directly dependent on this deformation of the church's Christian witness).

*De facto,* it is fair to say that Anglican councils, in this history, have never had any real authority at all; *nor were they designed to have any!* And Anglicans have known, understood, and at least sensed this. Until the twentieth century, it can be argued, no major decision about the faith has ever been made by an Anglican council. Instead, the Church of England has instinctively and also intentionally *adapted* itself to its structures of "unsanctified council" through three principal strategies: the strategy of avoidance of debate, the strategy of individualized struggle, and the strategy of unencumbered fellowship. The first two strategies are clear to most people. Avoiding debate, for instance, found an exemplary instance in the proroguing of Convocation for almost 150 years in the face of the explosive conflict known as the "Bangorian Controversy" of the early 18th century. This is a model that continues to be followed more locally through tabling of divisive motions at diocesan synods, transferring disagreement to endless rounds of commissions and so on. Individualized struggle, in turn, represents the common attempt — often finding its term in legal battles in the civil courts (cf. the so-called "Gorham Case" of 1847) — to expend efforts of resistance and sometimes aggression in matters of discipline, worship, and doctrine in a way that carefully avoids common counsel and decision-making on a contested or troubling issue, thereby avoiding determinative precedent.

The strategy of unencumbered fellowship as a way of dealing with unsanctified council deserves, however, a lengthier examination, since it is just this means that has proven the vessel of Anglicanism's providential transformation in the hands of God's ecclesial re-ordering for the sake of communion. For it is the Lambeth Conference itself — and the concrete "Communion" that has found its life in its wake — that has its origins in this strategy, quite explicitly. Tracing the origins of this peculiar council provides a glimpse at how the church is rightly "girded and carried where it does not wish to go" (cf. John 21:18) — one of the great dominical promises made to Christian hope.

The first Lambeth Conference was held in 1867, at the behest of Archbishop Charles Longley. Longley was acceding to the request, initially, of the Canadian bishops for a national synod of bishops that would include the English colonies. The hope was to clarify the nature of the Anglican Church as the legal connections between England and her colonies were beginning to unravel. At the same time, some of the Canadian bishops were concerned with firming up doctrinal commitments in the church, a concern that resonated with many English bishops. Of particular worry were views afoot that seemed to question the inerrant inspiration of Scripture and the temporally unending punishments of hell — views being propagated in a notorious anthology published in 1860, entitled *Essays and Reviews*. The call for an Anglican "General Council," then, arose out of a desire to make clear decisions about doctrine and discipline.

Low-church and evangelical leaders immediately set out to oppose such a council. They were worried that doctrinal decisions would be made that were both unnecessary and wrong, and certainly hurtful to true Christianity. When the topic was debated at Convocation, Arthur Stanley, the Dean of Westminster, stood up and attacked the whole notion of an Anglican general council, on the key Protestant principle that any council of the church must lack intrinsic authority. "He reminded his audience . . . that Gregory of Nazianzus had said he had never known a synod of bishops from which any good had come . . . that the council of Ephesus was disgraced by bribery; that of Chalcedon by disorder and violence; the council of Constance by treachery and murder" and so on.[13] To imagine a council of measly Anglican bishops making decisions about doctrines that even these earlier councils had eschewed was frightening, Stanley argued.

---

13. Alan M. G. Stephenson, *The First Lambeth Conference, 1867* (London: S.P.C.K., 1967), pp. 171-73.

Look, after all, at what the first American Episcopal Church's convention had done: throw out the Athanasian Creed from the Prayer Book!

Anglo-Catholics, on the other side, began to worry at the proposed council's potential crackdown on their liturgical innovations, and eventually a coalition of opposition formed of sufficient strength as to force Archbishop Longley to redefine the character of Lambeth altogether. It would not be a "council," it would not be a "synod"; it would, instead, be a "conference." Longley's letter of invitation to the first Lambeth Conference says this: "Such a meeting would not be competent to make declarations or lay down definitions on points of doctrine. But united worship and common counsels would greatly tend to maintain practically the unity of the faith; whilst they would bind us in straiter bonds of peace and brotherly charity."[14]

And in fact, when the first Lambeth Conference had been convened, the only outcome was an "encyclical letter" by the bishops that urged the faithful to prayer and vigilance, and whose only doctrinal content was an attack on Roman Catholics (the pope, the Virgin Mary), and an affirmation of Anglicanism's adherence to the faith and order of the "primitive church." It is certainly revealing of a mindset; but it does not constitute the church "speaking in council" in any traditional sense. For Anglicanism, at its core, had no mechanism to grasp such a sense.

Yet, as the Windsor Report has noted with some detail, this is not how the Lambeth Conferences developed.[15] And we have sought to emphasize at length in this volume how this has been so, and the theological character that both emerged and gave rise to this development from deep within the providential movement of evangelization and growth itself. As it has turned out, not only Anglican Churches, but throughout the twentieth century, the history of the larger church can be read as the story of a yearning to so break out of the box of unsanctified council altogether. The desire for the church to come together in the Spirit, joining holy people, and *therefore* witnessing with authority, fueled several generations, across denominations, who had witnessed the horror, sorrow, and hopelessness of two world wars, and so many other tragedies before which the church had proved powerless and hidden. The ecumenical movement leading to the World Council of Churches, and, in Roman Catholicism, to Vatican II is

---

14. Randall Davidson, ed., *The Origin and History of the Lambeth Conferences of 1867 and 1878: With the Official Reports and Resolutions* (London: S.P.C.K, 1888), p. 8.

15. The Windsor Report, paras. 100-02, 105-07, and Appendix One, paras. 3 and 4.

the concrete result of both this yearning: a yearning for a common gospel to speak to a world "hungry and athirst," amid "the misery of its pride and bestiality, of its hatred, its guilt and its perplexity" (Adolf Deissmann, 1927 Lausanne Faith and Order Conference); and a yearning for a unity of Christian witness that could be founded only on "interior conversion" and "holier lives" (Vatican II, *Decree on Ecumenism*, n. 7).

But both the WCC and the vision of Vatican II have foundered, to differing degrees, to the extent that the "routinization" of these movements has been perceived as negating or at least sapping the Holy Spirit's sanctifying power in their midst. Instead of saints, we have had bureaucrats renewing the church. It is, nonetheless, important to acknowledge the direction of this work, because it witnesses to a worldwide desire for the church to *act* like the church of Jesus himself. Thus Lambeth itself underwent a gradual, but striking shift in the nature of its work, leading away from the explicitly non-doctrinal principles of its establishment: in 1920, Lambeth stoked the postwar desire for ecumenical change with a world-wide appeal for Christian Reunion; in 1930 and 1948, it provided reports and resolutions regarding the doctrine of God, human creation, and marriage; in 1958 it offered a public teaching accepting contraception; and this has moved, as we now know, to considerable and pointed teachings on discipline, mission, morals, and ecclesial authority itself. None of these formulations were ever called "binding" — as we know, and with all the difficulties that the legal lack of definition given to life in communion has entailed — but they sprang from a prayer for missing authority in the midst of an aimless and certainly destructive secular world.

## The Witness of Holiness

It is important to be able to identify this prayer. In part it has been submerged in the seemingly louder publicizing of renewed nationalisms and theological assertions from around the world. The well-documented shift of the Christian church to newer nations and peoples, for instance, has now become a commonplace, along with the widely-disseminated discussions of the political shift in decision-making that this represents.[16] The current

16. Walbert Buhlmann already pointedly exposed this shift in the mid-1970s, with his widely read book *The Coming of the Third Church* (Maryknoll, N.Y.: Orbis Books, 1977),

struggles within the Anglican Communion especially now represent, for many, a kind of public drama exhibiting this development in terms of a narrative of adversarial encounter and almost oedipal transition. But what has not been sufficiently appreciated — indeed, apologists for the reloca- tion of ecclesial power have been loath to examine this altogether — are the rather towering challenges to ecclesial integrity the new distributions of power represent, especially in the context of the pressures to internal Chris- tian life that new economic arrangements around the world instigate. For the numerical growth of non-Western churches, astoundingly rapid and extensive as it is, is also bound up with well-documented cultural transfor- mations tied to globalized development. These have brought with them so- cial changes of a stark and often frighteningly punctuated extreme. The jux- taposition of the single-generational shift of ecclesial power to the "South" with the profoundly destructive and weakly opposed reach of the AIDS pandemic in many of the same locales disturbingly exemplifies a kind of topsy-turvy reshuffling of social forms that defies clear parsing.

Elements of Christian life are neither slowly appropriated and assimi- lated in many of these new regions, nor simply freshly transplanted. Rather, they are being shaped within a context of global forms, often eco- nomic forms (of extraordinary wealth juxtaposed to much more extensive and crushing poverty), characterized by technologically-driven evange- lism, artificial types of community driven by imported and focalized re- sources, and externally initiated methods of mass communication and re- sponse. No one is sure of either the meaning or the outcome to these critical social disjunctures that have drawn lines of pragmatic continuity (but unclear meaning) between American consumer religion and tradi- tional cultures. But the deep forms of ecclesial life that have characterized both the yearning and the resistances of the church's history for two mil- lennia are undoubtedly being subjected to enormous forces of dispute in the newer and growing churches outside the West, and in ways that cannot yet be adequately understood.

Some of the economic pressures at work are those that clearly move in the direction of ecclesial division. This parallels the period of the

which built its analysis on the reality that, by Paul VI's pontificate, the majority of Catholics lived in non-Western nations. Philip Jenkins's *The Next Christendom* and Alister McGrath's *The Future of Christianity* (Oxford: Blackwell, 2002) have renewed and updated this socio- logically detailed transformation, pointing now especially to some of the "power" changes implied.

sixteenth-century European Reformation, and although moving with an unmatched pace and breadth, there has been little attempt to study, let alone understand well, the character of these similarities. Sectarianism, in any case, has had a historical record of correlation with secularization.[17] And while there have been many attempts at undermining the thesis that "modernization" — economically, educationally, and politically — tends to weaken the hold of traditional religious belief, there are clear patterns that have emerged of distinctions in levels of social well-being as tied to religious adherence and commitment.[18] The combination of forces pulling the newer churches in opposing directions — of sectarian subversion of belief and social instability feeding the search for committed communal belief, all within the caldron of wildly disruptive economic changes — therefore points to extraordinarily rough sailing ahead for the coherence of ecclesial structures in these areas. This does not mean that these newer churches are bound to stop evangelizing and growing. But it does portend internal conflicts of a serious religious nature, most dangerous where they are least noted. Bishop Nathaniel Garang, of the Sudanese Diocese of Bor, recently spoke to the extraordinarily difficult challenge now emerging — for himself and other Anglicans of his country — to preaching the gospel of Christ in a situation of social "blessing" rather than in the longstanding context of civil conflict that has provided the landscape for the Sudanese church's growth over the past several decades. "Israel's departure from God became irresistible once she entered the Land of Promise."[19]

None of this, however, is simply a repeat of the dynamics of Western European transformation in the early modern epoch. If the prayer for the "missing authority" of sanctified council has not been entirely submerged,

17. Cf. Steve Bruce's *A House Divided: Protestantism, Schism, and Secularization* (New York: Routledge, 1990) and *Religion and Modernization: Sociologists and Historians Debate the Secularization Thesis* (Oxford: Clarendon Press, 1992).

18. The groundbreaking work in reorienting the discussion is Pippa Norris and Ronald Inglehart, *Sacred and Secular: Religion and Politics Worldwide* (Cambridge: Cambridge University Press, 2004), whose studies of a wide-ranging set of cross-cultural/national data clearly establish a correlation between "existential security" and levels and forms of religious commitment. Norris and Inglehart's conclusions are far more complex, predictively, than previous versions of the secularization argument allowed. But their overall thrust underlines the probability of the newer churches' strength of purpose coming under almost simultaneous assault from within and without right at the start. This appears to be a novel phenomenon.

19. Unpublished talk at the Diocese of Colorado, Denver, October, 2002.

it is because the strange and awesome growth of the newer churches has been not only tied to global economic shifts, but has also been firmly bound to situations of embedded suffering, political violence and endemic religious conflict. The "land of Promise" remains still something hoped for by most Christians of the world and therefore only a distant temptation. And in these situations, still very much present and living, the younger churches have seen their growth and the metamorphosis of their social character go hand in hand with an inescapable engagement with martyrdom and persecution.[20] The scale of this experience, as well as the complexity of its location within political life, is one that makes it hard to analyze comparatively. But it exposes a unique character to the uncertainties bound up with the globalization of Christianity: it infuses it, or rather unveils within it, the presence of an almost frightening working out of the Holy Spirit's life, constructing an almost invisible architecture of holiness within the corners of the otherwise contested center of ecclesial life. Pope Benedict XVI entered his papacy with repeated statements of concern over Europe's declining Christian life, and his remarks have been injected with a deep religious anxiety about the world's future as a whole.[21] But it is just in the midst of this kind of anxiety that the Spirit's illumination through the suffering of faith provides its fuel for hope and renewal. Humiliation uncovers the treasures hid by the Spirit beneath the mounds of enculturated Christendom, lifts them up, and burnishes them for a new day.

This is the anxiety, as well as the yearning, within which there has arisen a search for saints who might supply the authority that has been lacking the common gathering of Christian witness. It is a search, in a sense, for the means by which true communion can be found and founded. The agony of Anglicanism lies squarely at the center of this larger

---

20. Cf. Robert Royal, *The Catholic Martyrs of the Twentieth Century: A Comprehensive World History* (New York: Crossroad Publishing, 2000); Paul Marshall, *Their Blood Cries Out: The Worldwide Tragedy of Christians Who Are Dying for Their Faith* (Dallas: Word Publishing, 1997). While the methodology has been disputed by some, most recent references to martyrdom and persecution are based on David Barrett's "Annual Statistical Table on Global Mission," published each January in the *International Bulletin of Missionary Research,* and on the more synthetic material in David Barrett, George T. Kurian, and Todd M. Johnson, eds., *World Christian Encyclopedia* (New York: Oxford University Press, 2001).

21. Cardinal Ratzinger's homily of April 18, 2005, before the conclave, reiterated themes he has stressed for many years, including an almost resigned, but hopeful, prospect of Europe's Christian faithful dwindling to a resolute and resilient remnant in waiting.

quest. For from the 1970s on, the search for the sanctified authority that might reengage communion has been partly responsible for the increasing openness to, sometimes fervent embrace of, non-Western Christian leaders by their Western colleagues. In Anglicanism this finally reached a level of explicitness that required the mechanisms of ecclesial government and relationship simply to stop, take note, and now begin the painful process of their own transformation. How else explain the extraordinary and completely unexpected lopsided vote at Lambeth in 1998 on the resolution regarding human sexuality? Many bishops, whose position on the matter was publicly known to be other than that vote's substance, nonetheless joined voices with its traditionalist stance.

Behind all this was the perceived power of presence given by bishops whose churches and personal lives were formed by a context of struggle and sacrifice of another order than that in the West. Bishops from Mozambique, South Africa, Nigeria, the Sudan, Rwanda, the Congo, and elsewhere, rightly or wrongly, were heard speaking and praying, and in their words there was apprehended an echo from long ago: "are they servants of Christ? I am a better one, with far greater labors . . ." (2 Cor. 11:23). It was the smell of demonstrated holiness that, almost out of respect, led many bishops to permit the articulations of Scripture on certain matters to rest within the context of the traditional readings performed by non-Western churches. Communion was crouching by the door, and leapt.

To be sure, the sanctity of these leaders was, in a sense, immediately contested by the subsequent rejection among many Westerners of the "council" as authoritative altogether. But although the rejection was based on a certain plausible legal reading of the Lambeth Conferences, in fact the "moral authority" of the conference, and this one in particular, reasserted itself and grew in the face of these questions, exactly in the measure that the sanctity of its advocates among the non-Western bishops was gradually acknowledged with explicitness. In this way, the Lambeth Conference was simply transformed into an "authoritative council" by the sheer demand for and receipt of the communion the sanctified witness of its proponents offered. For the first time, in a way revealed by the very openness of its dispute, the Anglican Communion *as communion* became visible. While pundits claimed that the struggle evidenced a Communion fast disappearing, the struggle has served instead to articulate "cataleptically" that very communion as asserting itself in the midst of a church that until this point had flailed at apprehending it from a distance only. And thus the local struggle has become the tremendous promise for the larger church.

It has been the burden of this volume to trace some of the elements at work in this struggle. What is at stake in it — even in its almost provincial enactment by ECUSA and the larger Anglican world — is something, however, that touches the character of the whole church's future. Joining martyrdom and reconciliation — the Christian witness given within the cultural oppositions to the Gospel and the growth of the church in her culture-spanning ways — the church discovers the "meeting together of mercy and truth" (Psalm 85:10), the council of God's redemption in Christ. Together, they form the peculiar embodiment of the church's *historical* vocation to live in communion, which turns out to be a form of life that bears the assaults of its own history in a certain kind of hope.

## Communion and God's Time

We have discussed the virtues of this vocation, ones summed up in the vision of the church given by Paul in Ephesians 4 and 5; we have spoken at length of the ecclesial structures that uphold and are informed by these virtues, described in terms of the Christian tradition of "conciliarity," whose concrete mechanisms are geared to nothing else except the mutual subjection in which Christ is both recognized and exalted; we have alluded to the "witness" — even to the technical degree of martyrdom — that such subjection provides and requires, and through which fruit is borne by the embrace of the church's poverty. In all of this, we have sought to sketch, through the particularities of one church's paradigmatic destiny, the entry into the particular way that "time" is lived in God's church. For "communion" is, in the end, another way of speaking of God's time as it is assumed by the Body of Christ.

For all of Anglicanism's historical avoidance of council — through strategies of denial, individualism, and feigned fellowship — she has evidenced a single and common underside of grace within it all. Each of these strategies, in fact, has sought to buy time or take time apart from the issues involved themselves. They were strategies of time itself. And time, within the church's life, *is* a gift from God filled with potency (cf. 2 Peter 3:8-9). Divinely speaking, "time" is the embodiment of God's patience and of God's providence. And "taking time," at the least, can be a conscious opening to God's patient and active providence in the church's midst as it is re-fashioned in the form of mutual subjection.

This is not an idiosyncratic observation about Anglicanism; and it is one useful to consider for the church Catholic as a whole. As opposed to other Protestant denominations, the Anglican Church has been dragged by conflict and weakening, by denial and humiliation, into the apprehension of her vocation as a communion. It is an astonishing evolution — and therefore perhaps a divine sign — given the innate character of her origins and habits. And in doing so, she has been nurtured by two distinct self-interpretations: first, that change ought to take place slowly, if at all. This is the conservative Anglican principle of "order," paradoxically articulated in the midst of Reformation by Cranmer[22] and by the end of Elizabeth's reign entrenched as an ecclesial principle governing all aspects of Anglican life. The second self-interpretive principle in Anglicanism did not get explicitly articulated until well into seventeenth century, but it has stuck, grown roots, and spread: that is the principle of "antiquity," according to which the basis of our common life and teaching must and does cohere with the shape of the early church. Even the first Lambeth Conference spoke of its identity in these terms (i.e. the "primitive church" of the first four councils).

These two principles — changing only through orderliness, and tying the church to the past — are both potentially principles of "God's time." They represent ecclesial fruit to be shared with all the world. For once embraced, they give the life of the church over to patience and to a providential ordering that takes heed of the shape of the past as a molding gift from God's hand. And they orient the church as Christ's body toward the posture of receipt. The "church as communion" towards which the church of the world both yearns and tends in God's promise, is one in which the sanctifying gifts of the Spirit will be exercised within the common body in a way that *intentionally* embraces such forms of "temporal virtue." And the promise will lead us, thus virtuously, into the midst of debates over Scripture, sexuality, women's ordination, and the use of our resources for the common good, "in the form of a servant." That form, in turn, through which the church takes council, will be given a "new body," "changing our lowly body to be like his glorious body, by the power which enables him

---

22. See above, Chapter 4, on his Preface and essay "On Ceremonies" in the 1549 *Book of Common Prayer*.

even to subject all things to himself" (Phil. 3:21). Such is the great promise of God in Christ Jesus.

The Council of Trent took almost twenty years to convene, and another twenty years just to do its business. On top of that, it took another 120 years to be implemented in Europe. It is our impatience, we believe, that in part has driven away the Spirit's communal gifts from our midst in our own day. Yet still they press themselves into view from behind the shadows of the humiliated. And we are convinced that what is at stake now, in reclaiming some measure of humble and holy subjection one to another through this time, is our capacity to witness to God's hope in Christ within an unbelieving and broken world for which God wills an unexpected healing.

# Index

American Catholicism, 25-56; and American concerns with Newman's "Catholicism," 40-46; and American national character, 29-33, 44-45; and anti-Catholicism in American history, 46, 46n.36, 51; and Cain, 32-33, 32nn.15-16, 45-46, 54; and "Cainite" primordialism, 33-34; and catholic character of American Anglicanism, 47-49; and children of Cain, 32-33, 32n.15, 54; connection to Church of England, 47, 47n.37; defining catholicism, 33-40; and ECUSA's self-image, 25-26; Episcopal Catholicism, 47-53; and Gnosticism, 30, 30n.8; mutual views of Episcopalians and Roman Catholics, 51, 239; Newman on the Anglican church in America, 34-40, 47; the "new world" and the re-creationism, 31-32; and nineteenth-century Episcopal missionaries, 49-52; pneumatic emphasis, 44-45, 44n.32; and primordialism, 32n.16, 42-43; and Protestantism, 30, 30n.9; and sectarianism, 43-44; self-assertions of "apostolic succession," 47, 50;

and violence-laden orientations, 27-28, 54

Anglican Church of Canada: and episcopal authority, 135; and liberal culture, 3; and Windsor Report, 200-202, 205-8. *See also* Windsor Report (TWR)

Anglican Church of Korea, 129-30

Anglican Consultative Council (ACC), as "instrument of unity," 8n.1, 191-96

Anglican–Roman Catholic International Commission's Report on Authority, 106n.17

Anti-Catholicism, 46, 46n.36, 51

Anti-conciliarism and the yearning for communion, 285-90; English Reformation, 286-87; history of Anglican councils and authority, 285-90

Anti-Federalists, 42, 52

Apostles' Creed, 108n.22, 128, 168

Apostolic Succession, 47, 50, 154-55

Archbishop of Canterbury: fellowship of churches bound by communion with, 122-23; as "instrument of unity," 8n.1, 9-10, 165-66, 191-96

Arendt, Hannah, 137, 140-41

Arnold, Matthew, 70, 71n.4